D0357448

Oracle8i™ DBA: Backup and Recovery

Debbie Wong

Oracle8i™ DBA: Backup and Recovery Exam Cram

The Coriolis Group, LLC
14455 N. Hayden Road
Suite 220
Scottsdale, Arizona 85260

(480)483-0192
FAX (480)483-0193
www.coriolis.com

Library of Congress Cataloging-in-Publication Data
Wong, Debbie.
    Oracle8i DBA : backup and recovery / by Debbie Wong.
        p.   cm. -- (Exam cram)
    Includes index.
        ISBN 1-58880-045-8
        1. Electronic data processing personnel--Certification.   2. Database management--Examinations--Study guides.   3. Oracle (Computer file)
I. Title.   II. Series.
QA76.3 .W67   2001
005.75'85--dc21   2001032381
                                                                        CIP

President and CEO
Roland Elgey

Publisher
Steve Sayre

Associate Publisher
Katherine R. Hartlove

Acquisitions Editor
Sharon Linsenbach

Product Marketing Manager
Jeff Johnson

Project Editor
Julie McLaughlin

Technical Reviewer
Robert Freeman

Production Coordinator
Todd Halvorsen

Cover Designer
Laura Wellander

Layout Designer
April Nielsen

Printed in the United States of America
10 9 8 7 6 5 4 3 2 1

The Coriolis Group, LLC • 14455 North Hayden Road, Suite 220 • Scottsdale, Arizona 85260

A Note from Coriolis

Our goal has always been to provide you with the best study tools on the planet to help you achieve your certification in record time. Time is so valuable these days that none of us can afford to waste a second of it, especially when it comes to exam preparation.

Over the past few years, we've created an extensive line of *Exam Cram* and *Exam Prep* study guides, practice exams, and interactive training. To help you study even better, we have now created an e-learning and certification destination called **ExamCram.com**. (You can access the site at **www.examcram.com**.) Now, with every study product you purchase from us, you'll be connected to a large community of people like yourself who are actively studying for their certifications, developing their careers, seeking advice, and sharing their insights and stories.

We believe that the future is all about collaborative learning. Our **ExamCram.com** destination is our approach to creating a highly interactive, easily accessible collaborative environment, where you can take practice exams and discuss your experiences with others, sign up for features like "Questions of the Day," plan your certifications using our interactive planners, create your own personal study pages, and keep up with all of the latest study tips and techniques.

We hope that whatever study products you purchase from us—*Exam Cram* or *Exam Prep* study guides, *Personal Trainers, Personal Test Centers*, or one of our interactive Web courses—will make your studying fun and productive. Our commitment is to build the kind of learning tools that will allow you to study the way you want to, whenever you want to.

Visit ExamCram.com now to enhance your study program.

Help us continue to provide the very best certification study materials possible. Write us or email us at **learn@examcram.com** and let us know how our study products have helped you study. Tell us about new features that you'd like us to add. Send us a story about how we've helped you. We're listening!

Good luck with your certification exam and your career. Thank you for allowing us to help you achieve your goals.

ExamCram.com Connects You to the Ultimate Study Center!

Look for these other products from The Coriolis Group:

Oracle 8i DBA: Architecture and Administration Exam Cram
by Peter Sharman

Oracle 8i DBA: Performance Tuning Exam Cram
by Zulfiqer Habeeb

Oracle 8i DBA: Network Administration Exam Cram
by Barbara Ann Pascavage

Oracle 8i DBA: SQL and PL/SQL Exam Cram
by Michael Ault

MCSE SQL Server 2000 Database Design Exam Cram
by Richard McMahon and Sean Chase

Also recently published by Coriolis Certification Insider Press:

MCSE Exchange 2000 Design Exam Prep
by Michael Shannon and Dennis Suhanovs

Citrix CCEA MetaFrame 1.8 for Windows Exam Cram
by Anoop Jalan, Gene Beaty, and Travis Guinn

Server+ Exam Prep
by Drew Bird and Mike Harwood

CCSA Exam Cram
by Tony Piltzecker

To my parents, who gave my brothers and me the greatest gift of all—life.
You will always be the wind beneath our wings.
To you, the reader, I hope that you find what you are looking for,
and I urge you to remember that in the electronic virtual world,
it is those who help the most who receive the most benefit.

๏

About the Author

Debbie Wong is an IT professional whose experience includes system analysis and design, application development, database administration, customer support, and project management. She has spent the majority of her career developing and maintaining host, pc-LAN, and Web based database systems to accommodate her clients' distinct business needs.

Debbie began her Oracle certification history with Oracle6's Database Administration and Application Developer certification exams, and then served as a cut-score committee member and recipient of Chauncey/ETS Oracle7 certification. She is currently an Oracle Certified Professional (OCP) DBA for Oracle7.3, Oracle8, and Oracle8i. Additionally, she is an OCP-certified Application Developer.

Debbie is an active participant in local, regional, and international Oracle user groups. She has presented at MAOP, ECO, ODTUG, IOUW/IOUG-A, UKOUG, and Oracle OpenWorld conferences.

Acknowledgments

I would like to thank, in particular, the dedicated professionals at the Coriolis Group: Acquisitions Editor Sharon Linsenbach and Project Editor Julie McLaughlin. Without their patience, excellent support, and know-how, this book would never have gotten off the drawing board. I would also like to thank those behind the scenes: Production Coordinator Todd Halvorsen, Cover Designer Laura Wellander, and Layout Designer April Nielsen.

Many thanks to Robert Freeman for doing an excellent job tech reviewing the book. Additionally, thanks to Julie Grim for copyediting, Charlotte Zuccarini for proofreading, and Christina Palaia for indexing.

Sincere thanks to Jason Evans, VP Communications at Self Test Software, for providing some of the sample questions.

Heartfelt thanks to my uncle for bringing our family to this land of opportunity.

Special thanks to Elaine Schuetz, a great friend and an Oracle expert who patiently mentored me over the years. Your thoughtfulness, encouragement, and support provided the solid foundation upon which I stand.

Special thanks to Marlene Theriault, my Oracle, for your encouragement, inspiration, and willing support. Your believing in me (more than I believed in myself) has made this second book a reality.

Thank you to my family, friends, manager, and co-workers for tolerating my stressful moments, for putting up with me through months of grouchy days and sleepless nights, and for making this book a reality. Your encouragement, positive attitude, and unparalleled moral support have kept me motivated throughout this challenging project. You guys are the greatest!

Last but not least, thanks to you for purchasing this book.
—*Debbie Wong*

Contents at a Glance

Table of Contents

Chapter 7
Physical Backups without Oracle Recovery Manager 137

Introduction

Welcome to *Oracle8i DBA: Backup and Recovery Exam Cram*. This book will help you in preparing to take—and pass—the last of the five-part series of exams for the Oracle 8i Certified Professional-Database Administrator (OCP-DBA) certification. In this introduction, I'll talk about Oracle's certification programs and how the *Exam Cram* series can help you prepare for Oracle8i's certification exams.

Exam Cram books help you understand and appreciate the subjects and materials you need to pass Oracle certification exams. These books are aimed strictly at test preparation and review and do not teach you everything you need to know about a topic. Instead, I present and dissect the questions and problems that you're likely to encounter on a test.

To completely prepare yourself for any Oracle test, I recommend that you begin by taking the Self-Assessment included in this book immediately following this Introduction. This tool will help you evaluate your knowledge base against the requirements for an OCP-DBA under both ideal and real circumstances.

Based on what you learn from that exercise, you might decide to begin your studies with either some classroom training or reading one of the many DBA guides that are available from Oracle or third-party vendors. I also strongly recommend that you install, configure, and work with the software that you'll be tested on because nothing beats hands-on experience and familiarity when it comes to understanding the questions you're likely to encounter on a certification test. Book learning is essential, but hands-on experience is the best teacher of all.

The Oracle Certified Professional (OCP) Program

The OCP program for DBA certification currently includes five separate tests, and Table 1.1 shows the required exams for the OCP certification:

➤ *Introduction to Oracle: SQL and PL/SQL (Exam 1Z0-001)*—Test 1 is the base test for the series. The knowledge that is tested in Test 1 will serve as the foundation for all the other DBA tests. This test focuses on Structured Query Language (SQL) and PL/SQL language constructs, syntax, and usage. It covers

Table 1   Oracle8i OCP-DBA Requirements

Oracle8i

All 5 of these tests are required	
Exam 1Z0-001	Introduction to Oracle: SQL and PL/SQL
Exam 1Z0-023	Oracle8i: Architecture and Administration
Exam 1Z0-024	Oracle8i: Performance Tuning
Exam 1Z0-025	Oracle8i: Backup and Recovery
Exam 1Z0-026	Oracle8i: Network Administration

If you are currently an OCP certified in Oracle8, you need take only the upgrade exam (Oracle8i: New Features for Administrators, Exam 1Z0-020) to be certified in Oracle8i. If you have passed Introduction to Oracle: SQL and PL/SQL during your pursuit of Oracle8 certification, you do not need to retake it for Oracle8i certification.

Data Definition Language (DDL) and Data Manipulation Language (DML). Also covered are basic data modeling, database design, and basic Oracle Procedure Builder usage.

➤ *Oracle8i: Architecture and Administration (Exam 1Z0-023)*—Test 2 deals with all levels of database administration in Oracle8i. Topics include architecture, startup and shutdown, database creation, management of database internal and external constructs (such as redo logs, rollback segments, and tablespaces), and all other Oracle structures. Database auditing, use of National Language Support (NLS) features, and use of SQL*Loader and other utilities are also covered.

➤ *Oracle8i: Backup and Recovery (Exam 1Z0-025)*—Test 3 covers one of the most important parts of the Oracle DBA's job: database backup and recovery operations. This test focuses on backup and recovery motives, architecture as it relates to backup and recovery, backup methods, failure scenarios, recovery methodologies, archive logging, supporting 24x7 shops, troubleshooting, and using Oracle8i's standby database features. The test also includes Oracle's Recovery Manager (RMAN).

➤ *Oracle8i: Performance Tuning (Exam 1Z0-024)*—Test 4 covers all aspects of tuning an Oracle8i database (which includes application as well as database tuning). The test relies on knowledge in diagnosis of tuning problems; optimal configurations for databases; shared pool tuning; buffer cache tuning; Oracle block usage; tuning rollback segments and redo mechanisms; monitoring and detecting lock contention; tuning sorts; tuning in online transaction processing (OLTP), DSS, and mixed environments; and load optimization.

➤ *Oracle8i: Network Administration (Exam 1Z0-026)*—Test 5 covers all parts of the Net8 product: Net8 Assistant, Oracle Names Server, the listener process, name-resolution methods, Multithreaded Server (MTS), Connection Manager, Advanced Security Option, configuration files, and troubleshooting.

To obtain an OCP certificate in database administration, you must pass all five exams. You do not have to take the tests in any particular order, although it is usually better to do so because the knowledge that is tested does build from each exam. The core exams require you to demonstrate competence with all phases of Oracle8i database activities. If you already have your Oracle8 certification, you need to take only one exam—Oracle8i DBA: New Features for Administrators (Exam 1Z0-020)—to upgrade your status. If you have already passed some of the equivalent Oracle8 exams, you can take the Oracle8i version for the remaining exams plus the Oracle8i DBA: New Features for Administrations (Exam IZ0-020) for Oracle8i DBA-OCP.

It's not uncommon for the entire process to take a year or so, and many individuals find that they must take a test more than once to pass. The primary goal of the *Exam Cram* series is to make it possible, given proper study and preparation, to pass all of the OCP-DBA tests on the first try.

Finally, certification is an ongoing activity. After an Oracle version becomes obsolete, OCP-DBAs (and other OCPs) typically have six months to get recertified on current product versions. (If you do not get recertified within the specified time period, your certification becomes invalid.) Because technology keeps changing and new products continually supplant old ones, this should come as no surprise.

The best place to keep tabs on the OCP program and its various certifications is on the Oracle Web site. The current root URL for the OCP program is **www.oracle.com/education/certification/**. This site changes frequently, so if this URL doesn't work, try using the Search tool on Oracle's site (**www.oracle.com**) with either "OCP" or the quoted phrase "Oracle Certified Professional Program" as the search string. This will help you find the latest and most accurate information about the company's certification programs.

Taking a Certification Exam

Alas, testing is not free. You'll be charged $125 for each test you take, whether you pass or fail. In the United States and Canada, Sylvan Prometric administers tests. Sylvan Prometric can be reached at 1-800-891-3926, any time from 7:00 A.M. to 6:00 P.M., Central Time, Monday through Friday. If you can't get through, try 1-612-896-7000 or 1-612-820-5707.

To schedule an exam, call at least one day in advance. To cancel or reschedule an exam, you must call at least one day before the scheduled test time, or you may be charged the $125 fee. When calling Sylvan Prometric, please have the following information ready:

➤ Your name, organization, and mailing address

➤ The name of the exam you want to take

➤ A method of payment. (The most convenient approach is to supply a valid credit card number with sufficient available credit. Otherwise, payments by check, money order, or purchase order must be received before a test can be scheduled. If the latter methods are required, ask the Sylvan representative for more details.)

An appointment confirmation will be sent to you by mail (if you register more than five days before an exam) or by fax (if fewer than five days). A Candidate Agreement letter, which you must sign to take the examination, will also be provided.

On the day of the test, try to arrive at least 15 minutes before the scheduled time. You must supply two forms of identification, one of which must be a photo ID.

All exams are completely closed book. In fact, you will not be permitted to take anything with you into the testing area. I suggest that you review the most critical information about your test immediately prior to entering the room. (*Exam Cram* books provide a brief reference—the Cram Sheet, located inside the front of this book—that lists in distilled form the essential information from the book.) You will have some time to compose yourself, to mentally review this critical information, and even to take a sample orientation exam before you begin the real thing. I suggest you take the orientation test before your first exam. They're all more or less identical in layout, behavior, and controls, so you probably won't need to do this after the first test.

When you complete an Oracle8i certification exam, the testing software will tell you whether you've passed or failed. Results are broken into several topic areas. Whether you pass or fail, I suggest you ask for—and keep—the detailed report that the test administrator prints for you. You can use the report to help you prepare for another go-round, if necessary. Even if you pass, the report shows areas you may need to review to keep your edge. If you need to retake an exam, you'll have to call Sylvan Prometric, schedule a new test date, and pay another $125.

Tracking OCP Status

Oracle generates transcripts that indicate the exams you have passed and your corresponding test scores. After you pass the necessary set of five exams, you'll be certified as an Oracle8i DBA. Official certification can take anywhere from four to six weeks (although generally four weeks), so don't expect to get your credentials overnight. After you are certified, you will receive a package with a Welcome Kit that contains a number of elements:

➤ An OCP-DBA certificate, suitable for framing.

➤ A license agreement to use the OCP logo. After the agreement is sent into Oracle and your packet of logo information is received, it allows you to use the logo for advertisements, promotions, documents, letterhead, business cards, and so on. An OCP logo sheet, which includes camera-ready artwork, comes with the license.

Many people believe that the benefits of OCP certification go well beyond the perks that Oracle provides to newly anointed members of this elite group. I am starting to see more job listings that request or require applicants to have an OCP-DBA certification, and many individuals who complete the program can qualify for increases in pay and/or responsibility. As an official recognition of hard work and broad knowledge, OCP certification is a badge of honor in many IT organizations.

How to Prepare for an Exam

At a minimum, preparing for OCP-DBA exams requires that you obtain and study the following materials:

➤ The Oracle8i Documentation Set on CD-ROM. This documentation is also available free of charge at **http://technet.oracle.com**.

➤ The exam prep materials (especially the Candidate Guide), practice tests, and self-assessment exams on the Oracle certification page (**www.oracle.com/education/certification**). Find the materials, download them, and use them!

➤ This *Exam Cram* book. It's the first and last thing you should read before taking the exam.

In addition, you'll probably find any or all of the following materials useful in your quest for Oracle8i DBA expertise:

➤ *OCP Resource Kits*—Oracle has a CD-ROM with example questions and materials to help with the exam; generally, if you request them from your Oracle representatives, they will provide these free. The discs have also been offered free for the taking at most Oracle conventions, such as IOUGA-Alive! and Oracle OpenWorld.

➤ *Classroom training*—Oracle, TUSC, LearningTree, and many others offer classroom and computer-based training material that you will find helpful in preparing for the exam. But a word of warning: These classes are fairly expensive (in the range of $300 per day). However, they do offer a condensed form of learning to help you "brush up" on your Oracle knowledge. The tests are closely tied to the classroom training provided by Oracle, so I would suggest at least taking the introductory classes to get the Oracle-specific (and classroom-specific) terminology under your belt.

➤ *Other publications*—You'll find direct references to other publications and resources in this book, and there's no shortage of materials available about Oracle8i DBA topics. To help you sift through some of the publications out there, each chapter ends with a "Need to Know More?" section that provides pointers to exhaustive resources covering that chapter's subject matter.

➤ *The Oracle Administrator and PL/SQL Developer*—These online references are available from RevealNet, Inc., an Oracle and database online reference provider. These online references provide instant lookup on thousands of database and developmental topics and are an invaluable resource for studying and learning about Oracle. Demo copies can be downloaded from **www.revealnet.com**. Also available at the RevealNet Web site are the DBA and PL/SQL Pipelines, online discussion groups where you can obtain expert information from Oracle DBAs worldwide. The costs of these applications run about $400 each (current pricing is available on the Web site) and are worth every cent.

These required and recommended materials represent an unparalleled collection of sources and resources for Oracle8i DBA topics and software. In the section that follows, I explain how this book works and give you some good reasons why this book should also be on your required and recommended materials list.

About This Book

Each *Exam Cram* chapter follows a regular structure, along with graphical cues about especially important or useful material. Here's the structure of a typical chapter:

➤ *Opening hotlists*—Each chapter begins with lists of the terms, tools, and techniques that you must learn and understand before you can be fully conversant with the chapter's subject matter. I follow the hotlists with one or two introductory paragraphs to set the stage for the rest of the chapter.

➤ *Topical coverage*—After the opening hotlists, each chapter covers a series of topics related to the chapter's subject. Throughout this section, I highlight the material that is most likely to appear on a test using a special Exam Alert layout, like this:

This is what an Exam Alert looks like. Normally, an Exam Alert stresses concepts, terms, software, or activities that will most likely appear in one or more certification test questions. For that reason, any information found offset in this Exam Alert format is worthy of unusual attentiveness on your part. Indeed, most of the facts appearing in the Cram Sheet appear as Exam Alerts within the text.

Occasionally, in *Exam Crams*, you'll see tables of commands or values. The contents of these tables are worthy of extra study because they contain informational tidbits that might show up in a test question.

Even if material isn't flagged as an Exam Alert, *all* the contents of this book are associated, at least tangentially, to something test related. This book is tightly focused for quick test preparation, so you'll find that what appears in the meat of each chapter is critical knowledge.

I have also provided tips that will help build a better foundation of knowledge for database administration. Although the information may not be on the exam, it is highly relevant and will help you in your daily work as an Oracle8i DBA.

 This is how tips are formatted. Keep your eyes open for these, and you'll become an Oracle8i DBA guru in no time!

➤ *Practice Questions*—This section presents a series of mock test questions and explanations of both correct and incorrect answers.

➤ *Details and resources*—The "Need to Know More?" section at the end of each chapter provides direct pointers to Oracle and third-party resources that offer further details on the chapter's subject matter. In addition, these sections try to rate the quality and thoroughness of each topic's coverage. If you find a resource you like in this collection, use it (but don't feel compelled to use all these resources). On the other hand, I recommend only the resources that I use on a regular basis, so none of my recommendations will be a waste of your time or money.

The bulk of the book slavishly follows this chapter structure, but I would like to point out a few other elements. Chapter 16 includes a sample test that provides a good review of the material presented throughout the book to ensure you're ready for the exam. Chapter 17 provides an answer key to the sample test. Additionally, you'll find the glossary and an index that you can use to define and track down terms as they appear in the text.

Finally, look for the Cram Sheet, which appears inside the front of this *Exam Cram* book because it is a valuable tool that represents a condensed and compiled collection of facts, figures, and tips that I think you should memorize before taking the test. Because you can dump this information out of your head onto a piece of paper before answering any exam questions, you can master this information by brute force, remembering it only long enough to write it down after you walk into the test room. You might even want to look at it in the car or in the lobby of the testing center just before you walk in to take the test.

How to Use This Book

If you're prepping for a first-time test, I've structured the topics in this book to build upon each other. Therefore, some topics in later chapters make more sense if you've read earlier chapters. That's why I suggest you read this book from front to back for your initial test preparation.

If you need to brush up on a topic or you have to prepare for a second try, use the index or table of contents to find the topics and questions that you need to study. Beyond the tests, I think you'll find this book useful as a tightly focused reference to some of the most important aspects of topics associated with being a DBA, as implemented under Oracle8i.

Given the entire book's elements and its specialized focus, I've tried to create a tool that you can use to prepare for—but especially to pass—the OCP-DBA Backup and Recovery exam. Please share your feedback on the book with me, especially if you have ideas about how I can improve it for future test-takers. I'll consider everything you say carefully, and I try to respond to all suggestions and questions. You can reach me via email at **dw4ocpbook@yahoo.com**, or you can send your questions or comments to **learn@examcram.com**. Please remember to include the title of the book in your message; otherwise, I'll be forced to guess which book you're writing about. Also, be sure to check out the Web pages at **www.examcram.com**, where you'll find information updates, commentary, and certification information.

Thanks, and enjoy the book!

Self-Assessment

I've included a Self-Assessment in this *Exam Cram* to help you evaluate your readiness to tackle Oracle8i Oracle Certified Professional-Database Administrator (OCP-DBA) certification. It should also help you understand what you need to master the topic of this book—namely, Exam IZ0-025 (Test 3), Oracle8i: Backup and Recovery. But before you tackle this Self-Assessment, let's talk about the concerns you might face when pursuing an Oracle8i OCP-DBA and who an ideal Oracle8i OCP-DBA candidate might be.

Oracle8i OCP-DBAs in the Real World

In the next section, I describe an ideal Oracle8i OPC-DBA candidate, knowing full well that only a few actual candidates meet this ideal. In fact, this description of the ideal candidate might seem downright scary. But take heart, because although the requirements to obtain an Oracle8i OCP-DBA might seem pretty formidable, they are by no means impossible to meet. However, you should be keenly aware that it does take time, is expensive, and requires a substantial effort.

You can get all the real-world motivation you need from knowing that many others have gone before you. You can follow in their footsteps. If you're willing to tackle the process seriously and do what it takes to obtain the necessary experience and knowledge, you can take—and pass—the certification tests. In fact, the *Exam Crams* and the companion *Exam Preps* are designed to make it as easy as possible for you to prepare for these exams. But prepare you must!

The same, of course, is true for other Oracle certifications, including:

➤ Oracle8 OCP-DBA, which is like the Oracle8i OCP-DBA certifications

➤ Application Developer, Oracle Developer Rel. 2 OCP, which is aimed at software developers and requires five exams

➤ Oracle8 Database Operator OCP, which is aimed at database operations staff and requires only one exam

➤ Oracle Java Developer, which is aimed at Java developers and requires five exams

The Ideal Oracle8i OCP-DBA Candidate

Just to give you some idea of what an ideal Oracle8i OCP-DBA candidate is like, here are some relevant statistics about the background and experience such an individual might have. Don't worry if you don't meet these qualifications (or, indeed, if you don't even come close) because this world is far from ideal, and where you fall short is simply where you'll have more work to do. The ideal candidate will have:

➤ Academic or professional training in relational databases, Structured Query Language (SQL), performance tuning, backup and recovery, and Net8 administration.

➤ Three-plus years of professional database administration experience, including experience installing and upgrading Oracle executables, creating and tuning databases, troubleshooting connection problems, creating users, and managing backup and recovery scenarios.

I believe that well under half of all certification candidates meet these requirements. In fact, most probably meet less than half of these requirements (that is, at least when they begin the certification process). But because all those who have their certifications already survived this ordeal, you can survive it, too—especially if you heed what this Self-Assessment can tell you about what you already know and what you need to learn.

Put Yourself to the Test

The following series of questions and observations is designed to help you figure out how much work you'll face in pursuing Oracle certification and what kinds of resources you may consult on your quest. Be absolutely honest in your answers, or you'll end up wasting money on exams you're not ready to take. There are no right or wrong answers, only steps along the path to certification. Only you can decide where you really belong in the broad spectrum of aspiring candidates.

Two things should be clear from the outset:

➤ Even a modest background in computer science will be helpful.

➤ Hands-on experience with Oracle products and technologies is an essential ingredient to certification success.

Educational Background

1. Have you ever taken any computer-related classes? [Yes or No]

   If Yes, proceed to Question 2; if No, proceed to Question 4.

2. Have you taken any classes on relational databases? [Yes or No]

   If Yes, you will probably be able to handle Oracle's architecture and network administration discussions. If you're rusty, brush up on the basic concepts of databases and networks.

   If No, consider some basic reading in this area. I strongly recommend a good Oracle database administration book such as *Oracle8i Administration and Management* by Michael R. Ault (Wiley, 1999) or *Oracle DBA 101* by Marlene Theriault, et al. (Osborne McGraw-Hill, 1999). If these don't appeal to you, check out reviews for other similar titles at your favorite online bookstore.

3. Have you taken any networking concepts or technologies classes? [Yes or No]

   If Yes, you will probably be able to handle Oracle's networking terminology, concepts, and technologies (but brace yourself for frequent departures from normal usage). If you're rusty, brush up on basic networking concepts and terminology.

   If No, you might want to check out the Oracle TechNet Web site (**http://technet.oracle.com**) and read some of the papers and documentation on backup and recovery. If you have access to the Oracle MetaLink Web site, you can review the white papers at that site as well.

4. Have you done any reading on relational databases or networks? [Yes or No]

   If Yes, review the requirements from Questions 2 and 3. If you meet those, move on to the next section, "Hands-On Experience."

   If No, consult the recommended reading for both topics. This kind of strong background will be of great help in preparing you for the Oracle exams.

Hands-On Experience

Another important key to success on all of the Oracle tests is hands-on experience, especially with Oracle Enterprise Manager. If I leave you with only one realization after taking this Self-Assessment, it should be that there is no substitute for time spent installing, configuring, and using the various Oracle products upon which you'll be tested repeatedly and in depth.

5. Have you installed, configured, and worked with Net8? [Yes or No]

   If Yes, make sure you understand basic concepts as covered in Exam IZ0-023, Oracle8i: Architecture and Administration (Test 2) and advanced concepts as covered in Exam IZ0-024, Oracle8i: Performance Tuning (Test 4). You should also study the Net8 configuration and administration for Exam IZ0-026, Oracle8i: Network Administration (Test 5).

If you haven't worked with Oracle, obtain a copy of Oracle8i or Personal Oracle8i. Then, learn about the database and backup and recovery operations.

You can download the candidate certification guide, objectives, practice exams, and other information about Oracle exams from the Oracle Certification page at **www.oracle.com/education/certification/**. To get hands-on experience, sign up at **http://technet.oracle.com** and download free software, such as Personal Oracle8i. Better yet, join a TechNet Technology Track for $200, and get CD copies of Oracle products and upgrades for a year.

Before you take any OCP exam, make sure you've spent enough time performing backup and recoveries to understand how to perform those operations. This will help you in the exam—as well as in real life.

Testing Your Exam-Readiness

Whether you attend a formal class on a specific topic to get ready for an exam or use written materials to study on your own, some preparation for the Oracle certification exams is essential. At $125 a try, pass or fail, you want to do everything you can to pass on your first try. That's where studying comes in.

I have included a practice exam in this book, so if you don't score that well on the test, you can study more and then tackle the test again. The Coriolis Group also has exams that you can take online through the **ExamCram.com** Web site at **www.examcram.com**. If you still don't hit a score of at least 80 percent after these tests, you'll want to investigate the other practice test resources I mention in this section.

For any given subject, consider taking a class if you've tackled self-study materials, taken the test, and failed anyway. If you can afford the privilege, the opportunity to interact with an instructor and fellow students can make all the difference in the world. For information about Oracle classes, visit the Training and Certification page I've previously mentioned (**www.oracle.com/education/certification/**).

If you can't afford to take a class, visit the Training and Certification page anyway because it also includes free practice exams that you can download. Even if you can't afford to spend much at all, you should still consider investing in some low-cost practice exams from commercial vendors because they can help you assess your readiness to pass a test better than any other tool.

6. Have you taken a practice exam on your chosen test subject? [Yes or No]

If Yes—and you scored 80 percent or better—you're probably ready to tackle the real thing. If your score isn't above that crucial threshold, keep at it until you break that barrier.

If No, obtain all the free and low-budget practice tests you can find (or afford) and get to work. Keep at it until you can comfortably break the passing threshold.

 There is no better way to assess your test readiness than to take a good-quality practice exam and pass with a score of 80 percent or better. When preparing, shoot for 80-plus percent just to leave room for the "weirdness factor" that sometimes shows up on Oracle exams.

Assessing Your Readiness for Oracle8i DBA: Backup and Recovery (Test 3)

In addition to the general exam-readiness information in the previous section, other resources are available to help you prepare for the Oracle8i: Backup and Recovery exam. For starters, visit the RevealNet Pipeline (**www.revealnet.com**) or **http://technet.oracle.com**. These are great places to ask questions and get good answers, or simply to observe the questions that others ask (along with the answers, of course).

Oracle exam mavens also recommend checking the Oracle Knowledge Base from RevealNet. You can get information on purchasing the RevealNet software at **www.revealnet.com**.

For Oracle8i: Backup and Recovery preparation in particular, I recommend that you check out one or more of these books as you prepare for the exam:

➤ Velpuri, Rama and Anand Adkoli. *Oracle8i Backup and Recovery Handbook.* Oracle Press, Berkeley, CA, 2000.

➤ Ault, Michael R. *Oracle8i Administration and Management.* John Wiley and Sons, New York, NY, 1999.

Stop by your favorite bookstore or online bookseller to check out either one of these books.

One last note: I cannot stress enough the importance of hands-on experience in the context of the Backup and Recovery exam. As you review the material for this exam, you'll realize that hands-on experience with Oracle8i commands, tools, and utilities is invaluable.

Onward, through the Fog!

After you have assessed your readiness, undertaken the right background studies, obtained the hands-on experience that will help you understand the product and technologies at work, and reviewed the many sources of information to help you prepare for a test, you will be ready to take a round of practice tests. When your scores come back positive enough to get you through the exam, you will be ready to go after the real thing. If you follow this assessment regimen, you'll not only know what you need to study, but when you're ready to make a test date at Sylvan. Good luck!

Oracle OCP Certification Exams

Terms you'll need to understand:

✓ Radio button
✓ Checkbox
✓ Exhibit
✓ Multiple-choice question formats
✓ Process of elimination

Techniques you'll need to master:

✓ Assessing your exam-readiness
✓ Preparing to take a certification exam
✓ Practicing (to make perfect)
✓ Mastering the art of careful reading
✓ Making the best use of the testing software
✓ Budgeting your time
✓ Saving the hardest questions until last
✓ Guessing (as a last resort)

As experiences go, taking tests is not something that most people eagerly antici-
pate, no matter how well prepared they are. In most cases, however, familiarity
helps ameliorate test anxiety. In plain English, this means you probably won't be
as nervous when you take your fourth or fifth Oracle certification exam as you
will be when you take your first.

Whether it's your first test or your tenth, understanding the exam-taking par-
ticulars (how much time to spend on questions, the setting you'll be in, and so
on) and the testing software will help you concentrate on the material rather than
on the environment. Likewise, mastering a few basic test-taking skills should
help you recognize—and perhaps even outfox—some of the tricks you're bound
to find on the Oracle exam.

In this chapter, I'll explain the testing environment and software, as well as some
proven test-taking strategies you should be able to use to your advantage.

Assessing Exam-Readiness

Before you take any Oracle exam, I strongly recommend that you read through
and take the Self-Assessment included with this book (it appears just before this
chapter). This will help you compare your knowledge base to the requirements
for obtaining an Oracle Certified Professional (OCP) designation, and it will
also help you identify parts of your background or experience that might be in
need of improvement, enhancement, or further learning. If you get the right set
of basics under your belt, obtaining Oracle certification will be that much easier.

After you've gone through the Self-Assessment, you can address those areas where
your background or experience might not measure up to that of an ideal certification
candidate. But you can also tackle subject matter for individual tests at the same time,
so you can continue making progress while you're catching up in some areas.

After you've worked through this *Exam Cram*, read the supplementary materials,
and taken the practice test at the end of the book, you'll have a pretty clear idea of
when you should be ready to take the real exam. Although I strongly recommend
that you keep practicing until your scores top the 80 percent mark, 85 percent
would be a good goal to give yourself some margin for error in a real exam situation (where stress will play more of a role than when you practice). After you hit
that point, you should be ready to go. But if you get through the practice exam in
this book without attaining that score, you should keep taking practice tests and
studying the materials until you get there. You'll find more information about
how to study and prepare in the Self-Assessment. But now, on to the exam itself!

The Testing Situation

When you arrive at the Sylvan Prometric testing center where you've scheduled your test, you'll need to sign in with a test coordinator. You'll be asked to produce two forms of identification, one of which must be a photo ID. After you've signed in and your time slot arrives, you'll be asked to leave any books, bags, or other items you brought with you, and you'll be escorted into a closed room. Typically, the room will be furnished with one to six computers, and each workstation will be separated from the others by dividers designed to keep you from seeing what's happening on someone else's computer.

You'll be furnished with a pen or pencil and a blank sheet of paper or, in some cases, an erasable plastic sheet with an erasable felt-tip pen. You're allowed to write down any information you want on this sheet. I suggest that you memorize as much as possible of the material that appears on the Cram Sheet (inside the front of this book) and then write down that information on the blank sheet as soon as you sit in front of the test machine. You can refer to the sheet any time you like during the test, but you'll have to surrender it when you leave the room.

Most test rooms feature a wall with a large window from which the test coordinator will monitor the room. The test coordinator will have loaded the Oracle certification test that you've signed up for—IZ0-025—and you'll be permitted to start as soon as you're seated in front of the machine.

All Oracle certification exams permit you to take up to a certain maximum amount of time (usually 90 minutes). The computer maintains an on-screen counter/clock so that you can check the time remaining any time you like. Each exam consists of 60 to 70 questions that are randomly selected from a pool of questions.

 The passing score varies per exam and the questions selected. For the Oracle8i: Backup and Recovery Exam, the passing score is 70 percent. You must get 42 questions correct out of 60 total questions.

All Oracle certification exams are computer generated and use a multiple-choice or fill-in-the-blank format. Although this might sound easy, the questions are constructed not just to check your mastery of basic facts and figures about Oracle8i DBA topics, but also to evaluate one or more sets of circumstances or requirements. Often, you'll be asked to give more than one answer to a question; likewise, you might be asked to select the best or most effective solution from a range of choices, all of which technically are correct. The tests are quite an adventure, and they involve real thinking. This book will show you what to expect and how to deal with the problems, puzzles, and predicaments you're likely to find on the tests (in particular, the Oracle8i: Backup and Recovery Exam, 1Z0-025).

Test Layout and Design

A typical test question is depicted in Question 1. It's a multiple-choice question that requires you to select a single correct answer. Following the question is a brief summary of each potential answer and why it is either right or wrong.

Question 1

What mode must the database be in to perform an online backup?

○ a. NOARCHIVELOG

○ b. HOT_BACKUP_ENABLED

○ c. ARCHIVE_LOG

○ d. ARCHIVELOG

Answer d is correct. The database must be in ARCHIVELOG mode in order to perform online backups. Answer a is incorrect because NOARCHIVELOG mode specifically excludes the possibility of doing online backups. Answers b and c are not valid backup modes and are therefore incorrect.

This sample question corresponds closely to those you'll see on Oracle certification tests. To select the correct answer during the test, you position the cursor over the radio button next to the appropriate answer and click the mouse to select that choice. The only difference between the certification test and this question is that the real questions are not immediately followed by the answers.

Next, I'll examine a question in which one or more answers are possible. This type of question provides checkboxes, rather than radio buttons, for marking all appropriate selections.

Question 2

> Which of the following are different backup types in Oracle? [Choose three]
>
> ❑ a. Logical
>
> ❑ b. Conditional
>
> ❑ c. Physical
>
> ❑ d. Relational
>
> ❑ e. Archivelog

Answers a, c, e are correct. A logical backup is a backup of the data itself in the database. A physical backup is a backup of the physical data files of a database. An archivelog backup is a backup of the archived redo logs that are generated by a database in ARCHIVELOG mode. Answers b and d are both incorrect because they are not backup terms.

For this type of question, all the parts to the answer must be selected to answer the question correctly.

The third type of question is a fill-in-the-blank format that requires you to enter a specific word or words. For this type of question, you will have a rectangular box in which you will have to type the correct answer. This is the most difficult type of question because it does not allow for the process of elimination. Although the answers will usually be simple and consist of only one word, that word must be spelled correctly.

Question 3

> **ALTER TABLESPACE** *<tablespace_name>* _____ **BACKUP** is
> used to put a tablespace in online backup mode.

The correct answer is **BEGIN**. It is important that you type only the word "BEGIN". Issuing the command **ALTER TABLESPACE** *<tablespace_name>* **BEGIN BACKUP** will put the tablespace listed into online backup mode.

The number of fill-in-the-blank questions is usually very small. You might see only one or two questions of this type on the exam.

These three basic types of questions can appear in many forms, and they constitute the foundation on which all the Oracle certification exam questions rest. More complex questions might include so-called exhibits, which are usually tables or data-content layouts of one form or another. You'll be expected to use the information displayed in the exhibit to guide you in answering the question.

Other questions involving exhibits might use charts or diagrams to help document a workplace scenario that you'll be asked to troubleshoot or configure. Paying careful attention to such exhibits is the key to success. Be prepared to toggle between the picture and the question as you work. Often, both are complex enough that you might not be able to remember all of either one. Use your sheet to write down any notes on the exhibit that will help you to answer the question.

Using Oracle's Test Software Effectively

A well-known test-taking principle is first to read over the entire test from start to finish, but to answer only those questions that you feel absolutely sure of on this pass. On subsequent passes, you can dive into more complex questions, knowing how many such questions you have remaining and the time you have to spend on those questions.

Fortunately, Oracle test software makes this approach easy to implement. At the top of each screen, you'll find a checkbox that permits you to mark that question for a later visit. (Note that marking questions makes review easier, but you can return to any question by clicking the Forward and Back buttons repeatedly until you get to the question.) As you read each question, if you answer only those you're sure of and mark for review those that you're not sure of, you can keep going through a decreasing list of open questions as you knock off the trickier ones in order.

There's at least one potential benefit to reading through the test before answering the trickier questions. Sometimes you find information in later questions that sheds light on earlier ones. Other times, information you read in later questions might jog your memory about Oracle8i facts, figures, or behavior that also will help with earlier questions. Either way, you'll come out ahead if you defer those questions about which you're not absolutely sure.

Keep working on the questions until you are absolutely sure of all your answers or until you know you'll run out of time. If you still have unanswered questions and time is running out, you'll want to zip through them and guess. Not answering a question at all guarantees only that you'll get no credit for it, and a guess has at least a chance of being correct. (Oracle scores blank answers and incorrect answers as equally wrong.)

Taking Testing Seriously

The most important advice I can give you about taking any Oracle test is this: Read each question carefully. Some questions are deliberately ambiguous; some use double negatives; others use terminology in incredibly precise ways. I've taken numerous practice tests and real tests, and I've found that it is very easy to misread a question or to read something into a question that is beyond what is being asked.

Here are some suggestions on how to deal with the tendency to jump to an answer too quickly:

➤ Make sure you read every word in the question. If you find yourself jumping ahead impatiently, return to the beginning of the question and start over.

➤ As you read, try to restate the question in your own terms. If you can do this, you should be able to pick the correct answer(s) much more easily.

➤ When returning to a question after your initial read-through, reread every word again. Otherwise, the mind falls quickly into a rut. Sometimes seeing a question afresh after turning your attention elsewhere lets you see something you missed before, but the strong tendency is to see only what you've seen before. Try to avoid this natural tendency at all times.

➤ If you return to a question more than twice, try to articulate to yourself what you don't understand about the question, why the answers don't appear to make sense, or what appears to be missing. If you chew on the subject for a while, your subconscious might provide the details that are lacking, or you might notice a "trick" that will point to the right answer.

Question-Handling Strategies

Based on the tests I've taken, a couple of interesting trends in the answers have become apparent. For those questions that take only a single answer, usually two or three of the answers will be obviously incorrect, and two of the answers will be plausible. Of course, only one can be correct. Unless the answer leaps out at you (and if it does, reread the question to look for a trick, because sometimes those are the ones you're most likely to get wrong), begin the answering process by eliminating those that are obviously wrong.

Things to look for in the "obviously wrong" category include spurious command choices or table or view names, nonexistent software or command options, and terminology you've never seen before. If you've done your homework for a test, no valid information should be completely new to you. In that case, unfamiliar or bizarre terminology probably indicates a bogus answer.

Numerous questions assume that the default behavior of a particular Oracle utility (such as the listener control utility) is in effect. It's essential, therefore, to know and understand the default settings for the listener, Oracle Names, Connection Manager, Multithreaded Server (MTS), Intelligent Agent, and the Advanced Security Option (ASO). If you know the defaults and understand what they mean, this knowledge will help you cut through many knots.

When dealing with questions that require multiple answers, you must know and select all of the correct options to get credit. This, too, qualifies as an example of why careful reading is so important.

As you work your way through the test, another counter that Oracle provides will come in handy: the numbers of questions completed and questions outstanding. Budget your time by making sure that you've completed one-fourth of the questions one-quarter of the way through the test period (between 14 and 15 questions in the first 22 or 23 minutes). Check again three-quarters of the way through (between 44 and 45 questions in the first 66 to 69 minutes).

If you're not through after 85 minutes, use the last five minutes to guess your way through the remaining questions. Remember that guesses are potentially more valuable than blank answers because blanks are always wrong and a guess might turn out to be right. If you haven't a clue about any of the remaining questions, pick answers at random or choose, for example, all a's or all b's. The important thing is to submit a test for scoring that has an answer for every question.

 At the very end of your test period, you're better off guessing than leaving questions blank or unanswered. If you have to guess, go with your first impression because that is often the correct answer.

Mastering the Inner Game

In the final analysis, knowledge breeds confidence, and confidence breeds success. If you study the materials in this book carefully and review all of the questions at the end of each chapter, you should be aware of those areas for which additional studying is required.

Next, follow up by reading some or all of the materials recommended in the "Need to Know More?" section at the end of each chapter. The idea is to become familiar enough with the concepts and situations that you find in the sample questions to be able to reason your way through similar situations on a real test. If you know the material, you have every right to be confident that you can pass the test.

After you've worked your way through the book, take the practice test in Chapter 16. The test will provide a reality check and will help you identify areas that you need to study further. Make sure you follow up and review materials related to the questions you miss before scheduling a real test. Only when you've covered all the ground and feel comfortable with the whole scope of the practice test should you take a real test.

If you take the sample test (Chapter 16) and you don't score at least 80 percent correct, you'll want to practice further. At a minimum, download the practice tests and the self-assessment tests from the Oracle Education Web site's certification page.

As with any sample test , you need to beware of becoming so familiar with the test itself that you are answering the questions by rote. If you find yourself answering the questions before you finish reading them, you have become too familiar with the test, and it is no longer helpful.

Armed with the information in this book and with the determination to increase your knowledge, you should be able to pass the certification exam. But, if you don't work at it, you'll spend the test fee more than once before you finally do pass. If you prepare seriously, the exam should go flawlessly. Good luck!

Additional Resources

By far, the best source of information about Oracle certification tests comes from Oracle itself. Because its products and technologies—and the tests that go with them—change frequently, the best place to go for exam-related information is online.

If you haven't already visited the Oracle certification pages, do so now. As of the writing of this chapter, the certification page resides at **www.oracle.com/ education/certification/**. (See Figure 1.1.)

Note: The certification page might not be there by the time you read this, or it might have been replaced by something new and different because things change regularly on the Oracle site. Should this happen, please read the sidebar titled "Coping with Change on the Web" later in this chapter.

The menu options in the left column of the page point to the most important sources of information in the certification pages. Here's what to check out:

➤ *News/Events*—This section provides the latest information on Oracle OCP exams.

➤ *Why Certify?*—This section provides a narrative of the benefits of certification.

➤ *OCP Tracks*—This section contains a list of the Oracle Certified Professional Program Tracks.

➤ *Exam Registration*—This section provides information on how to register online or by phone.

➤ *Day of Exam*—This section provides you with the basic information on procedures at the exam site.

➤ *Partners/Alliance*—This section is for those interested in the OCP Partner programs.

➤ *Candidate Guides*—This is a direct link to the page that lists the OCP Tracks and Candidate Guides. I suggest you closely review the DBA Candidate Guide for details on what topics are covered in the exams.

➤ *Practice Tests*—This link provides you with the option of going to a page to fill out a form and download a free sample set of questions.

➤ *OCP Members Only*—This site is currently being constructed. At the time of writing, it provides a method to download the OCP logo. It also provides instructions for contacting Sylvan Prometric if you have not received your OCP certification within 30 days of passing the exams.

These are just the high points of what's available in the Oracle certification pages. As you browse through them—and I strongly recommend that you do—you'll probably find other things I didn't mention here that are every bit as interesting and helpful.

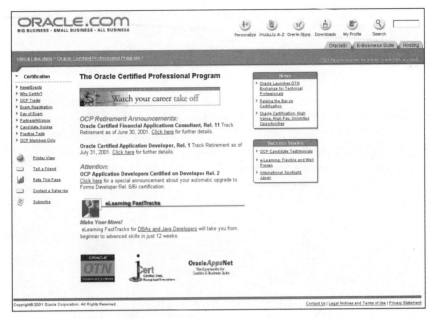

Figure 1.1   The Oracle Certification page should be your starting point for further investigation of the most current exam and preparation information.

Coping with Change on the Web

Sooner or later, all the specifics I've shared with you about the Oracle certification pages, and all the other Web-based resources I mention throughout the rest of this book, will go stale or will be replaced by newer information. In some cases, the URLs you find here might lead you to their replacements; in other cases, URLs will go nowhere, leaving you with the dreaded "404 File not found" error message.

When that happens, please don't give up. There's always a way to find what you want on the Web, if you're willing to invest some time and energy. Most large or complex Web sites—and Oracle's qualifies on both counts—offer a search engine. As long as you can get to Oracle's home page (and I'm sure that it will stay at **www.oracle.com** for a long while yet), you can use this tool to help you find what you need.

The more specific or focused you can make a search request, the more likely it is that the results will include information you can use. For instance, you can search the string "training and certification" to produce a lot of data about the subject in general, but if you're looking for the Candidate Guide for the Oracle DBA tests, you'll be more likely to get there quickly if you use a Boolean search string such as this:

```
"DBA" AND "candidate guide"
```

Likewise, if you want to find the training and certification downloads, try a string such as this one:

```
"training and certification" AND "download"
```

Finally, don't be afraid to use general search tools such as **www.search.com**, **www.altavista.com**, or **www.excite.com** to search for related information. So, if you can't find something where this book says it lives, start looking around. If worse comes to worst, you can always email me! I just might have a clue. My email address is **dw4ocpbook@yahoo.com**.

Backup and
Recovery Considerations

Terms you'll need to understand:

✓ Availability

✓ Downtime

✓ Backup

✓ Recovery

✓ Disaster

✓ Disaster recovery plan

Techniques you'll need to master:

✓ Understanding business considerations

✓ Understanding operational considerations

✓ Understanding technical considerations

✓ Understanding Oracle Server's high availability features

✓ Understanding the importance of testing your backup and recovery strategy

In today's complex networked computing environments, enterprise databases house data that represents a valuable asset for public and private organizations. Data takes many forms—purchase orders, customer names, inventory items, taxes due, and so on. The loss of data, even for a short period of time, can translate into thousands of dollars of lost revenue and productivity.

In every database system, system failure is always a possibility. In the event of a system failure or catastrophe, the data must be recovered accurately and quickly. An Oracle database backup makes this possible; it is a copy of data that can be used to recover the original data if it is lost. The recovery process varies depending on the type of failure, the component of the database affected by the failure, and the availability of backups. Planning and implementation of an effective backup and recovery strategy are critical tasks performed by the Oracle database administrators (DBAs). Without an effective backup strategy, the recoverability of the database will be severely limited. To protect organizations against system failures and related data loss, a large percentage of planning, developing, and testing efforts on any computing system should be spent on backup and recovery considerations.

Creating an Effective Backup and Recovery Strategy

Every database computing environment is unique and has its own requirements. Business, operational, and technical considerations are important factors in defining an effective backup and recovery strategy for a particular site. It is important that these considerations are communicated to the appropriate level of management so that corporate resources are dedicated to ensuring a successful backup and recovery strategy. An effective backup and recovery strategy will protect the database from different types of failures and will ensure high availability, minimal downtime, and complete data recovery.

When you're creating an effective backup and recovery strategy, you should keep in mind three important factors:

➤ Business considerations

➤ Operational considerations

➤ Technical considerations

Whatever backup approach you choose, it is important that you gain appropriate management support. All parties involved should understand the ramifications of the different backup approaches and their potential effects on recoverability.

Note: An effective backup and recovery strategy should evolve with the business to meet ongoing needs.

Business Considerations

Any level of system downtime affects a business. To determine the costs associated with downtime and data loss, DBAs should address three business issues:

➤ What is the minimum downtime an organization can tolerate?

➤ What is the maximum amount of data an organization can afford to lose?

➤ How critical is the data to the business?

After the costs of downtime and data loss have been determined, DBAs can direct their efforts toward maximizing database availability, minimizing data loss, and preventing system failure. Maximizing database availability can be accomplished using effective recovery techniques and procedures. Minimizing data loss can be achieved through effective backup methodologies. Failure can be prevented through enhanced understanding of backup and recovery structures and appropriate database configuration. As business needs change over time, an organization should regularly review its backup and recovery strategy to incorporate new or changed business needs.

Operational Considerations

Two issues affect operational needs for backup and recovery:

➤ Business needs

➤ Database volatility

Business Needs

Different types of businesses have different operational needs. An online catalog business, for instance, may require around-the-clock database availability. It must be continuously available 24 hours a day and seven days a week. Every second the database is not operational can lead to lost revenues and dissatisfied customers. If no downtime can be tolerated, *online (hot) backups*, in which the database is backed up while it is still online, should be considered. On the other hand, the database for a professional membership organization is less mission critical, and there are periods of time that the database could be shut down for maintenance operations. In this case, the DBA should consider *offline (cold) backups*, in which the database is shut down first and the database files backed up. Database backup and recovery configurations should be tailored to support different business operational needs.

Database Volatility

Database volatility concerns how often changes occur to the data and the structure of the database. Changes can be triggered from the following database operations:

➤ Inserting, updating, or deleting rows in existing tables

➤ Adding new tables

➤ Creating or dropping tablespaces

➤ Adding or renaming data files

➤ Adding, renaming, or dropping an online redo log group or member

Frequent backups are critical for any recovery approach. The frequency of backups should be based on how often changes occur to the data and the structure of the database. If the database sustains high update activity, database backup frequency should be proportionally high. On the other hand, a static database may be backed up less frequently. Highly volatile databases generally require more frequent backups than static read-only databases.

Technical Considerations

Effective use of system resources is the key to backup and recovery. The types of backups affect available system storage space. The two types of backups are typically referred to as physical or logical backups. The *physical backups* can be taken while the database is online (open) or offline (closed) and involve making physical copies of operating system files associated with the database. The *logical backups* are copies of data and structural definitions in a proprietary Oracle binary format other than the format of the physical database files. The logical backups are typically generated by the Oracle EXPORT utility and are used by the Oracle IMPORT utility. These utilities are covered in more detail in Chapter 13. Physical backups require greater storage space requirements than logical backups do. Logical backups may affect the load on system resources because they are performed while the database is online and accessible to other database users.

The amount of modification activity sustained by the database will affect how frequently backups are made. If frequent backups must be made, as for a 24×7 business, this will increase the load on system resources. If the data can be recreated easily or is available from an alternate source such as a flat file, less frequent backups are required and therefore have less impact on system resources. Different database configurations dictate the availability of the database and the types of backups that are performed. Each backup type has different needs for system resources.

A thorough understanding of the business, operational, and technical requirements will ensure an effective backup and recovery strategy that will protect the database from different types of failures and that will ensure high availability, minimal downtime, and complete data recovery.

Disaster Recovery Plans

As organizations deploy a greater number of mission-critical applications over distributed networks, the organizations become more vulnerable to potential disasters. A *disaster* is any event that renders an organization unable to provide critical business functions for some predetermined period of time. A disaster could be one of the following:

➤ Natural disaster (flood, fire, snowstorm, earthquake, and so on)

➤ Blackout

➤ Hardware failure

➤ Viruses

➤ Theft

➤ Key personnel departure/critical illness of essential staff

Disaster recovery is the ability to recover from a disaster and to resume business functions in a timely manner. Disaster recovery has gained importance in recent years due to the expanding role of computers and the increasing occurrences of various types of disasters.

A *disaster recovery plan* is the document that defines the resources, actions, tasks, and data required to manage the business recovery process in the event of a business interruption. The plan is designed to assist in restoring the business process following a catastrophic event by minimizing risk and optimizing recovery time. Many people don't bother creating disaster recovery plans because they believe their businesses are not at high risk for disaster. The World Trade Center and the Oklahoma Federal Building were not high-risk areas, but each was hit with events that crippled many businesses. Any disaster can affect the availability, integrity, and confidentiality of critical business resources and can leave an organization paralyzed.

A disaster recovery plan should include these four components:

➤ Data

➤ Equipment

➤ Facilities

➤ Personnel

Data

One of the cardinal rules in using computers is to back up your files regularly. Even the most reliable computer is apt to break down eventually. Backups should include data files in addition to complete system backups. It is also prudent to perform a backup before and after a major upgrade. The type of media used will depend on your needs. Common choices are tapes and CDs. Tapes support a large capacity and are reusable. CDs have lower storage capacity but are more durable and easier to use for partial restorations. To protect archive storage media from damage, you should acquire a sturdy fire and waterproof box. Keep one backup in an offsite storage facility that would allow you rapid access to your data. You will also need to have a reasonable schedule to regularly update the offsite data.

Equipment

Critical machines used by the organization should be documented. Vital information should include what the machine does, the vendor, and information about the central processing unit (CPU), hard drive, controller, type of power supply, serial number, operating system, and so on. Determine how long replacements will take to acquire and from whom you will acquire them. Depending on the organization's system availability, you may need to consider an alternate replacement system.

Facilities

Determine what processes you will have to go through if a building-wide disaster takes place. A timeline for safety inspection and restoration of data and power should be developed. Make sure the processes fit within your business' operational requirements. Your organization should also investigate alternate facilities in the case of total destruction.

Personnel

Personnel are the most important resource in an organization. How will the loss of key personnel, like the DBA, affect the business? During a disaster, knowledgeable personnel can save the company time and money. Key personnel should not be totally irreplaceable in the case of an emergency. Properly documented processes and cross-training for redundancy will not only minimize the effects of a disaster, but will also typically improve business processes. Educate everyone in the organization on the location and use of the disaster recovery plan so that everyone will be prepared to cope if disaster strikes.

Disaster recovery plans should be a key part of any system setup. The time and money spent to set up a plan is worth it in the long run. Testing the disaster recovery plan is as critical as the plan itself. An untested disaster recovery plan is of little or no value. Testing enables your organization to assess the effectiveness of a disaster recovery plan before a real disaster strikes.

Oracle Server Features for High Availability

Oracle Server has optional features—Oracle Parallel Server, Oracle Standby Database, and Oracle Fail Safe—that enable organizations to maintain high database availability.

The *Oracle Parallel Server (OPS) feature* consists of two or more database instances that share one physical database. The database's data files reside on a set of raw disks so that each database instance can access the same data files. If one of the database instances goes down, the surviving database instance can still access the data files and provide data access to users. Further detail can be found in the *Oracle8i Parallel Server Concepts* manual.

The *Oracle Automated Standby Database* is a replica of a production database. This replica database can be kept on-site or off-site. In the event of a catastrophic failure that renders the primary database unrecoverable, the standby database can be activated. The standby database is implemented on another server that has the same operating system (OS) version, OS patch level, and Oracle relational database management system (RDBMS) version as the primary database. Oracle standby databases are covered in more detail in Chapter 14.

The *Oracle Fail Safe feature* is available only on the Windows NT or Windows 2000 platform. This feature works with the Windows cluster technology to provide database failover capability. Only one database instance is operational at any given time. When the operational instance fails, the other instance activates. Further details can be found in the *Oracle Fail Safe Concepts and Administration* manual.

Testing a Backup and Recovery Strategy

To ensure the effectiveness of a backup and recovery strategy, a DBA should test the strategy in a dummy test environment before and after moving to a production environment. Testing offers numerous benefits:

➤ It ensures the integrity of backups.

➤ It ensures that the backup and recovery methods are sound.

➤ It ensures that the backup and recovery strategy meets ongoing business needs.

➤ It minimizes problems before they occur in a production environment.

➤ It helps the DBA staff maintain familiarity with backup and recovery procedures so that they can react quickly and effectively and so that errors are less likely to occur in a crisis situation.

➤ It enables streamlining of the overall backup and recovery process.

A test plan should be developed and executed in support of this testing effort. The purpose of a test plan is to define the test domain, test strategy, test exit and entrance criteria, and to test configurations to verify and validate functionality. When creating a test plan, you should aim to accomplish the following:

➤ Set test objectives.

➤ Describe items to be tested.

➤ Determine testing resources.

➤ Compose schedules.

➤ Design the test process and create a test case design specification.

➤ Define test cases and create scenarios.

➤ Create a test procedures specification.

➤ Evaluate scripts using walkthrough or inspection.

➤ Execute test cases.

➤ Record test results.

➤ Analyze test results.

➤ Generate management-level summary reports.

Upon successful execution of a backup and recovery test plan, the backup and recovery methodology can be promoted to the production environment.

Practice Questions

Question 1

What is the DBA's most important responsibility?

○ a. Keeping the database organized

○ b. Keeping up-to-date backups

○ c. Maximizing database availability for users

○ d. Preventing users from corrupting the database

The correct answer is c. The database is of no value to the organization if it is not available for use. Answers a, b, and d are responsibilities of the DBA, but not the most important responsibility.

Question 2

How will offline physical backups affect your database in comparison to online backups?

○ a. They will increase disk space requirements.

○ b. The backups will not be valid.

○ c. They will increase recovery time from a media failure.

○ d. They will increase the DBA staff's maintenance effort.

The correct answer is a. A physical backup copies each database file to the target backup location. The number of files involved in the copy operation can affect available disk space. Answer b is not correct because offline physical backups are valid backups unless testing indicates they are not valid. Answer c is incorrect because offline physical backups don't increase recovery time from a media failure. Answer d is incorrect because offline physical backups are easier to manage than online backups.

Question 3

> Your company has a relatively static database that is refreshed monthly. Recovery time is not an issue with the business users. Which backup approach should you follow?
>
> ○ a. Perform backups less frequently than a company with high data update activity.
>
> ○ b. Perform backups more frequently than a company with high data update activity.
>
> ○ c. Perform backups each time the database is changed.
>
> ○ d. Backups are not necessary because the data does not change frequently.

The correct answer is a. Depending on the required recovery time, a fairly static database will need less frequent backups than a highly volatile database. Answer b is incorrect because a static database does not require more frequent backups than a volatile database. Answer c is incorrect because a static database that is refreshed monthly does not require taking a backup each time the database is changed. Answer d is incorrect because backups are still necessary, but not as frequently as for a static database that doesn't change often.

Question 4

> What is the main objective for conducting a thorough analysis of the business, operational, and technical needs for backup and recovery?
>
> ○ a. To facilitate effective management decisionmaking by providing information that fosters understanding of all backup and recovery ramifications
>
> ○ b. To maintain optimal database configuration
>
> ○ c. To ensure the backup and recovery strategy is sound
>
> ○ d. To prepare a static backup and recovery strategy

The correct answer is a. A thorough analysis of the business, operational, and technical needs provides management with information so that an effective decision can be made and appropriate resources can be dedicated for the execution of the backup and recovery strategy. Answers b and c are incorrect because they are secondary objectives. Answer d is incorrect because a backup and recovery strategy should not be static. It should evolve with the business.

Question 5

How will minimizing recovery time affect the business?

○ a. It reduces the need to regularly update the backup and recovery strategy.

○ b. It reduces the cost of downtime.

○ c. It reduces the amount of data loss.

○ d. It helps to prevent failures from occurring.

The correct answer is b. A reduction in recovery time will shorten total downtime and thus reduce the costs associated with downtime. Answer a is incorrect because minimizing recovery time does not affect how often the backup and recovery strategy is updated. Answer c is incorrect because the amount of data loss depends on the availability of valid backups. Answer d is incorrect because appropriate database configuration, not minimization of recovery time, prevents failures from occurring.

Question 6

What are the components to develop in a disaster recovery plan? [Choose all correct answers]

❑ a. Data

❑ b. Equipment

❑ c. Facilities

❑ d. Personnel

❑ e. None of the above

The correct answers are a, b, c, and d. There are four components to develop in a disaster recovery plan: data, equipment, facilities, and personnel.

Question 7

> You are the newly hired DBA for a pizza delivery company. What should you do to ensure that the previous DBA's backup and recovery plan is valid?
>
> ○ a. Place 100 percent reliance on the documentation for the plan if it looks like it should work.
>
> ○ b. Throw away the previous DBA's plan and write your own from scratch.
>
> ○ c. Test the backup and recovery plan to make sure that a complete recovery is possible.
>
> ○ d. Make sure that the documentation is correct.

The correct answer is c. All backup and recovery plans should be tested to ensure their validity and effectiveness. Answer a is incorrect because a DBA should not rely solely on documentation to determine validity. Answer b is incorrect because only testing can validate the backup and recovery plan. Answer d is incorrect because testing is required before a DBA can be sure that the documentation is correct.

Question 8

> What is the main goal of backup and recovery?
>
> ○ a. Performing backups only when absolutely necessary
>
> ○ b. Backing up all files
>
> ○ c. Keeping backed up files offsite
>
> ○ d. Minimizing data loss and downtime

The correct answer is d. An effective backup and recovery strategy will minimize data loss and downtime. Answers a, b, and c are incorrect because they are supplementary goals.

Question 9

> What is the benefit of regularly testing the validity of your backup and re-covery strategy?
>
> ○ a. Testing reduces the likelihood of media failures.
>
> ○ b. Testing helps to identify business, operational, and technical needs that may have changed over time.
>
> ○ c. Testing is the only way to ensure optimal database configuration.
>
> ○ d. Testing helps management determine the costs associated with downtime.

The correct answer is b. Testing helps to assess the effectiveness of the backup and recovery strategy and to identify any new or changed requirements. Answer a is incorrect because testing does not affect the likelihood of media failures. Answer c is incorrect because testing is not the only way to ensure optimal database configuration. Answer d is incorrect because the costs associated with downtime depend on business, operational, and technical factors and not testing.

Question 10

> Which Oracle Server optional features support high availability database requirements? [Choose two]
>
> ❏ a. Automated Standby Database
>
> ❏ b. Parallel Query
>
> ❏ c. Parallel Server
>
> ❏ d. Snapshots

The correct answers are a and c. The Automated Standby Database and Parallel Server optional features enable organizations to maintain high availability of the databases. Answer b is incorrect because it enables almost all database operations to be parallelized, but it does not impact database availability. Answer d is incorrect because it provides support to dynamically replicate data between distributed databases, but it does not impact database availability.

Need to Know More?

 Arnold, Richard. *Disaster Recovery Plan.* John Wiley & Sons, New York, NY, 1993. ISBN 0-47155-696-3. This book contains a fully developed disaster recovery plan designed to minimize the effect of a disaster. It offers a methodology to create and test a recovery plan that will cover most contingencies.

 Loney, Kevin and Marlene Theriault. *Oracle8i DBA Handbook.* Oracle Press, Berkeley, CA, 1999. ISBN 0-07212-188-2. This comprehensive guide for DBAs includes general backup and recovery concepts.

 Velpuri, Rama. *Oracle8i Backup and Recovery Handbook.* Oracle Press, Berkeley, CA, 2000. ISBN 0-072-12717-1. This book provides information on how to maximize uptime and recover data without compromising mission critical systems. Actual corporate scenarios and case studies are included.

 http://technet.oracle.com. This site provides the best information on Oracle's products and technologies. You can also purchase the following manuals online:

Bauer, Mark. *Oracle8i Parallel Server Concepts Release 2.* Oracle Corporation, Redwood City, CA, 1999. Part No. A76968-01. This manual provides information on Oracle Parallel Server concepts. It describes parallel processing fundamentals, synchronization processing among instances, and how Oracle Parallel Server is implemented.

Dialeris, Connie. *Oracle8i Backup and Recovery Guide Release 2.* Oracle Corporation, Redwood City, CA, 1999. Part No. A76993-01. This manual is designed to help DBAs understand what backup and recovery is and how to perform backup, restore, and recovery procedures.

Oracle Fail Safe Concepts and Administration Release 2.0.5. Oracle Corporation, Redwood City, CA, 1997. Part No. A57521-01. This manual describes how to configure and manage Oracle Fail Safe.

 www.revealnet.com. This site from RevealNet provides Oracle administration reference software.

Oracle Recovery Structures and Processes

....

Terms you'll need to understand:

- ✓ Oracle database
- ✓ Oracle instance
- ✓ Database buffers
- ✓ Redo log buffers
- ✓ Shared pool
- ✓ Large pool
- ✓ Program Global Area
- ✓ System Global Area
- ✓ Background processes
- ✓ Online redo log
- ✓ Redo log group

- ✓ Log switch
- ✓ Archived redo log
- ✓ User process
- ✓ Server process
- ✓ Multiplexed control files
- ✓ Checkpoint
- ✓ Fast-Start Checkpointing
- ✓ Fast-Start Parallel Rollback
- ✓ Fast-Start On-Demand Rollback
- ✓ Multiplexed online redo logs

Techniques you'll need to master:

- ✓ Understanding architectural components for backup and recovery
- ✓ Understanding the importance of redo logs, checkpoints, and archives
- ✓ Understanding the file synchronization process during checkpoints

- ✓ Understanding the benefits of multiplexing control files and redo logs
- ✓ Understanding deferred transaction recovery

The backup and recovery functionality of Oracle relies on many components of the Oracle Server architecture. The pertinent architectural components include memory structures, background processes, and the physical database structure, as shown in Figure 3.1. A good understanding of key database structures and backup and recovery concepts will help you protect data against potential failure and will facilitate an effective recovery process in the event of a problem. Key database structures and backup and recovery concepts you should focus on include the following:

➤ Architectural components of the Oracle Server architecture

➤ Importance of redo logs, checkpoints, and archived redo logs

➤ File synchronization process during checkpoints

➤ Multiplexing control files and redo logs

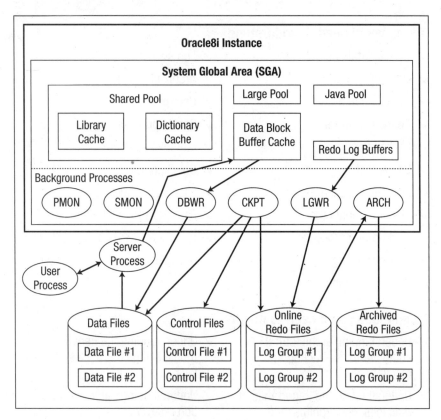

Figure 3.1 The basic Oracle8i architecture.

Architectural Components for Backup and Recovery

An Oracle server is comprised of an *Oracle instance* and an *Oracle database*. An Oracle instance is a set of memory structures and background processes that access a set of database files. An instance is not operationally effective without the user processes that submit information requests and the server processes that fulfill the requests. Multiple database instances could access a single database by using the Parallel Server option. An Oracle database is subdivided into a *physical* and a *logical* structure. This division enables the management of physical data storage to be independent from the access to logical storage structures. Oracle provides numerous data dictionary views to get information on the database and the instance.

Memory Structures

Oracle creates and uses memory structures to accomplish many tasks. One of the main tasks is to share program code and data among users. The *System Global Area (SGA)* is a shared memory region that holds data and control information for a database instance. Oracle allocates the SGA when an instance is started. The SGA is deallocated when the instance is shut down. The SGA is composed of the following memory elements:

➤ Database buffers

➤ Redo log buffers

➤ Shared pool

➤ Large pool

➤ Java pool

➤ Program Global Area (PGA)

Database Buffers

Database buffers in the SGA hold the most recently used data blocks that are read from the database files. *Database buffer cache* refers to the set of database buffers in an instance. The database buffer cache contains modified and unmodified blocks. Because the database buffer cache cannot hold all of the database's data blocks in memory concurrently, Oracle uses the least recently used (LRU) algorithm to manage the available memory space. The LRU algorithm allows the most frequently used data blocks to remain in memory, which reduces the amount of disk input/output (I/O) and improves database performance.

Redo Log Buffers

The *redo log buffer* of the SGA holds redo entries that contain the changes made to the database by database transactions. Redo entries are written to the online redo log files by the Log Writer (LGWR) process so that they can be used in the roll-forward operations if database recovery is needed. Oracle optimizes the writing of the redo log entries to the online redo log files using batch writes. The size in bytes of the redo log buffers is specified in the **LOG_BUFFER** parameter of the init.ora file.

Shared Pool

The *shared pool* holds the library cache, the data dictionary cache, and session information. The library cache contains information about statements that are issued against the database. The parse tree and the execution plan for the issued statement are kept in the library cache. The library cache fosters the sharing of commonly used *Structured Query Language (SQL)* statements. The data dictionary cache holds information about database objects that are stored in the data dictionary tables. Data dictionary information includes table descriptions, index descriptions, data file names, user account details, privileges, and the like. Oracle manages the data dictionary cache using the LRU algorithm. If the size of the data dictionary cache is inadequate, Oracle repetitively queries the data dictionary tables for information needed by the database. These repetitive queries are known as *recursive calls*. Recursive calls affect database performance because, if the data dictionary information is not found in memory due to limited cache size and cache management using the LRU algorithm, Oracle will need to get the same information repetitively. These additional queries require additional consumption of system resources, which will affect database performance. The size in bytes of the shared pool is specified in the **SHARED_POOL_SIZE** parameter of the init.ora file.

Large Pool

The *large pool* is an optional Oracle8i memory area. It is used to allocate sequential I/O buffers from shared memory. Recovery Manager uses the large pool for performing backup and restore operations. The large pool does not have an LRU list. If the **LARGE_POOL_SIZE** init.ora parameter is not set, Oracle attempts to allocate shared memory buffers from the shared pool in the SGA. If the **LARGE_POOL_SIZE** is set but is not adequate, the allocation fails, and the buffer requester responds as follows:

➤ The log archiving operation fails, and an error is returned.

➤ Recovery Manager writes a message to the alert file, and I/O slaves are not used for the operation.

The large pool has the following init.ora parameters:

➤ LARGE_POOL_SIZE—If unspecified, the large pool does not exist. If specified, the size of memory is allocated from the SGA.

➤ BACKUP_TAPE_IO_SLAVES—If set to TRUE, Recovery Manager's backup and restore operations will use an I/O slave to perform asynchronous I/O when reading and writing to tape. Asynchronous I/O is an Input/Output mechanism that allows processes to proceed with the next operation without having to wait after issuing a write. Asynchronous I/O improves system performance by minimizing the wasted idle time and Database Writer (DBWR) won't be blocked on each I/O. Asynchronous I/O capability is operating system specific.

➤ If not specified, synchronous tape I/O will be in effect. This parameter needs to be set when performing duplexed backups. Recovery Manager will configure as many slaves as required for the requested number of backup copies when this parameter is set.

➤ DBWR_IO_SLAVES—If nonzero, the numbers of I/O slaves used by the ARCn process, LGWR process, and Recovery Manager are set to four. I/O slaves are typically used to simulate asynchronous I/O on platforms that don't support it or that implement it inefficiently. I/O slaves can be used along with asynchronous I/O.

Java Pool
The *Java Pool* contains the shared parts of each Java class. This includes read-only memory, such as methods. The init.ora parameter **JAVA_POOL_SIZE** controls the size of the Java pool which defaults to 20MB. The more Java classes and code that are actually in use in your database instance, the more Java pool is required. For organizations that don't use the Java Virtual Machine (JVM) in the database, the **JAVA_POOL_SIZE** should be reduced to avoid wasted memory.

Program Global Area (PGA)
The PGA is a memory area reserved for a user process. The PGA memory is private to the user process and is not shareable. If the multi-threaded server configuration is in effect, part of the PGA may exist in the SGA. The multi-threaded server configuration allows multiple user processes to use the same server process, resulting in reduction of the overall database memory require-

ments. If the multi-threaded server configuration is used, the user session information is stored in the SGA as opposed to the PGA, and the size of the shared pool will need to be increased to accommodate the additional share memory requirements.

Background Processes

Oracle creates a set of background processes for each database instance. The number of background processes vary depending on the database's configuration. The processes are automatically managed by Oracle. The main background processes include the following:

➤ System Monitor (SMON)

➤ Process Monitor (PMON)

➤ Database Writer (DBWR)

➤ Log Writer (LGWR)

➤ Checkpoint (CKPT)

➤ Archiver (ARCH)

System Monitor—SMON

Upon starting the database, the *SMON process* performs instance recovery and will use the online redo log files when needed. Under the Parallel Server configuration, SMON of one instance can also perform instance recovery for other failed instances. SMON performs garbage collection by eliminating transactional items that are no longer needed by the system. In addition, SMON recovers temporary segments when they are not being used, and it coalesces contiguous free extents into larger free chunks.

Note: SMON coalesces free space only in tablespaces whose default PCTINCREASE storage value is nonzero.

Process Monitor—PMON

The *PMON background process* performs process recovery for failed user processes. It frees up the resources that the failed process was holding. PMON wakes up periodically to check on dispatcher and server processes and restarts them as needed.

Database Writer—DBWR

The *DBWR process* manages the database buffer cache. It writes changed blocks (dirty buffers) from the database buffer cache to the data files in batch. When the database checkpoint event (discussed in the "Checkpoint" section later in this chapter) occurs, the DBWR process performs the synchronization of the database buffer cache and the data files. Multiple DBWR processes can be configured to run concurrently for systems that sustain high data modification rates. The init.ora parameter **DB_WRITER_PROCESSES** can be used to specify the number of DBWR processes. Using multiple DBWR processes improves write performance and reduces contention for systems that are heavily modified. When using multiple DBWR processes, the operating system names of the processes should follow this convention: DBWn, DBWn+1, DBWn+2, and so on. If you run three DBWR processes, for instance, the names could be DBW0, DBW1, and DBW2. The maximum number of DBWR processes is 10.

Log Writer—LGWR

The *LGWR process* writes the redo log entries from the redo log buffer to the online redo log files. LGWR performs writes in batches and writes under the following conditions: (a) when a transaction commits; (b) when the redo log is one-third full; (c) when the three seconds timeout occurs; (d) before DBWR performs its write operation of modified blocks associated with this redo batch; and (e) when the redo log file to be written has been archived when the database is in ARCHIVELOG mode. LGWR writes are triggered when transactions commit, and the log buffer fills up. The online redo log files are sequentially written. If the online redo log files are mirrored, LGWR writes to the mirrored sets of logs simultaneously.

Checkpoint—CKPT

The *CKPT process* is responsible for notifying DBWn at checkpoints so that all modified data blocks in the SGA from the last checkpoint are written out to the data files. The CKPT process is always enabled, and it records the most recent checkpoint in the data file headers and the control file upon checkpoint completion.

Archiver—ARCH

The *archiver* is an optional process. The archiver copies the online redo log files to a designated archival destination. This process is critical in the backup and recovery of a database in ARCHIVELOG mode where 24×7 availability needs to be maintained.

The archiver process is triggered when a log switch occurs. When a database is run in ARCHIVELOG mode, the database makes a copy of each redo log file before overwriting it. When using the archiver, contention may be experienced on the redo log disk during heavy transaction processing because LGWR is trying to write to one redo log file while ARCH is trying to read from another. Placing redo log groups on different disks can resolve this issue. If the archive log destination disk is full, the database freezes until free space is available for the archived redo log files. The init.ora parameter **LOG_ARCHIVE_DEST** can be set to specify the archival destination location.

User Processes

A *user process* is created when a tool, such as SQL*Plus, Oracle Forms, and the like, is invoked by the user. User process can exist on the client machine or the server machine, and they provide the interface for database users to interact with the database.

Server Processes

Oracle creates *server processes* to receive requests from the user processes and to carry out the requests. For example, if a user requests data that is not currently in the database buffer cache of the SGA, the associated server process will read the pertinent data blocks from the data files into the SGA. When a valid database connection is established with a database that is not using the multi-threaded server option, a server process is created on the machine holding the instance.

Physical Database Structure

An Oracle database's physical structure consists of the physical operating system files. An Oracle instance comprises three main file types: one or more control files, one or more data files, and two or more redo log files. These files must be considered when you're creating the backup strategy.

Control Files

Control files are binary files used by the Oracle server to store its configuration information. Control files record the physical structure and state of the database while preserving internal consistency and integrity. Additionally, control files guide recovery operations. The following information exists within a control file:

➤ The name of the database

➤ The name and location of all the database files

➤ The name and location of all the redo log files

➤ The timestamp of database creation

➤ Checkpoint synchronization information

➤ Log sequence information

➤ Redo thread information

➤ Auxiliary backup information when Recovery Manager is used

Note: An Oracle instance typically uses only one redo thread unless the parallel option is in effect.

Control files are required to mount, open, and maintain the database. These files are critical to the database, so multiple copies are typically stored online. Control files should be backed up every time structural changes are made to the database.

 Control files are typically stored on different physical disks to minimize the potential loss due to disk failures. Oracle recommends a minimum of two control files on different disks.

The names of the database's control files are specified in the **CONTROL_FILES** init.ora parameter.

Data Files

Data files are the backbone of the database instance. They are the physical files that make up the tablespaces—the logical structures in which tables, indexes, and the like exist. Each tablespace consists of one or more separate physical data files. Each Oracle database has one or more physical data files, but a data file can be associated with only one database.

Every database instance must contain at least one data file for the **SYSTEM** tablespace. After a data file has been added to a tablespace, the data file cannot be removed from the tablespace or associated with any other tablespace. Data files can be resized after they are created, and they can also be set to extend automatically when the database runs out of space.

A database's data files contain all the data for the database. The data may be in one of two states: committed or uncommitted. The data files contain only committed data when the Normal, Immediate, or Tranactional option is exercised for a clean instance shutdown. During a clean instance shutdown, all uncommitted data is rolled back, and a database checkpoint event is triggered to force all committed data to disk. During a running instance, data files can contain uncommitted data when data in the memory cache has been modified, but not committed, and has been forced to disk when more space is needed in the memory cache. Redo logs and rollback segments may be used to synchronize the data files during the recovery process from a failure condition.

Redo Log Files

The *redo log files* contain all changes made to the database. The database changes that generate redo entries in the redo log files may be triggered by the following sample database transactions:

➤ INSERT

➤ UPDATE

➤ DELETE

➤ CREATE TABLE

➤ DROP TABLE

➤ CREATE INDEX

➤ DROP INDEX

Redo log files include online redo logs and archived redo logs. Online redo logs record redo log entries as they occur. Redo log entries are used to reconstruct all changes made to the database. Redo log entries are stored in the redo log buffer of the SGA of an Oracle instance. Whenever a transaction is committed, the LGWR background process writes the committed transaction's redo log entries from the redo log buffer to the current online redo log file. Redo log entries can also be written to an online redo log file when the redo log buffers are full. Every Oracle database instance must contain at least two online redo log files. One of the required online redo log files must be available for writing. If a member of a redo log group is unavailable for writing, messages are written to the LGWR trace file and to the alert file. You can issue the **ALTER DATA-BASE ADD LOGFILE** command to create additional log file groups. You can issue the **ALTER DATABASE DROP LOGFILE** command to drop an online redo log group.

Figure 3.2 illustrates the online redo log writing process. The LGWR process writes to the online redo log files in a circular fashion. The LGWR process starts by writing to the current online redo log file. When the current online redo log file is filled, the LGWR process starts writing to the next available online redo log file. A log switch occurs when LGWR stops writing to one redo log and begins writing to another. At a log switch, the current redo log group is assigned a log sequence number that identifies the information stored in that redo log group and is also used for synchronization. Log sequence numbers are unique throughout the logical life of a database until they are explicitly reset. When the last available redo log file is filled, the LGWR process returns to the first online redo log file and overwrites the content. A database administrator (DBA) can manually force a log switch using the **ALTER SYSTEM SWITCH LOGFILE** command.

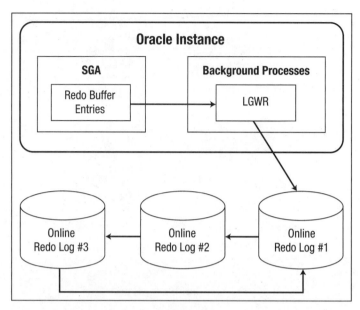

Figure 3.2   The online redo log writing process.

Note: Each redo log entry is assigned a System Change Number (SCN) to uniquely identify the committed transactions.

 The contents of an online redo log file should never be modified.

The mode in which the database runs dictates the existence of archived redo logs. An archived redo log is essentially a copy of its online redo log group. Archived logs are essential in the backup and recovery process because, along with a valid database backup, they guarantee that all committed data can be recovered in the event of a failure.

Oracle provides numerous data dictionary views to get information on the redo log files:

➤ **V$LOG**—Provides information on the number of members in each log group, the group number, log sequence number, size of the group, number of mirrors, status (CURRENT or INACTIVE), checkpoint change numbers, and other details:

```
SQL> desc V$LOG
 Name                              Null?    Type
 ----                              -----    ----
 GROUP#                                     NUMBER
 THREAD#                                    NUMBER
 SEQUENCE#                                  NUMBER
 BYTES                                      NUMBER
 MEMBERS                                    NUMBER
 ARCHIVED                                   VARCHAR2(3)
 STATUS                                     VARCHAR2(16)
 FIRST_CHANGE#                              NUMBER
 FIRST_TIME                                 DATE
```

➤ **V$LOGFILE**—Provides information on the names, status (STALE or IN-VALID), and group of each log file member:

```
SQL> desc V$LOGFILE
 Name                              Null?    Type
 ----                              -----    ----
 GROUP#                                     NUMBER
 STATUS                                     VARCHAR2(7)
 MEMBER                                     VARCHAR2(513)
```

➤ **V$LOG_HISTORY**—Provides information on log history from the control file:

```
SQL> desc V$LOG_HISTORY
 Name                              Null?    Type
 ----                              -----    ----
 RECID                                      NUMBER
 STAMP                                      NUMBER
 THREAD#                                    NUMBER
 SEQUENCE#                                  NUMBER
 FIRST_CHANGE#                              NUMBER
 FIRST_TIME                                 DATE
 NEXT_CHANGE#                               NUMBER
```

➤ **V$ARCHIVE_DEST**—Provides information on the location of the archived redo log destinations, status, and whether archiving success must be achieved:

```
SQL> desc V$ARCHIVE_DEST
Name                              Null?     Type
----                              -----     ----
ARCMODE                                     VARCHAR2(12)
STATUS                                      VARCHAR2(8)
DESTINATION                                 VARCHAR2(256)
```

Logical Database Structure

The *logical database structure* is comprised of two main constructs:

➤ One or more tablespaces

➤ Schema objects

Tablespaces

A *tablespace* is a logical storage structure that contains one or more data files. The logical storage structures, including tablespaces, segments, and extents, affect how the physical space is used. Tablespaces should be created judiciously, with the backup and recovery strategy kept in mind. The following are some guidelines for creating tablespaces:

➤ System and user data should be stored separately under different tablespaces to simplify backup and recovery operations.

➤ Temporary segments should exist in a dedicated tablespace so that they can be recreated instead of recovered if the tablespace is lost. Temporary segments are used by Oracle for temporary storage, such as sorting result sets. Temporary segments don't contain any business data that is expected to persist beyond the duration of a user's session. In the practical DBA world, temporary segments are typically recreated instead of recovered.

➤ Index data should be stored in a dedicated tablespace so that it can be recreated rather than recovered.

➤ Data subject to frequent changes should be stored in a dedicated tablespace so that backups can be performed more frequently, which results in reduced recovery time.

➤ A table or index can be divided into partitions based on a range of key values. Each partition can be operated on independently and stored in its own tablespace. For example, a table partition can be backed up and recovered without affecting the other partitions.

➤ Read-only data should be stored in a dedicated tablespace to reduce overall backup time because a backup is needed only when the tablespace is made read-only. When read-only data is centralized in a dedicated tablespace and the tablespace is designated as **READONLY**, a backup of this tablespace will be taken. Subsequent backups are not needed for the **READONLY** tablespace because the data doesn't change, and the initial tablespace backup can be used to recover the read-only data. When read-only data is interspersed with data subject to change in a tablespace, the read-only data is backed up each time that the tablespace is backed up. Centralizing read-only data in a dedicated tablespace reduces overall backup time because the read-only data is backed up less frequently.

➤ Rollback segments should exist in a dedicated tablespace to simplify backup and recovery operations.

Schema Objects

A *schema* is a set of database objects that inherits the name of its creator. Schema objects are logical structures, such as tables, views, indexes, sequences, synonyms, stored procedures, and so on.

 You will need to be familiar with the following **V$** views: **V$SGA**, **V$INSTANCE**, **V$PROCESS**, **V$BGPROCESS**, **V$DATABASE**, **V$DATAFILE**, and **V$CONTROLFILE**. Familiarize yourself with these views by querying the data they contain.

Dynamic Performance Views

Oracle provides numerous data dictionary views to get information on the database and instance:

➤ **V$SGA**—Provides information on the memory sizes for the shared pool, log buffer, data buffer cache, and fixed memory sizes:

```
SQL> desc V$SGA
   Name                              Null?    Type
   ----                              -----    ----
   NAME                                       VARCHAR2(20)
   VALUE                                      NUMBER
```

➤ **V$INSTANCE**—Provides information on the status of the instance. Information available includes the following: instance name, instance mode, startup time, and host name:

```
SQL> desc V$INSTANCE
 Name                             Null?      Type
 ----                             -----      ----
 INSTANCE_NUMBER                             NUMBER
 INSTANCE_NAME                               VARCHAR2(16)
 HOST_NAME                                   VARCHAR2(64)
 VERSION                                     VARCHAR2(17)
 STARTUP_TIME                                DATE
 STATUS                                      VARCHAR2(7)
 PARALLEL                                    VARCHAR2(3)
 THREAD#                                     NUMBER
 ARCHIVER                                    VARCHAR2(7)
 LOG_SWITCH_WAIT                             VARCHAR2(11)
 LOGINS                                      VARCHAR2(10)
 SHUTDOWN_PENDING                            VARCHAR2(3)
```

➤ **V$PROCESS**—Provides information on the background and server processes for the instance:

```
SQL> desc V$PROCESS
 Name                             Null?      Type
 ----                             -----      ----
 ADDR                                        RAW(4)
 PID                                         NUMBER
 SPID                                        VARCHAR2(9)
 USERNAME                                    VARCHAR2(15)
 SERIAL#                                     NUMBER
 TERMINAL                                    VARCHAR2(16)
 PROGRAM                                     VARCHAR2(64)
 BACKGROUND                                  VARCHAR2(1)
 LATCHWAIT                                   VARCHAR2(8)
 LATCHSPIN                                   VARCHAR2(8)
```

➤ **V$BGPROCESS**—Provides information on the background processes for the instance:

```
SQL> desc V$BGPROCESS
 Name                             Null?      Type
 ----                             -----      ----
 PADDR                                       RAW(8)
 NAME                                        VARCHAR2(5)
 DESCRIPTION                                 VARCHAR2(64)
 ERROR                                       NUMBER
```

➤ **V$DATABASE**—Provides database status and recovery information. Information available includes the unique database identifier, the database name, the database creation date, the control file creation date and time, the last database checkpoint, and other details:

```
SQL> desc V$DATABASE
 Name                             Null?     Type
 ----                             -----     ----
 DBID                                       NUMBER
 NAME                                       VARCHAR2(9)
 CREATED                                    DATE
 RESETLOGS_CHANGE#                          NUMBER
 RESETLOGS_TIME                             DATE
 PRIOR_RESETLOGS_CHANGE#                    NUMBER
 PRIOR_RESETLOGS_TIME                       DATE
 LOG_MODE                                   VARCHAR2(12)
 CHECKPOINT_CHANGE#                         NUMBER
 ARCHIVE_CHANGE#                            NUMBER
 CONTROLFILE_TYPE                           VARCHAR2(7)
 CONTROLFILE_CREATED                        DATE
 CONTROLFILE_SEQUENCE#                      NUMBER
 CONTROLFILE_CHANGE#                        NUMBER
 CONTROLFILE_TIME                           DATE
 OPEN_RESETLOGS                             VARCHAR2(11)
 VERSION_TIME                               DATE
```

➤ **V$DATAFILE**—Provides the names and locations of the data files that comprise the database. Information available includes file sequence number, file name, file size, creation date, online or offline status, read-write state, last data file checkpoint, and other details:

```
SQL> desc V$DATAFILE
 Name                             Null?     Type
 ----                             -----     ----
 FILE#                                      NUMBER
 CREATION_CHANGE#                           NUMBER
 CREATION_TIME                              DATE
 TS#                                        NUMBER
 RFILE#                                     NUMBER
 STATUS                                     VARCHAR2(7)
 ENABLED                                    VARCHAR2(10)
 CHECKPOINT_CHANGE#                         NUMBER
 CHECKPOINT_TIME                            DATE
```

```
UNRECOVERABLE_CHANGE#                    NUMBER
UNRECOVERABLE_TIME                       DATE
LAST_CHANGE#                             NUMBER
LAST_TIME                                DATE
OFFLINE_CHANGE#                          NUMBER
ONLINE_CHANGE#                           NUMBER
ONLINE_TIME                              DATE
BYTES                                    NUMBER
BLOCKS                                   NUMBER
CREATE_BYTES                             NUMBER
BLOCK_SIZE                               NUMBER
NAME                                     VARCHAR2(513)
```

➤ **V$CONTROLFILE**—Provides the name and status of control files:

```
SQL> desc V$CONTROLFILE
Name                         Null?    Type
----                         -----    ----
STATUS                                VARCHAR2(7)
NAME                                  VARCHAR2(513)
```

Importance of Redo Logs, Checkpoints, and Archives

Online redo log group archiving is performed by either the ARCH background process when automatic archiving is started or by a user process that issues SQL statements to archive the online redo log group manually. The ARCH process archives a redo log group after the group becomes inactive and the log switch to the next online redo log group has completed. At this point, a record is created in the database's control file identifying the archived redo log file. The group of online redo log files being archived cannot be reused and written to by the LGWR process until the ARCH process has concluded and released a lock on the redo log files. This ARCH locking process guarantees that the LGWR process does not accidentally overwrite a redo log file that needs to be archived. When the ARCH process has finished archiving the redo log files, a second record is written to the database's control file identifying the success of the archiving process.

DBAs can start multiple archiver processes and can specify multiple archive destinations for an instance. DBAs can specify the destinations as local or remote and required or desirable. If a remote destination is specified, the remote file server (RFS) process will be started at the remote site to receive the file and to store it at the specified location.

The ARCH process uses the **LOG_ARCHIVE_DEST_n** parameter to specify one or more destinations of the archived redo log files. The following sample code illustrates the **LOG_ARCHIVE_DEST_1** initialization parameter setting:

```
LOG_ARCHIVE_DEST_1
  = "LOCATION=/u01/oradata/DBSALES/arch/dest1 MANDATORY"
```

You can issue the following sample SQL statements to add a second archive log destination:

```
SQL> ALTER SYSTEM SET LOG_ARCHIVE_DEST_2 = "LOCATION=/u02/oradata/
DBSALES/arch/dest2 OPTIONAL REOPEN=60"
SQL> ALTER SYSTEM ARCHIVE LOG STOP;
System altered.
SQL> ALTER SYSTEM ARCHIVE LOG START;
System altered.
```

This destination is usually a storage device separate from the Oracle database. The ARCH process can write out multiple copies of an online redo log group—the multiple archive log destination feature. A missing archived redo log file renders all subsequent archived redo log files useless. The archiving of online redo logs has two key advantages during backup:

➤ A database backup, together with online and archived redo log files, guarantees that all committed transactions can be recovered in the event of an operating system or disk failure.

➤ A backup taken while the database is open and in normal use can be used if an archived redo log is kept permanently.

File Synchronization Process during Checkpoints

During a checkpoint, the DBWR process writes all modified buffers in the database buffer cache to disk, and LGWR writes all log buffer entries to disk if there is redo in the log buffer associated with that particular checkpoint. The checkpoint event ensures that all modified data blocks since the last checkpoint have been written to disk and that all entries can be committed or rolled back, depending on the commit status of the transaction. The checkpoint event synchronizes the write operations of DBWR and LGWR. Checkpoints occur during the following database events:

➤ When an online redo log file fills (known as a log switch)

➤ When a specified number of seconds passed between the most recent redo entry and the checkpoint position (specified in the **LOG_CHECKPOINT_ TIMEOUT** init.ora parameter)

➤ When a specified number of operating system (OS) blocks have been written to the redo log files between the most recent redo entry and the checkpoint position (specified in the **LOG_CHECKPOINT_INTERVAL** init.ora parameter)

➤ When manually instructed by a DBA using the **ALTER SYSTEM CHECK-POINT** command

➤ When a tablespace is taken offline

➤ When an online backup is initiated

➤ When Fast-Start Checkpointing is in effect and the DBWR writes buffers more frequently to meet a DBA-specified instance or crash recovery time

➤ When the instance shuts down using the Normal or Immediate option

At each checkpoint event, the checkpoint number is updated in every database file header and in the control file by the CKPT process. The checkpoint number serves as a synchronization indicator for the data, redo, and control files. The database is in a consistent state if all the database files contain the same checkpoint number. During database startup, the control file is used to confirm that all files are at the same checkpoint number. Any discrepancy in the checkpoint numbers in the file headers leads to failure and requires recovery operations.

Checkpoints minimize the time spent in performing instance recovery because, at every checkpoint, all modified data is written to disk, and the redo log entries before the last checkpoint are no longer needed during the roll-forward process of instance recovery. The init.ora parameter **LOG_CHECKPOINTS_ TO_ ALERT** can be specified to log the checkpoints to the alert file and to determine if the target checkpoint frequency has been achieved.

Fast-Start Checkpointing

Pre-Oracle8i, the DBA had a hard time controlling instance recovery time because it was dependent on the transaction load at the time of failure. In Oracle8i, *Fast-Start Checkpointing* enables DBAs to control recovery performance during instance or crash recovery. However, it doesn't improve the performance of media recovery.

The time required for crash or instance recovery is proportional to the number of data blocks that need to be read or written during the roll-forward phase. You can specify the maximum number of data blocks that will need to be processed during the roll-forward phase. Oracle8i then adjusts the checkpoint write rate accordingly. Because instance failure recovery time is mostly dependent on data file I/O, Fast-Start Checkpointing enables DBAs to establish service-level agreements with business users.

The dynamic initialization parameter **FAST_START_IO_TARGET** can be set to limit the number of data blocks that need to be read for instance or crash recovery. After this parameter is set, Oracle8i will examine the redo log blocks and will calculate the target redo blocks. It will then force DBWR to write dirty buffers to advance the checkpoint position to meet the calculated target redo blocks. **FAST_START_IO_TARGET** is used in conjunction with **LOG_CHECKPOINT_INTERVAL** and **LOG_CHECKPOINT_TIMEOUT** to derive the optimal checkpoints.

Multiplexing Control Files and Redo Logs

To protect against single-point media failures, Oracle provides the capability to multiplex or mirror an instance's online redo logs and control files. When multiplexing online redo log files, the LGWR process simultaneously writes the same redo log information to multiple identically sized online redo log files. Figure 3.3 illustrates this process. The prerequisites for multiplexing online redo log files are as follows:

➤ Each group should have at least two redo log members per group, with each member on a different disk.

➤ All members of a group should hold identical information and should be the same size.

➤ Each group should have the same number of members.

➤ Group members should be updated concurrently.

You can change the locations of the online redo log files by renaming the online redo log files. Specifically, perform the following steps:

1. Issue the following SQL command to initiate a log switch:

```
ALTER SYSTEM SWITCH LOG FILE;
```

2. Copy the redo log file from the source location to the target location using an OS copy utility (**cp** in Unix or **copy** in Windows NT).

3. Issue the **ALTER DATABASE RENAME FILE** command to make the change in the control files.

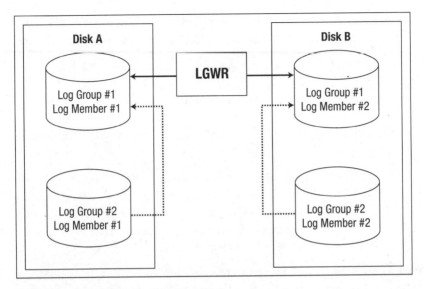

Figure 3.3 The multiplexing of online redo logs.

You can use the **ALTER DATABASE ADD LOGFILE MEMBER TO** command to add new members to existing redo log file groups. Optionally, you may issue the **ALTER DATABASE DROP LOGFILE MEMBER** command to drop an online redo log member if it becomes Invalid.

Oracle also supports multiplexing of control files. This functionality protects the control files against a single point of failure. An instance cannot start with a corrupted control file. The secondary control file ensures the Oracle instance always has a valid and current control file available in case the primary control file gets corrupted. The recommended configuration consists of at least two control files on different disks.

Deferred Transaction Recovery

Instance recovery restores a database to a consistent state prior to instance failure. The two main phases of instance recovery are roll forward (redo) and rollback (undo). The roll-forward phase applies all changes recorded in the log file to the data blocks. The rollback phase removes the uncommitted data from the files. *Deferred Transaction Rollback*, which was first introduced in Oracle 7.3.1, enables a database to be opened as soon as the roll-forward phase has been completed. The rollback phase is performed under the following conditions:

1. The SMON process periodically scans the rollback segments and rolls back dead transactions.

2. The user process, upon encountering row lock(s) held by a dead transaction, will recover the transaction to free up the row lock(s) so that processing can continue.

Deferred rollback could be time consuming when parallel transactions are terminated abnormally becauseof the serial nature of the rollback operation. The Fast-Start Parallel Rollback feature of Oracle8i allows SMON to use parallel query slaves to complete the rollback activity. Parallel rollback is automatically in effect when SMON determines that the dead transaction had generated 100 or more rollback blocks.

Fast-Start Parallel Rollback can be set using the dynamic initialization parameter **FAST_START_PARALLEL_ROLLBACK**. The valid values are **FALSE**, **LOW**, or **HIGH**. **FALSE** specifies no parallel recovery servers. **LOW** specifies the 2***CPU_COUNT** number of parallel recovery servers. **HIGH** specifies the 4***CPU_COUNT** number of parallel recovery servers.

Oracle8i provides the following dynamic performance views to monitor the progress of Fast-Start Parallel Rollback and the applicable rollback processes:

➤ **V$FAST_START_SERVERS**—Provides information about the parallel query slave processes. The **STATE** attribute can be **RECOVERING** or **IDLE**:

```
SQL> desc V$FAST_START_SERVERS
 Name                              Null?     Type
 ----                              -----     ----
 STATE                                       VARCHAR2(11)
 UNDOBLOCKSDONE                              NUMBER
 PID                                         NUMBER
```

➤ **V$FAST_START_TRANSACTIONS**—Provides information on the status of Fast-Start Parallel Rollback. The USN (undo segment number) attribute indicates from which rollback segment the rollback is taking place. The **UNDOBLKSDONE** and **UNDOBLKSTOTAL** indicate the amount of rollback completed and the total amount of rollback to be done:

```
SQL> desc V$FAST_START_TRANSACTIONS
 Name                              Null?     Type
 ----                              -----     ----
 USN                                         NUMBER
 SLT                                         NUMBER
 SEQ                                         NUMBER
 STATE                                       VARCHAR2(16)
 UNDOBLOCKSDONE                              NUMBER
 UNDOBLOCKSTOTAL                             NUMBER
```

```
PID                              NUMBER
CPUTIME                          NUMBER
PARENTUSN                        NUMBER
PARENTSLT                        NUMBER
PARENTSEQ                        NUMBER
```

Fast-Start Parallel Rollback improves the performance of transaction rollbacks done by SMON. This feature does not mitigate the problem of a user transaction having to wait for resources held by a dead transaction that SMON has not yet cleaned up. In On-Demand Parallel Rollback, the server process will perform the following actions when it encounters data to be rolled back: (a) roll back the block the user transaction is trying to access and (b) passes the remaining block recovery to SMON, which may use parallel operations.

Practice Questions

Question 1

Which of the following architectural components is made up of background processes and memory buffers?

○ a. The SGA

○ b. The Oracle instance

○ c. The Oracle database

○ d. The PGA

The correct answer is b. An Oracle instance is comprised of memory structures and background processes. Answer a is incorrect because the SGA is the shared memory area that contains memory buffers. Answer c is incorrect because the Oracle database is made up of the physical database files and the logical storage structures. Answer d is incorrect because the PGA is a memory area reserved for a user process.

Question 2

What three main types of database files constitute an Oracle database?

○ a. Data files, redo log files, and alert log file

○ b. Data files, parameter file, and control file

○ c. Data files, redo log files, and parameter file

○ d. Data files, redo log files, and control file

The correct answer is d. An Oracle database is composed of one or more control files, one or more data files, and two or more redo log files. Answers a, b, and c are incorrect because an alert log file or a parameter file are supplementary files in an Oracle database.

Question 3

The database initialization parameter file sets the characteristics of which Oracle architectural component? [Choose three]

❑ a. Background processes

❑ b. Oracle instance

❑ c. SGA

❑ d. Oracle database

The correct answers are a, b, and c. DBAs can use database initialization parameters to set the characteristics of background processes, such as designate the archival directory location. DBAs can use the initialization parameters to set instance-wide characteristics, such as the default date format. DBAs can also use database initialization parameters to adjust memory structure settings in the SGA; for example, they can set the number of database buffers in memory, how much space is initially allocated for a context area when it is created, the maximum number of database users, and so on. Answer d is incorrect because the database initialization parameters cannot be used to set the physical and logical storage characteristics of the Oracle database.

Question 4

Which SGA component contains copies of data blocks read from disk?

○ a. Shared pool

○ b. Large pool

○ c. Database buffer cache

○ d. Redo log buffer

The correct answer is c. When user-requested data is not found in the database buffer cache of the SGA, an associated server process will read the pertinent data blocks from the data files into the database buffer cache. Answer a is incorrect because the shared pool holds the library cache and the data dictionary cache. Answer b is incorrect because the large pool is used to allocate sequential I/O buffers from shared memory. Answer d is incorrect because the redo log buffers hold redo entries that contain the changes made to the database by database transactions.

Question 5

> Which background process is responsible for freeing resources held up by a failed user process?
>
> ○ a. SMON
>
> ○ b. PMON
>
> ○ c. CKPT
>
> ○ d. ARCH

The correct answer is b. The PMON process performs process recovery for failed user processes. It frees the resources that the failed process was holding up. Answer a is incorrect because the SMON process performs instance recovery and free space coalescing. Answer c is incorrect because the CKPT process is responsible for notifying the DBWn at checkpoints so that all modified data blocks in the SGA from the last checkpoint are written out to the data files. Answer d is incorrect because the ARCH process is responsible for copying the online redo log files to a designated archival destination.

Question 6

> Which five background processes will cause the instance to fail if one of them fails? [Choose five]
>
> ❑ a. DBWR
>
> ❑ b. LGWR
>
> ❑ c. CKPT
>
> ❑ d. SMON
>
> ❑ e. ARCH
>
> ❑ f. PMON

The correct answers are a, b, c, d, and f. On instance startup, the background processes are started. If DBWR, LGWR, CKPT, SMON, or PMON processes fail, the instance will fail to start. Answer e is incorrect because a failed ARCH process does not cause the instance to fail.

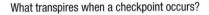

Question 7

> What transpires when a checkpoint occurs?
>
> O a. SMON coalesces contiguous free extents into larger free chunks.
>
> O b. DBWR writes all modified data blocks in the database buffer cache to disk to advance the checkpoint position far enough to meet recovery considerations.
>
> O c. PMON frees resources held by failed user processes.
>
> O d. LGWR writes all modified data blocks in the database buffer cache to disk.

The correct answer is b. During a checkpoint event, the DBWR process writes all modified data blocks in the database buffer cache of the SGA to the database files to advance the checkpoint position far enough to meet recovery considerations, and the LGWR process writes all redo log entries in the log buffer to disk. Answers a and c are incorrect because they are triggered independent of a checkpoint. Answer d is incorrect because the LGWR process writes the redo log entries from the redo log buffer to the online redo log files.

Question 8

> During which of these events is a checkpoint signaled?
>
> ○ a. When a user commits a transaction
>
> ○ b. When the **SHUTDOWN ABORT** command is issued by the DBA
>
> ○ c. When the DBA adds a new data file
>
> ○ d. When a log switch is needed

The correct answer is d. Checkpoints occur during the following database events:

➤ When an online redo log file fills (known as a log switch)

➤ When a specified number of seconds passed between the most recent redo entry and the checkpoint position (specified in the **LOG_CHECKPOINT_ TIMEOUT** init.ora parameter)

➤ When a specified number of OS blocks have been written to the redo log files between the most recent redo entry and the checkpoint position (specified in the **LOG_CHECKPOINT_INTERVAL** init.ora parameter)

➤ When manually instructed by a DBA using the **ALTER SYSTEM CHECK-POINT** command

➤ When a tablespace is taken offline

➤ When an online backup is initiated

➤ When the instance shuts down using the Normal or Immediate option

Answers a, b, and c are incorrect because they don't trigger a checkpoint.

Question 9

> Which of these architectural components is found only for a database that takes online backups?
>
> ○ a. Archived redo log files
>
> ○ b. Redo log files
>
> ○ c. Data files
>
> ○ d. Control files

The correct answer is a. When a database is running in ARCHIVELOG mode, online backups can be made. Answers b, c, and d are incorrect because online backups can be made only when the database is archiving redo log files.

Question 10

> Which background process is responsible for performing the roll-forward phase during instance recovery?
>
> ○ a. LGWR
>
> ○ b. PMON
>
> ○ c. DBWn
>
> ○ d. SMON

The correct answer is d. SMON performs the roll-forward phase during instance recovery. All committed and uncommitted changes recorded in the log files are applied to the data files. Answers a, b, and c are incorrect because they have no role during the roll-forward phase of instance recovery.

Need to Know More?

 Loney, Kevin and Marlene Theriault. *Oracle8i DBA Handbook*. Oracle Press, Berkeley, CA, 1999. ISBN 0-07212-188-2. This comprehensive guide for DBAs includes general backup and recovery concepts.

 Velpuri, Rama. *Oracle8i Backup and Recovery Handbook*. Oracle Press, Berkeley, CA, 2000. ISBN 0-072-12717-1. This book provides information on how to maximize uptime and recover data without compromising mission critical systems. Actual corporate scenarios and case studies are included.

 http://technet.oracle.com. This site provides the best information on Oracle's products and technologies. You can also purchase the following manuals online:

Dialeris, Connie. *Oracle8i Backup and Recovery Guide Release 2*. Oracle Corporation, Redwood City, CA, 1999. Part No. A76993-01. This manual provides guidance on data protection techniques and offers strategies for data storage, backup, and restore for Oracle 8i.

Leverenz, Lefty. *Oracle8i Concepts Release 2*. Oracle Corporation, Redwood City, CA, 1999. Part No. A76965-01. This manual describes all features of the Oracle8i server running on all operating systems.

Lorentz, Diana. *Oracle8i Reference Release 2*. Oracle Corporation, Redwood City, CA, 1999. Part No. A 76961-01. This manual describes the architecture, processes, structures, and other concepts of Oracle8i and provides detailed information on static and dynamic data dictionary views.

 www.revealnet.com. This site from RevealNet provides Oracle administration reference software.

4

Oracle Backup and Recovery Configuration

Terms you'll need to understand:

- ✓ ARCHIVELOG mode
- ✓ NOARCHIVELOG mode
- ✓ Online backup
- ✓ Offline backup
- ✓ System Change Number (SCN)
- ✓ Dynamic performance views
- ✓ Manual archiving
- ✓ Automatic archiving
- ✓ ARCH background process
- ✓ Multiple archive destinations
- ✓ Multiple archive processes

Techniques you'll need to master:

- ✓ Understanding the Archive modes of a database
- ✓ Viewing the Archive mode of a database
- ✓ Issuing the **ARCHIVE LOG LIST** command
- ✓ Changing the Archive mode of a database
- ✓ Using the dynamic performance views relating to the archived redo log files
- ✓ Understanding recovery implications of NOARCHIVELOG mode
- ✓ Configuring a database for manual redo log archiving
- ✓ Configuring a database for automatic redo log archiving
- ✓ Setting up multiple archive destinations
- ✓ Setting up multiple archive processes

After gaining an understanding of the Oracle backup and recovery structures and processes, a database administrator (DBA) can proceed to configure Oracle for backup and recovery. Effective Oracle backup and recovery configuration requires an understanding of the following concepts:

➤ Archive modes of a database

➤ Recovery implications of NOARCHIVELOG mode

➤ Configuration of a database for redo log archiving

➤ Multiplexing of archived redo log files

➤ Setup of multiple archive destinations

➤ Setup of multiple archive processes

Archive Modes of a Database

An Oracle8i database instance can operate in two distinctive Backup modes: ARCHIVELOG and NOARCHIVELOG. The information on the Archive mode is stored in the control file associated with the database. Each mode determines the type of backup and recovery procedures that can be performed.

ARCHIVELOG Mode

ARCHIVELOG mode enables the archiving of the online redo log files so that a history of redo information is maintained. When the command to operate in ARCHIVELOG mode is issued, the control file is updated accordingly. Setting the database in ARCHIVELOG mode does not enable the ARCH background process. The ARCH background process must be explicitly started to support automatic archiving of the online redo log files.

A filled online redo log file cannot be overwritten until a checkpoint has taken place and the ARCH background process has archived it. The log sequence number of the archived redo log file is recorded in the control file. All changes to the database are stored in the archived redo log files.

 Be aware that when the archiving destination runs out of space, the database will hang until sufficient free space is available for more archived redo log files.

When ARCHIVELOG mode is in effect, complete recovery up to the point of disk and instance failure can be accommodated because the current redo information and the redo history (in the form of the archived redo logs) are available.

An Oracle8i database in the ARCHIVELOG mode enables online hot backups. *Online hot backups* are backups made while the database is open and in use.

A DBA should be aware of the following implications when configuring the database for ARCHIVELOG mode:

➤ The database is protected from media failures.

➤ Online hot backups can be made while the database is online. When a non-SYSTEM tablespace goes offline in the event of a media failure, other parts of the database remain available because full database restore is not needed. The data needed to recover the offline tablespace is in the redo history, which is composed of archived redo log files.

➤ The loss of any active rollback segment tablespace will cause the database to crash.

➤ You should increase the number of online redo log groups to ensure that the archiving of online redo log files is completed before the files are overwritten.

When the database is operating in ARCHIVELOG mode, the following options are available for performing media recovery:

➤ Incomplete recovery up to a particular point in time

➤ Incomplete recovery up to the end of a particular archived redo log file

➤ Incomplete recovery up to a particular *System Change Number (SCN)*

➤ Ability to use the archived redo log files in conjunction with the backup copies of the damaged data files to bring the data files up to date, irrespective of the database being online or offline

NOARCHIVELOG Mode

If the database is set up for NOARCHIVELOG mode, no redo history is maintained. The NOARCHIVELOG mode disables the archiving of the online redo log files. In this mode, an online redo log group becomes inactive after it fills up. As the checkpoint at the log switch completes, the group becomes available for reuse by the LGWR process. Recovery operations are limited because only the most recent changes made to the database stored in the groups of the online redo logs are available. Due to the recycling of online redo log files, a loss of transactions may result because older redo log files needed for recovery are no longer available. When redo log files are overwritten, media recovery is limited to the last full backup. This mode only protects a database from instance failure. By default, an Oracle database is configured for NOARCHIVELOG mode.

A DBA should be aware of the following implications when configuring the database for NOARCHIVELOG mode:

➤ Online hot backups cannot be performed.

➤ Data will be lost since the most recent full backup.

➤ Each database backup must include the complete set of control, redo log, and data files.

➤ Operating system backups of the database can be performed only when the database is shut down.

➤ Complete offline database backups affect database availability.

➤ If a tablespace becomes unavailable in the event of a failure, the database is inoperative until the tablespace has been dropped or until the whole database has been restored from backups.

Viewing the Archive Mode of a Database

To view the Archive mode of an Oracle8i database, a DBA can use tools, including Server Manager, Structured Query Language (SQL)*Plus Worksheet, or Instance Manager. Using Server Manager, Oracle responds with the following information after the **ARCHIVE LOG LIST** command has been issued:

```
C:\>svrmgrl

Oracle Server Manager Release 3.1.7.0.0 - Production

Copyright (c) 1997, 1999, Oracle Corporation. All Rights
    Reserved.

Oracle8i Enterprise Edition Release 8.1.7.0.0 - Production
With the Partitioning option
JServer Release 8.1.7.0.0 - Production

SVRMGR> connect internal
Password:
Connected.
SVRMGR> archive log list
Database log mode                No Archive Mode
Automatic archival               Disabled
Archive destination              C:\ORANT817\RDBMS
Oldest online log sequence       1564
Current log sequence             1566
SVRMGR>
```

The **ARCHIVE LOG LIST** command provides information on the Archive mode and the status of the archiving for the database. There are six **ARCHIVE LOG LIST** display elements:

➤ Database Log mode indicates the current archiving mode.

➤ Automatic archival indicates the status of the ARCH background process.

➤ Archive destination indicates the target location where archived redo log files will reside.

➤ Oldest online log sequence indicates the oldest online redo log sequence number.

➤ Next log sequence to archive indicates the next redo log to archive (applicable for ARCHIVELOG mode).

➤ Current log sequence indicates the sequence number of the current redo log file.

Figure 4.1 illustrates the SQL*Plus Worksheet with NOARCHIVELOG mode after the **ARCHIVE LOG LIST** command is issued. Figure 4.2 illustrates the Instance Manager with NOARCHIVELOG mode.

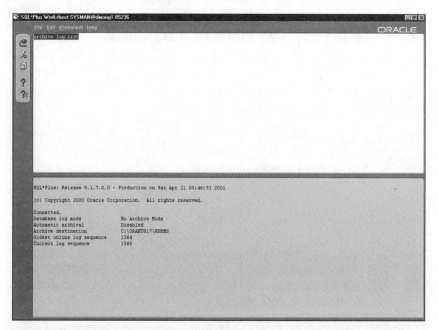

Figure 4.1   The SQL*Plus Worksheet with NOARCHIVELOG mode after issuing the **ARCHIVE LOG LIST** command.

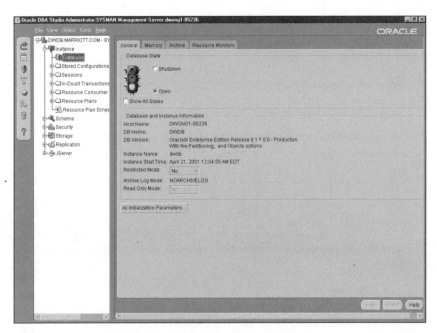

Figure 4.2 The Instance Manager with NOARCHIVELOG mode.

Changing the Archive Mode of a Database

The **ALTER DATABASE** command is used to change the Archive mode while the database is in a **MOUNT** state. A user must have the **ALTER SYSTEM** privilege to change the Archive mode of the database. To enable ARCHIVELOG mode for redo log files, issue the following command:

```
ALTER DATABASE ARCHIVELOG
```

To disable ARCHIVELOG mode for the redo log files, issue the following command:

```
ALTER DATABASE NOARCHIVELOG
```

 Know the database states associated with various commands because they are likely to appear on the exam. For example, the **ALTER DATABASE** command is used to change the Archive mode while the database is in a **MOUNT** state.

If the database is in NOARCHIVELOG mode, you can change the Archive mode by logging into Server Manager. Use the following Server Manager command line statements to change a database from NOARCHIVELOG mode to ARCHIVELOG mode:

```
SVRMGR> shutdown immediate;
Database closed.
Database dismounted.
ORACLE instance shut down.
SVRMGR>
SVRMGR> startup mount
ORACLE instance started.
Total System Global Area                    73164828 bytes
Fixed Size                                     75804 bytes
Variable Size                               56233984 bytes
Database Buffers                            16777216 bytes
Redo Buffers                                   77824 bytes
Database mounted.
SVRMGR>
SVRMGR> archive log list
Database log mode              No Archive Mode
Automatic archival            Disabled
Archive destination           C:\ORANT817\RDBMS
Oldest online log sequence    1572
Current log sequence          1574
SVRMGR>
SVRMGR> alter database archivelog;
Statement processed.
SVRMGR> alter database open;
Statement processed.
SVRMGR>
```

To verify that the Archive mode change took place, use Server Manager, SQL*Plus Worksheet, or Oracle DBA Studio. Figure 4.3 illustrates the enabled ARCHIVELOG mode from Oracle DBA Studio. In Server Manager, Oracle displays the following information after the **ARCHIVE LOG LIST** command has been issued:

```
SVRMGR> archive log list
Database log mode              Archive Mode
Automatic archival            Disabled
Archive destination           C:\ORANT817\RDBMS
Oldest online log sequence    1572
Next log sequence to archive  1574
Current log sequence          1574
SVRMGR>
```

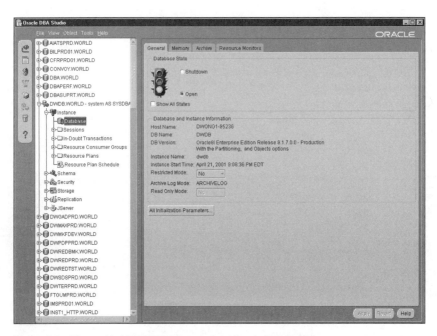

Figure 4.3　The enabled ARCHIVELOG mode from Oracle DBA Studio.

After the database Archive mode has been changed from NOARCHIVELOG to ARCHIVELOG, a full offline database backup must be made. This new backup will be the backup against which all future archived redo log files will apply. The previous backup is of no value because it was taken when the database was in NOARCHIVELOG mode.

If the database is in ARCHIVELOG mode, the Archive mode can be changed using Server Manager. The following Server Manager command-line statements can be issued to change a database from ARCHIVELOG mode to NOARCHIVELOG mode:

```
SVRMGR> connect internal
Password:
Connected.
SVRMGR> startup mount;
ORACLE instance started.
Total System Global Area                73164828 bytes
Fixed Size                                 75804 bytes
Variable Size                           56233984 bytes
Database Buffers                        16777216 bytes
Redo Buffers                               77824 bytes
Database mounted.
SVRMGR>
```

```
SVRMGR> archive log list
Database log mode                Archive Mode
Automatic archival               Disabled
Archive destination              C:\ORANT817\RDBMS
Oldest online log sequence       1573
Next log sequence to archive     1574
Current log sequence             1575
SVRMGR>
SVRMGR> alter database noarchivelog;
Statement processed.
SVRMGR>
SVRMGR> alter database open;
Statement processed.
SVRMGR>
```

To verify that the Archive mode change took place, use Server Manager, SQL*Plus Worksheet, or Oracle DBA Studio. In Server Manager, Oracle displays the following information after the **ARCHIVE LOG LIST** command has been issued:

```
SVRMGR> archive log list
Database log mode                No Archive Mode
Automatic archival               Disabled
Archive destination              C:\ORANT817\RDBMS
Oldest online log sequence       1573
Current log sequence             1575SVRMGR>
```

Dynamic Performance Views

Oracle provides numerous data dictionary views to get information on the archived redo log files, including the following:

➤ **V$ARCHIVED_LOG**—Provides information on the archived redo log files from the control file:

```
SQL> desc V$ARCHIVED_LOG;
 Name                           Null?     Type
 ----                           -----     ----
  RECID                                   NUMBER
  STAMP                                   NUMBER
  NAME                                    VARCHAR2(513)
  THREAD#                                 NUMBER
  SEQUENCE#                               NUMBER
  RESETLOGS_CHANGE#                       NUMBER
  RESETLOGS_TIME                          DATE
  FIRST_CHANGE#                           NUMBER
```

```
FIRST_TIME                                      DATE
NEXT_CHANGE#                                    NUMBER
NEXT_TIME                                        DATE
BLOCKS                                          NUMBER
BLOCK_SIZE                                       NUMBER
CREATOR                                         VARCHAR2(4)
REGISTRAR                                       VARCHAR2(4)
STANDBY_DEST                                    VARCHAR2(3)
ARCHIVED                                        VARCHAR2(3)
DELETED                                         VARCHAR2(3)
COMPLETION_TIME                                 DATE
SQL>
```

➤ **V$ARCHIVE_DEST**—Provides information on all archived log destinations for the current instance. Information available includes binding (**MANDATORY** or **OPTIONAL**), target (**PRIMARY** or **STANDBY**), status (**VALID, DEFERRED, ERROR,** or **INACTIVE**), and the destination specifications:

```
SQL> desc V$ARCHIVE_DEST
Name                              Null?      Type
----                              -----      ----
DEST_ID                                      NUMBER
STATUS                                       VARCHAR2(9)
BINDING                                      VARCHAR2(9)
NAME_SPACE                                   VARCHAR2(7)
TARGET                                       VARCHAR2(7)
REOPEN_SECS                                  NUMBER
DESTINATION                                  VARCHAR2(256)
FAIL_DATE                                    DATE
FAIL_SEQUENCE                                NUMBER
FAIL_BLOCK                                   NUMBER
ERROR                                        VARCHAR2(256)
SQL>
```

➤ **V$DATABASE**—Provides information on the current state of archiving:

```
SQL> desc V$DATABASE;
Name                              Null?      Type
----                              -----      ----
DBID                                         NUMBER
NAME                                         VARCHAR2(9)
CREATED                                      DATE
RESETLOGS_CHANGE#                            NUMBER
RESETLOGS_TIME                               DATE
PRIOR_RESETLOGS_CHANGE#                      NUMBER
```

```
PRIOR_RESETLOGS_TIME                        DATE
LOG_MODE                                    VARCHAR2(12)
CHECKPOINT_CHANGE#                          NUMBER
ARCHIVE_CHANGE#                             NUMBER
CONTROLFILE_TYPE                            VARCHAR2(7)
CONTROLFILE_CREATED                         DATE
CONTROLFILE_SEQUENCE#                       NUMBER
CONTROLFILE_CHANGE#                         NUMBER
CONTROLFILE_TIME                            DATE
OPEN_RESETLOGS                              VARCHAR2(11)
VERSION_TIME                                DATE
OPEN_MODE                                   VARCHAR2(10)
SQL>
```

➤ **V$LOG_HISTORY**—Provides log file history information from the control file. Information available includes the thread number of the archived log file, the sequence number of the archived log file, the lowest SCN, the highest SCN, the control file record identifier, and the control file record stamp:

```
SQL> desc V$LOG_HISTORY
 Name                           Null?      Type
 ----                           -----      ----
 RECID                                     NUMBER
 STAMP                                     NUMBER
 THREAD#                                   NUMBER
 SEQUENCE#                                 NUMBER
 FIRST_CHANGE#                             NUMBER
 FIRST_TIME                                DATE
 NEXT_CHANGE#                              NUMBER

SQL>
```

➤ **V$ARCHIVE_PROCESSES**—Provides status about the ARCH processes for the database instance. This view contains 10 rows for the possible archiver processes. Valid values for the **STATE** column are **ACTIVE, BUSY,** and **IDLE:**

```
SQL> desc V$ARCHIVE_PROCESSES
 Name                           Null?      Type
 ----                           -----      ----
 PROCESS                                   NUMBER
 STATUS                                    VARCHAR2(10)
 LOG_SEQUENCE                              NUMBER
 STATE                                     VARCHAR2(4)
SQL>
```

Recovery Implications of NOARCHIVELOG Mode

When the database is operating in NOARCHIVELOG mode, the following options are available for performing media recovery:

➤ The control files, data files, and redo log files from the most recent full database backup must be restored. This option performs media recovery using the physical operating system database files. However, the user may choose to perform media recovery using the logical backups instead.

➤ If logical backups using the Export utility are available, the Import utility can be used to restore lost data. This technique results in an incomplete recovery that may include lost transactions.

Configuring a Database for Redo Log Archiving

After the database is operating in ARCHIVELOG mode, the online redo log files can be archived manually or automatically. You can automate the archiving of the online redo log groups by setting the **LOG_ARCHIVE_START** initialization parameter to **TRUE**. This causes Oracle8i to start one or more ARCH background processes, copy online redo log files when they are filled, and manage the archiving process. The ARCH processes are disabled by default. The database should be shut down cleanly before you enable the archive process. For manual archiving, the DBA must use Server Manager, SQL*Plus Worksheet, or the Backup Management tool.

Oracle recommends enabling automatic archival of online redo log files.

One or more ARCHIVELOG destinations can be specified in the database initialization parameter file. The **LOG_ARCHIVE_FORMAT** parameter enables you to specify filename options: (a)**%s** or **%S** for including the log sequence number, (b) **%t** or **%T** for including the thread number, and so forth. The following code shows a sample parameter entry:

```
LOG_ARCHIVE_FORMAT=arch%s.dbf
```

You can use two methods to define multiple archive destinations to protect against media failure. The recommended method is to use the **LOG_ARCHIVE_ DEST_n** parameters to point to local disk storage or a remote database. You can specify up to five destinations by using a suffix from one to five. Local disk storage is defined by the **LOCATION** keyword. Remote database storage is defined by the **SERVICE** keyword. You can also specify whether the archive destination is **MANDATORY** or **OPTIONAL. MANDATORY** specifies that archiving must be successful before an online redo log can be reused. **OPTIONAL** specifies that an online redo log file can be reused even though archiving to this destination has not been successful. The optional **REOPEN** keyword enables you to define the retry time interval (default is 300 seconds) in the event of archiving failures. The following sample code shows **LOG_ARCHIVE_DEST_n** parameter usage:

```
log_archive_dest_1 =
"LOCATION=c:\orant817\database\archive MANDATORY REOPEN"
log_archive_dest_1 =
"LOCATION=c:\orant817\database\archive2 MANDATORY REOPEN=900"
log_archive_dest_2 = "SERVICE=dwdb2 OPTIONAL"
```

The second method to define multiple archiving destinations is to specify a primary location via the **LOG_ARCHIVE_DEST** parameter and to use the **LOG_ARCHIVE_DUPLEX_DEST** parameter to define a backup location. The **LOG_ARCHIVE_DEST** implies a local mandatory location and the **LOG_ARCHIVE_DUPLEX_DEST** implies an optional location. The limitation of this method is that it cannot be used to archive to a remote location.

 LOG_ARCHIVE_DEST_n parameter is only valid for Oracle8i Enterprise Edition. You may continue to use **LOG_ARCHIVE_DEST** under Oracle8i. However, you cannot use both **LOG_ARCHIVE_DEST_n** and **LOG_ ARCHIVE_DEST** because they are not compatible.

The initialization parameter **LOG_ARCHIVE_DEST_STATE_n** enables DBAs to change the state of an archive destination dynamically. The default state for an archive destination is **ENABLE**. To temporarily halt archiving to a mandatory destination, you can set the state of that destination to **DEFER**. You can define multiple destinations and set them to **DEFER** in the initialization parameter file. These destinations can be enabled on demand when other destinations encounter errors or require maintenance. This can be achieved by setting the initialization parameter or by using the **ALTER SYSTEM SET LOG_ARCHIVE_DEST_ STATE_N = ENABLE** command.

The following code sample illustrates **LOG_ARCHIVE_DEST_STATE_n** initialization parameter entry:

```
log_archive_dest_state_2 = ENABLE
log_archive_dest_state_3 = DEFER
```

 When the state of the archive destination is changed from **DEFER** to **ENABLE**, DBAs must manually archive any missed redo logs to this destination.

When configuring archiving, you can set the **LOG_ARCHIVE_MIN_ SUCCEED_DEST** parameter to specify the number of destinations that need to be successfully archived before an online redo log file can be overwritten. An online redo log can be reused under the following conditions:

➤ Archiving has been completed to all enabled mandatory target locations.

➤ The number of local destinations archived must be greater than or equal to the value of **LOG_ARCHIVE_MIN_SUCCEED_DEST** parameter.

Spawning Multiple Archiver Processes

A single ARCH process might not be sufficient to keep up with the generation of a large amount of redo logs. Oracle8i allows DBAs to define multiple archive processes dynamically using the **LOG_ARCHIVE_MAX_PROCESSES** parameter. The **LOG_ARCHIVE_MAX_PROCESSES** parameter enables DBAs to define up to 10 archive processes. An Oracle database instance will start with as many archiver processes as defined by this parameter, and the DBA can add or remove archive processes as needed.

To start the ARCH background process(es), issue the following SQL command in Server Manager or SQL*Plus Worksheet:

```
ARCHIVE LOG START
```

This SQL command initiates automatic archiving using the archive destination(s) specified in the **LOG_ARCHIVE_DEST_n** init.ora parameter(s). Invoke the **ARCHIVE LOG LIST** command to verify that automatic archiving has been started.

To stop automatic archiving, issue the following SQL statement in Server Manager or SQL*Plus Worksheet:

```
ARCHIVE LOG STOP
```

Enabling the Archival Process(es) (ARCn) in an Open Instance

Take the following five steps when enabling the ARCn process(es) in an open instance:

1. Open the database.

2. Verify that the database is operating in ARCHIVELOG mode, using the following code:

```
SVRMGR> archive log list
Database log mode                Archive Mode
Automatic archival               Disabled
Archive destination              c:\orant817\database\archive2
Oldest online log sequence       1573
Next log sequence to archive     1575
Current log sequence        \    1575
SVRMGR>
```

3. Invoke the ARCn process(es) using the following code to automatically archive redo log files:

```
SVRMGR> alter system archive log start to
  '/u02/oradata/TEST/log'; (Unix)
SVRMGR> alter system archive log start to
  'd:\orant\database\TEST\log'; (NT)
```

4. Verify that the ARCn process(es) is enabled using the following code:

```
SVRMGR> archive log list
Database log mode                Archive Mode
Automatic archival               Enabled
Archive destination              c:\orant817\database\archive2
Oldest online log sequence       1573
Next log sequence to archive     1575
Current log sequence             1575
SVRMGR>
```

5. The ARCn process(es) automatically copies the redo log files to the archival destination when they are filled.

When the ARCn process is not initiated through the init.ora parameter file, it must be restarted at each instance startup.

Enabling Archival Process at Instance Startup

The ARCn process(es) can be automatically started at instance startup by setting the LOG_ARCHIVE_START init.ora parameter. This makes manual archiving by the DBA unnecessary. When the LOG_ARCHIVE_START parameter is set to TRUE, the ARCn process(es) is automatically invoked at instance startup. When the LOG_ARCHIVE_START parameter is set to FALSE, the ARCn process is disabled at instance startup.

Selectively Archiving Redo Log Files

To selectively archive redo log files, the ALTER SYSTEM ARCHIVE LOG command requires that the OSDBA or the OSOPER role be enabled, and this command is used with the following options:

➤ THREAD—Specifies the thread of the redo log file group to be archived. This parameter applies to the Oracle Parallel Server option in Parallel mode.

➤ SEQUENCE—Specifies the log sequence number of the online redo log file group to archive manually. The ARCHIVE LOG LIST command can be used to retrieve archive log information.

➤ CHANGE—Specifies manual archiving based on the SCN. A log switch is triggered if the SCN is in the current redo log file group.

 If an SCN is specified with the **CHANGE** option and earlier unarchived redo log file groups exist, all unarchived redo log groups up to and including the specified group will be archived by Oracle.

➤ GROUP—Specifies the online redo log group to archive manually. The DBA_LOG_FILES data dictionary view can be used to retrieve the group number for the redo log file groups.

➤ CURRENT—Specifies the thread of the current redo log file group to be archived manually. This parameter will trigger a log switch.

 If a thread of the current redo log file group is specified with the **CURRENT** option and earlier unarchived redo log file groups exist, all unarchived redo log groups up to and including the specified group will be archived by Oracle.

➤ LOGFILE—Identifies the redo log file group member to be archived manually.

If a redo log file group is specified for the **LOGFILE** option and earlier unarchived redo log file groups exist, an error will be returned.

➤ **NEXT**—Archives the oldest unarchived online redo log file group.

➤ **ALL**—Specifies that all online redo log file groups are to be archived.

➤ **START**—Enables automatic archiving of redo log file groups.

➤ **TO**—Specifies the archival destination for the copies of the online redo log group.

➤ **STOP**—Disables automatic archiving of redo log file groups.

Manually Disable Archiving

Regardless of how the ARCn process(es) is started, use the Backup Management tool or the **ALTER SYSTEM** command in Server Manager to disable the archival process. The following steps detail how to manually disable the archival process:

1. Issue the following command to stop the ARCn background process(es):

```
SVRMGR> alter system archive log stop;
```

2. Modify the init.ora parameter file by setting the following parameter to disable automatic archiving:

```
LOG_ARCHIVE_START=FALSE
```

3. Make sure that the database is operating in NOARCHIVELOG mode after the ARCH process is disabled. Stopping the ARCH process has no effect on the Archive mode of the database. When all redo log file groups are filled and are not archived, the database will hang if it is in ARCHIVELOG mode.

The following code snippet shows how to stop automatic archiving from Server Manager or SQL*Plus Worksheet:

```
SVRMGR> archive log stop;
Statement processed.
SVRMGR> archive log list
Database log mode               Archive Mode
Automatic archival              Disabled
Archive destination             c:\orant817\database\archive2
```

```
Oldest online log sequence     1573
Next log sequence to archive   1575
Current log sequence           1575
SVRMGR>

SVRMGR> startup mount
ORACLE instance started.
Total System Global Area                    73164828 bytes
Fixed Size                                     75804 bytes
Variable Size                               56233984 bytes
Database Buffers                            16777216 bytes
Redo Buffers                                   77824 bytes
Database mounted.
SVRMGR> archive log list
Database log mode              No Archive Mode
Automatic archival             Disabled
Archive destination            C:\ORANT817\RDBMS
Oldest online log sequence     1573
Current log sequence           1575
SVRMGR>
```

Practice Questions

Question 1

Which archive mode is in effect for a default installation of Oracle Server?

○ a.   ARCHIVELOG mode with automatic archiving

○ b.   NOARCHIVELOG mode

○ c.   ARCHIVELOG mode with manual archiving

○ d.   None of the above

The correct answer is b. The default Oracle Server installation sets the database for NOARCHIVELOG mode. In this mode, no redo log history is maintained. Answers a, c, and d are incorrect because the default installation mode is the NOARCHIVELOG mode.

Question 2

> Which command can be issued to get the current log sequence number?
>
> ○ a. **ARCHIVE LOG ALL**
>
> ○ b. **LIST ALL ARCHIVE**
>
> ○ c. **ARCHIVE LIST**
>
> ○ d. **ARCHIVE LOG LIST**

The correct answer is d. The **ARCHIVE LOG LIST** command provides information on the Archive mode and the status of the archiving for the database. The **ARCHIVE LOG LIST** displayed elements include the following:

➤ **DATABASE LOG MODE**—Indicates the current archiving mode

➤ **AUTOMATIC ARCHIVAL**—Indicates the status of the ARCH background process

➤ **ARCHIVE DESTINATION**—Indicates the target location where archived redo log files will reside

➤ **OLDEST ONLINE LOG SEQUENCE**—Indicates the oldest online redo log sequence number

➤ **NEXT LOG SEQUENCE TO ARCHIVE**—Indicates the next redo log to archive (applicable for ARCHIVELOG mode)

➤ **CURRENT LOG SEQUENCE**—Indicates the sequence number of the current redo log file

Answers a, b, and c are invalid commands.

Question 3

Which backup method should you employ to enable complete recovery up to the point of media failure?

○ a. Operating system backup without archiving.

○ b. Logical backup using the conventional path of the EXPORT utility.

○ c. Operating system backup with archiving.

○ d. None of the backup methods enable complete recovery up to the point of media failure.

The correct answer is c. An operating system backup with archiving facilitates a complete recovery because the redo log history is available for reapplying all database transactions. Answer a is incorrect because an operating system backup without archiving only enables restoration to the last full backup. Answer b is incorrect because logical backups using the EXPORT utility only enable restoration to the point in time when the logical backups were made. Answer d is incorrect because an operating system backup with archiving will enable a complete recovery up to the point of media failure.

Question 4

What will happen if the **LOG_ARCHIVE_DEST_n** location which was designated as mandatory runs out of space?

○ a. The redo log files will be overwritten.

○ b. The database will hang.

○ c. Redo log file writing continues.

○ d. Archiving will stop.

The correct answer is b. When archiving is enabled, redo log files are not overwritten until they have been archived. When the archival destination designated as mandatory runs out of space, the ARCn background process(es) will fail, which causes the database to hang. Answer a is incorrect because the redo log files will be overwritten when sufficient free space is available in the **LOG_ARCHIVE_DEST_n** location and the target minimum copies are met. Answer c is incorrect because the redo log file writing will not continue until sufficient space is available in the **LOG_ ARCHIVE_DEST_n** location designated as mandatory. Answer d is incorrect because the ARCn process(es) will fail until sufficient free space is available in the **LOG_ARCHIVE_DEST_n** location designated as mandatory.

Question 5

> When a database is operating in ARCHIVELOG mode, when will the redo log files get overwritten due to the cyclical writing by the LGWR?
>
> ○ a. At the start of the checkpoint, after the redo log file is archived
> ○ b. At the start of the checkpoint, before the redo log file is archived
> ○ c. After the checkpoint completes, before the redo log file is archived
> ○ d. After the checkpoint completes, after the redo log file is archived

The correct answer is d. When operating in ARCHIVELOG mode, the redo log files cannot be reused until they have been archived. With automatic archiving, the ARCH background process copies the oldest unarchived redo log group to the archival location at a log switch. Each log switch triggers a checkpoint event. Answers a and b are incorrect because redo log files get overwritten after the checkpoint completes. Answer c is incorrect because redo log files get overwritten after the redo log file is archived.

Question 6

> What command needs to be issued to change the database to ARCHIVELOG mode?
>
> ○ a. **ALTER DATABASE**
> ○ b. **ALTER TABLESPACE**
> ○ c. **ALTER SYSTEM**
> ○ d. **ALTER SESSION**

The correct answer is a. The **ALTER DATABASE ARCHIVELOG** command is used to put the database in ARCHIVELOG mode while the database is in the MOUNT state. Answers b, c, and d are incorrect because those commands cannot be used to change the database mode to ARCHIVELOG.

Question 7

Which init.ora parameter should be set to specify the minimum number of redo log file copies that needs to be successfully created when duplexing archived redo log files?

- O a. **LOG_ARCHIVE_SUCCEED**
- O b. **LOG_ARCHIVE_MIN_SUCCEED_DEST**
- O c. **LOG_ARCHIVE_DUPLEX_DEST**
- O d. **LOG_ARCHIVE_DEST**

The correct answer is b. The **LOG_ARCHIVE_MIN_SUCCEED_DEST** parameter specifies the minimum number of redo log file copies that must be successfully written. The parameter can be set to one or two. Answer a is incorrect because it is an invalid parameter. Answers c and d are incorrect because they specify the primary and the duplex archived redo log file destinations.

Question 8

Which Server Manager command can be issued to check which Archive mode is in effect for the database?

- O a. **SELECT * FROM V$LOGFILE**
- O b. **SELECT * FROM V$DATAFILE**
- O c. **ARCHIVE LOG ALL**
- O d. **ARCHIVE LOG LIST**

The correct answer is d. The **ARCHIVE LOG LIST** command displays information about the Archive mode of the database. Answers a and b are incorrect because these **V$** views don't contain information about the Archive mode for a database. Answer c is incorrect because it is an invalid command.

Question 9

What can a DBA do to avoid archiving bottlenecks during month end when the update activities are high?

○ a. Increase the value of the **LOG_ARCHIVE_MAX_PROCESSES** parameter, shutdown, and restart the database.

○ b. Change to manual archiving for full control of creating archive log files.

○ c. Use the **ALTER SYSTEM SET LOG_ARCHIVE_MAX_ PROCESSES** command to temporarily increase the number of ARCn processes, and later reduce the number of ARCn processes.

○ d. Use the **ALTER SYSTEM** command to reset the **LOG_ARCHIVE_ MAX_PROCESSES** and the **LOG_ARCHIVE_MIN_PROCESSES** parameters for defining the upper and lower bound of ARCn processes.

The correct answer is c. Use the **ALTER SYSTEM SET LOG_ARCHIVE_ MAX_PROCESSES** command to temporarily increase the number of ARCn processes and then later to reduce the number when no longer needed. Answer a is incorrect because the **LOG_ARCHIVE_MAX_ PROCESSES** parameter can be dynamically changed without bringing down the database. Answer b is incorrect because manual archiving is not recommended. Answer d is incorrect because **LOG_ARCHIVE_MIN_PROCESSES** is an invalid parameter.

Question 10

What is the maximum number of archival destinations that can be specified for the **LOG_ARCHIVE_DEST_n** initialization parameter?

○ a. 10

○ b. 5

○ c. 3

○ d. 2

The correct answer is b. The maximum number of archival destinations is five. Answers a, c, and d are incorrect because they are higher or lower than five.

Need to Know More?

 Loney, Kevin and Marlene Theriault. *Oracle8i DBA Handbook*. Oracle Press, Berkeley, CA, 1999. ISBN 0-07212-188-2. This comprehensive guide for DBAs includes general backup and recovery concepts.

 Velpuri, Rama. *Oracle8i Backup and Recovery Handbook*. Oracle Press, Berkeley, CA, 2000. ISBN 0-072-12717-1. This book provides guidance on data protection techniques and offers strategies for data storage, backup, and restore for Oracle 8i.

 http://technet.oracle.com. This site provides the best information on Oracle's products and technologies. You can also purchase the following manuals online:

Dialeris, Connie. *Oracle8i Backup and Recovery Guide Release 2*. Oracle Corporation, Redwood City, CA, 1999. Part No. A76993-01. This manual provides guidance on data protection techniques and offers strategies for data storage, backup, and restore for Oracle 8i.

Leverenz, Lefty. *Oracle8i Concepts Release 2*. Oracle Corporation, Redwood City, CA, 1999. Part No. A76965-01. This manual describes all features of the Oracle8i server running on all operating systems.

Lorentz, Diana. *Oracle8i Reference Release 2*. Oracle Corporation, Redwood City, CA, 1999. Part No. A76961-01. This manual describes the architecture, processes, structures, and other concepts of Oracle8i and provides detailed information on static and dynamic data dictionary views.

 www.revealnet.com. This site from RevealNet provides Oracle administration reference software.

Oracle Recovery Manager Overview

. . . .

Terms you'll need to understand:

✓ Recovery Manager (RMAN)

✓ Backup and Recovery Wizards

✓ Oracle Enterprise Manager (OEM)

✓ **V$BACKUP_CORRUPTION**

✓ **V$COPY_CORRUPTION**

✓ Channel

✓ Recovery catalog

✓ Recovery catalog database

✓ Target database

✓ Incremental block-level backup

✓ Unused block compression

✓ **CONTROL_FILE_RECORD_ KEEP_TIME**

✓ Snapshot control file

Techniques you'll need to master:

✓ Understanding RMAN characteristics

✓ Understanding RMAN components, packages, interfaces, and startup process

✓ Understanding additional issues when using RMAN

✓ Understanding when to use RMAN

✓ Understanding the Backup and Recovery Wizards

✓ Understanding the recovery catalog

✓ Understanding the recovery catalog creation process

✓ Understanding control files and the resynchronization process with respect to RMAN

✓ Connecting to RMAN with or without a recovery catalog

This chapter provides information on a new feature introduced in Oracle8—the *Oracle Recovery Manager (RMAN)* utility. Specific topics discussed include the following:

➤ Overview of RMAN

➤ When to use RMAN

➤ Backup Manager overview

➤ Recovery catalog overview

➤ RMAN advantages and disadvantages, with the recovery catalog

➤ Recovery catalog creation

➤ Control file information with respect to RMAN

➤ Resynchronization of the control file

➤ Connections to RMAN

Overview of RMAN

RMAN is an Oracle-provided utility that enables database administrators (DBAs) to manage the backup, restore, and recovery processes for organizations. One of the key components of RMAN lies in the Oracle-proprietary operating system-independent scripting language that is covered in Chapter 6.

RMAN records all backup, restore, and recovery activities in the control file. The physical backup files are stored on a disk or tape. RMAN interfaces with the target Oracle server by creating server processes that provide connection, backup, restore, and recovery services through a Procedural Language/Structured Query Language (PL/SQL) interface. This has also been referred to as server-managed backup and recovery. You can access RMAN features using the command-line interface or the *graphical user interface (GUI)* through the Oracle Enterprise Manager's Backup Wizard tool.

RMAN Characteristics

The characteristics of RMAN include the following:

➤ It facilitates the backup of the database, tablespaces, data files, control files, and archived redo log files.

➤ It supports database storage of frequently run operations that are specified in the form of scripts.

➤ It supports incremental block level backups. This capability enables DBAs to associate backup time to the number of changes made to the database instead of to the size of the database.

➤ It reduces the size of the backup by compressing unused blocks.

➤ It allows the DBA to specify the number of open files and the size of backup pieces for each backup. This capability overcomes operating system (OS) limits on concurrent open files and enables a backup piece to reach the maximum file size supported by the OS or the Media Manager.

➤ It can be started from the Backup and Recovery Wizards or the operating system. The Unix cron utility or the Windows NT AT utility are typical operating system scheduling utilities used in conjunction with RMAN.

➤ It can detect corrupted blocks during backup and restore operations. RMAN writes corruption information in the database alert log file, the trace files, and the control file. You can also access the corruption information by querying the **V$BACKUP_CORRUPTION** and the **V$COPY_CORRUPTION** data dictionary views. The following code sample provides the view details:

```
SQL> desc v$backup_corruption
 Name                          Null?     Type
 ----                          -----     ----
 RECID                                   NUMBER
 STAMP                                   NUMBER
 SET_STAMP                               NUMBER
 SET_COUNT                               NUMBER
 PIECE#                                  NUMBER
 FILE#                                   NUMBER
 BLOCK#                                  NUMBER
 BLOCKS                                  NUMBER
 CORRUPTION_CHANGE#                      NUMBER
 MARKED_CORRUPT                          VARCHAR2(3)

SQL> desc v$copy_corruption
 Name                          Null?     Type
 ----                          -----     ----
 RECID                                   NUMBER
 STAMP                                   NUMBER
 COPY_RECID                              NUMBER
 COPY_STAMP                              NUMBER
 FILE#                                   NUMBER
 BLOCK#                                  NUMBER
 BLOCKS                                  NUMBER
 CORRUPTION_CHANGE#                      NUMBER
 MARKED_CORRUPT                          VARCHAR2(3)
```

➤ It supports distributed backup, restore, and recovery operations for the Oracle parallel server.

➤ It provides improved performance through automatic use of parallel operations, reduction of the amount of redo information generated during online database backups, input/output (I/O) restrictions on a read per file and per second basis, and tape streaming.

➤ It supports the use of third-party media management tools, such as Legato and Veritas, to interface with storage devices.

RMAN Components

RMAN is composed of the following components:

➤ *RMAN executable*—The RMAN executable invokes the RMAN command-line interface. RMAN interprets user requests and invokes applicable server processes to perform the desired actions.

➤ *RMAN processes*—These are the server processes invoked by RMAN that connect to the target database to perform backup, restore, and recovery operations through a PL/SQL interface.

➤ *Target database*—This is the database that requires the backup, restore, or recovery operation.

➤ *RMAN metadata*—This is the data that RMAN uses for backup, restore, and recovery operation. It is stored in the control file of the target database or in a database schema of another database. When the metadata is stored in a database schema, it is referred to as the recovery catalog.

➤ *Media management layer (MML)*—RMAN uses the MML to read from and write to tapes. Media and storage system vendors provide the media management software required to support tape storage.

➤ *Auxiliary database*—This is the duplicate of the target database that RMAN creates. The auxiliary database is an important component when performing tablespace point-in-time-recovery using RMAN.

➤ *Channel*—This is an RMAN resource allocation that establishes a connection from RMAN to the target database for backup, restore, or recovery operations. For each channel, RMAN creates a server process on the target database.

RMAN Packages

Upon running the catproc.sql script (which is executed every time a database is created) located in the $ORACLE_HOME/rdbms/admin directory, two sets of RMAN packages are created. These packages support RMAN functionality, such as querying information that RMAN needs from the recovery catalog or the target database control file, or interfacing with the OS for creating, restoring, and recovering backups of data files and archive log files. The following code sample extracted from the catproc.sql file shows the addition of RMAN support:

```
Rem on-disk versions of RMAN support
@@dbmsRMAN.sql
@@prvtrmns.plb
@@dbmsbkrs.sql
@@prvtbkrs.plb
```

The dbmsRMAN.sql and prvtrmns.plb files created the DBMS_RCVCAT and DBMS_RCVMAN packages. RMAN uses the DBMS_RCVCAT package to maintain information in the recovery catalog. The DBMS_RCVMAN package queries the recovery catalog or the control file.

The dbmsbkrs.sql and prvtbkrs.plb files created the DBMS_ BACKUP_ RE-STORE package. The DBMS_BACKUP_RESTORE package provides the interface to the Oracle server for creating and restoring backups of data files and archived log files. The Oracle server will read and write backups.

In Oracle8i, the RMAN packages are fixed and are a part of the Oracle kernel. Therefore, these packages are available when the database is in NOMOUNT state.

RMAN Startup Process

The RMAN startup process follows these steps:

1. The RMAN user process is created.

2. The RMAN user process creates two server processes—a default process and a polling process—that connect to the target database. The default process is responsible for SQL command executions, control file resynchronizations, and redo log file roll-forward operations. The polling process is responsible for locating *Remote Procedure Call (RPC)* completions. There is only one polling process per Oracle instance.

3. RMAN creates additional server processes for writing to disk or tape.

4. When a recovery catalog is being used, RMAN creates a server process that connects to a recovery catalog database and facilitates recovery catalog information retrieval and maintenance.

5. When a recovery catalog is not being used, RMAN retrieves the backup and recovery information from the database control file.

RMAN Interfaces

RMAN provides two ways to access its functionality:

➤ Command-line interface

➤ GUI interface

Command-Line Interface

In the RMAN command-line interface, RMAN behaves as a *Command-Line Interpreter (CLI)* with its own proprietary command language. The CLI interprets user requests in the form of RMAN commands. The CLI supports commands in both an interactive mode and a batch mode using command files.

GUI

The RMAN GUI is available through Oracle Enterprise Manager's (OEM's) Backup and Restore Wizards. It provides the same functionality as the command-line interface.

Things to Consider When Using RMAN

You should keep in mind the following issues when using RMAN:

➤ RMAN is not the only way to perform backup and recovery operations in Oracle8i. You could choose to perform backup, restore, and recovery operations using only operating system mechanisms or third party software.

➤ RMAN can use a catalog if one is available, but it is not a catalog.

➤ RMAN does not support backing up pre-Oracle8 databases.

➤ The *Enterprise Backup Utility (EBU)* is not compatible with RMAN. The EBU does not support Oracle8 or Oracle8i databases. It provides backup and recovery functionality for Oracle7 databases only. The EBU is not compatible with Oracle running on Windows NT systems.

➤ A recovery catalog is required when there is a need to store frequently run scripts, to track backup and restore information for historical purposes, or to use RMAN features.

➤ When a recovery catalog is not used, the DBA should perform the following actions:

  ➤ Multiplex control files and place them on different disks.

  ➤ Develop a backup and recovery strategy that includes control files.

  ➤ Maintain a detailed record of what was backed up and when the backup was performed and maintain a detailed record of all RMAN backup logs.

➤ Password files are needed to support remote administration and security needs.

➤ RMAN does not back up the following files:

> ➤ Init.ora file

> ➤ Password files

> ➤ Online redo log files

> ➤ Operating system files

➤ Because RMAN uses Oracle server processes to perform its work, the **PROCESSES** initialization parameter may require adjustment. Additionally, OS parameters (such as shared memory and semaphores under Unix) should be set accordingly.

➤ The **NLS_DATE_FORMAT** and the **NLS_LANG** environment variables should be set before invoking RMAN because these variables determine the format used for the time parameters in RMAN commands.

When to Use RMAN

Backups performed using OS mechanisms can also be performed by RMAN. A DBA should consider the advantages of using RMAN and site-specific requirements when determining when to use RMAN. The advantages of using RMAN include the following:

➤ It supports incremental block-level backups. Backup time is proportional to the number of changes made to the database instead of to the size of the database. Backups take less time because only changed blocks are backed up.

➤ It supports backup, restore, and recovery operations for the Oracle parallel server.

➤ It offers improved performance by the use of parallel operations, reduction of the amount of redo information generated during online database backups, definition of I/O restrictions, and tape streaming.

➤ It offers tight integration with third-party media management tools, such as Legato and Veritas, to interface with storage devices. Check your documentation for specific supported platforms.

➤ It detects corrupted blocks during backup and restore operations. RMAN writes corruption information in the database alert log file, trace files, and control file.

➤ Smaller backup files are required as a result of the compression of unused blocks.

RMAN does not offer the true compression for the backup pieces that third party compression tools do. You may experience an increase in storage requirements when converting from third party compression tools to RMAN.

➤ It enables the backup of the database, tablespaces, data files, control files, and archived redo log files.

➤ It supports database storage of frequently run operations that are specified in the form of scripts.

Backup and Recovery Wizards Overview

The Backup and Recovery Wizards are part of the DBA tools within the OEM administrative toolset. It provides a GUI that enables you to manage your database backup and recovery environment. Installation and configuration of OEM is required before you can use the Backup Manager.

The Backup and Recovery Wizards are client application programs that interface with the RMAN server processes in the target database. The DBA should set up a password file to support remote database administration and SYSDBA access required by the Backup and Recovery Wizards. *Oracle8i DBA: Architecture and Administration Exam Cram* provides detailed information on how to set up and use the password file. The Backup and Recovery Wizards can be used along with the RMAN command-line interface.

You must establish a connection to your target database that requires the backup, restore, or recovery operations before using the Backup and Recovery Wizards. To connect to the Backup Wizard using a recovery catalog, perform the following steps:

1. Start OEM.

2. In the Navigator window, highlight and connect to the target database that requires backup.

3. Invoke the Backup Wizard by right-clicking to get the pop-up menu. Then, highlight Backup Management and Backup... options. Figure 5.1 shows the pop-up menu to invoke the Backup Wizard, and Figure 5.2 shows an example Backup Wizard interface.

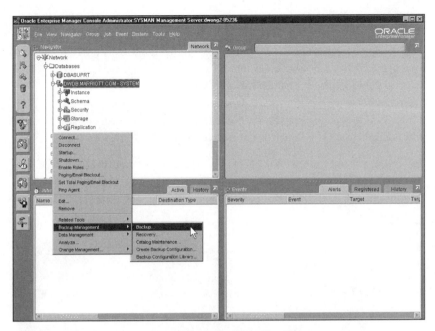

Figure 5.1   The OEM pop-up menu to the Backup Wizard interface.

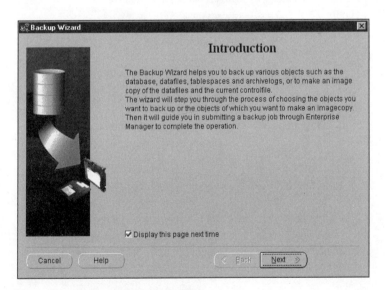

Figure 5.2   The Backup Wizard interface.

Recovery Catalog Overview

The recovery catalog is a central repository of information residing on a remote system that contains information about the structure and previous backups of the target database. It is maintained by the RMAN utility. The recovery catalog enables DBAs to store historical information on backup, restore, and recovery operations. Refer to Chapter 6 for detailed information on recovery catalog creation and maintenance. The information in a recovery catalog includes the following:

➤ The name and time of backup sets. A backup set is comprised of a backup of the data files or the archived redo log files for a single target database. The physical files contained in a backup set are called backup pieces.

➤ The name of and timestamp on the backup data files and datafile copies.

➤ Which archived redo log files have been created by the database and which backups were made by RMAN.

➤ The physical structure of the database. The information is initially populated from the database control file.

If a recovery catalog is used, essential information is stored in both the control file and in a separate database.

➤ Stored scripts that facilitate frequently executed commands.

The actual backups of data are stored as files on storage devices, such as disk or tape. The recovery catalog consists of a set of database objects in a specially created Oracle8i schema. The size of the recovery catalog schema depends on the following factors:

➤ The number of target databases that needs to be monitored.

The recovery catalog should not reside in the target database (database to be backed up) because the database can't be recovered in the mounted state. Make sure enough resources are available. Oracle recommends placing the recovery catalog in a separate tablespace.

➤ The number and size of the RMAN stored scripts.

➤ The number of archived redo log files and the data file backups for each target database and the amount of history you choose to maintain. The DBA needs to incorporate the recovery catalog into the enterprise's backup plan. RMAN can be used to back up the recovery catalog in Oracle8i. The recovery catalog is optional when you're using the RMAN utility.

If there are many target databases to back up, you should consider creating multiple recovery catalog databases to support them.

RMAN Advantages and Disadvantages with the Recovery Catalog

Using the recovery catalog with the RMAN utility offers these advantages:

➤ It supports the preservation of historical information about backup, restore, and recovery actions.

➤ It supports database storage of frequently executed scripts for backup, restore, and recovery operations.

➤ It supports tablespace point-in-time recovery.

➤ It supports incremental block level backups.

The disadvantages of using the recovery catalog with the RMAN utility include the following:

➤ The maintenance overhead of the remote database in which the recovery catalog resides can exceed available resources or may not be cost-effective.

➤ Using the recovery catalog can result in duplication of effort when automated backup, restore, and recovery are not required because existing procedures that are performed manually or through the OS are adequate.

➤ There is no requirement for RMAN features, such as tablespace point-in-time recovery or automatic recovery, when a current control file is not available.

Connecting to Oracle Recovery Manager

You have two options for connecting to the RMAN utility:

➤ With a recovery catalog

➤ Without a recovery catalog

Connecting to RMAN Using a Recovery Catalog

To connect to RMAN using a recovery catalog, perform the following steps:

1. Determine the target database that needs to be backed up.

2. Determine the recovery catalog database for the target database.

3. Use one of the following methods to connect to RMAN:

➤ For local RMAN connections, specify the following code samples at the OS prompt:

```
Unix:
$ ORACLE_SID=your_local_target_database_instance
$export ORACLE_SID
$ RMAN rcvcat RMAN/RMAN@remote_recovery_catalog_instance
RMAN> connect target (password file not in use)
Or
RMAN> connect target username_at_target_db/password
(password file in use)

NT:
C:\> set ORACLE_SID=your_local_target_database_instance
C:\> RMAN rcvcat RMAN/RMAN@remote_recovery_catalog_instance

Recovery Manager: Release 8.1.7.0.0 - Production

RMAN-06008: connected to recovery catalog database

RMAN> connect target (password file not in use)
Or
RMAN> connect target username_at_target_db/password
(password file in use)
```

➤ For RMAN connections initiated by a user with SYSDBA privileges, specify the following code samples at the OS prompt:

```
$ RMAN target username_with_sysdba_privileges/password
rcvcat RMAN/RMAN@remote_recovery_catalog_instance
```

➤ For remote RMAN connections, specify the following code samples at the OS prompt:

```
$ RMAN target username_at_remote_target_db/password rcvcat
RMAN/RMAN@remote_recovery_catalog_instance
```

The connect string for remote connections should be a valid Transparent Network Substrate (TNS) alias contained in the tnsnames.ora file.

Connecting to RMAN without Using a Recovery Catalog

To connect to RMAN without using a recovery catalog, perform the following steps:

1. Determine the target database that needs to be backed up.

2. Use one of the following methods to connect to RMAN:

   ➤ For local RMAN connections, specify the following code samples at the OS prompt:

   ```
   Unix:
   $ ORACLE_SID=your_local_target_database_instance
   $ export ORACLE_SID
   $ RMAN nocatalog
   RMAN> connect target (password file not in use)
   Or
   RMAN> connect target username_at_target_db/password
   (password file in use)

   NT:
   C:\> set ORACLE_SID=your_local_target_database_instance
   C:\> RMAN nocatalog

   Recovery Manager: Release 8.1.7.0.0 - Production
   RMAN-06009: using target database controlfile
   instead of recovery catalog

   RMAN> connect target (password file not in use)
   Or
   RMAN> connect target username_at_target_db/password
   (password file in use)

   RMAN-06005: connected to target database: ORCO
   RMAN>
   ```

   ➤ For RMAN connections initiated by a user with SYSDBA privileges, specify the following code samples at the OS prompt:

   ```
   $ RMAN target username_with_sysdba_privileges/password
   nocatalog
   ```

➤ For remote RMAN connections, specify the following code samples at the OS prompt:

```
$ RAN target username_at_remote_target_db/password nocatalog
```

 The target database must be mounted or open for RMAN to connect. If a recovery catalog is used, the catalog must be open.

To access online help for RMAN command-line arguments, you can type the following invalid RMAN command-line specification and get useful descriptions of valid RMAN command-line arguments and usages:

```
C:\>rman ?

Argument      Value           Description
--------      -----           -----------
target        quoted-string   connect-string for target database
rcvcat        quoted-string   connect-string for recovery catalog
debug         none            if specified, activate debugging mode
cmdfile       quoted-string   name of input command file
msglog        quoted-string   name of output message log file
trace         quoted-string   name of output debugging message log
                              file
append        none            if specified, msglog opened in append
                              mode
nocatalog     none            if specified, then no recovery catalog
-------------------------------------------------------------------
Both single and double quotes (' or ") are accepted for a
quoted-string.
Quotes are not required unless the string contains embedded
white-space.

RMAN-00571: ======================================================
RMAN-00569: =============== ERROR MESSAGE STACK FOLLOWS ===========
RMAN-00571: ======================================================
RMAN-00552: syntax error in command line arguments
RMAN-01006: error signaled during parse
RMAN-02001: unrecognized punctuation symbol "?"

C:\>
```

The preceding error messages resulting from issuing the invalid RMAN command-line specification can be ignored.

Recovery Catalog Creation

You can create the recovery catalog using tools such as the OEM toolset, SQL*Plus, or Server Manager from the command line. The following recovery catalog creation steps use Server Manager:

➤ Choosing a remote database where the recovery catalog will reside

➤ Determining the backup and resynchronization schedule for the recovery catalog

➤ Creating a tablespace for the catalog, which uses the following:

```
SVRMGR> create tablespace RMAN_data
datafile '<file specification>'
      size 20M autoextend on next 20M maxsize 60M;
```

➤ Creating an RMAN user, which uses the following:

```
SVRMGR> create user RMAN identified by RMAN
      2> default tablespace RMAN_data
      3> temporary tablespace temporary_data
      4> quota unlimited on RMAN_data;
```

➤ Granting the **RECOVER_CATALOG_OWNER** role to the RMAN user for maintaining and querying the recovery catalog, which uses the following:

```
SVRMGR> grant RECOVERY_CATALOG_OWNER to RMAN;
```

➤ Granting applicable DBA privileges to the RMAN user, which uses the following:

```
SVRMGR> connect internal as sysdba
Password:
Connected.
SVRMGR> grant dba, sysdba to RMAN;
Statement Processed.
SVRMGR>
```

 The target database must be set up for remote SYSDBA access to use RMAN against the target database.

Note: A password file must exist for granting the SYSDBA role.

➤ Connecting as the RMAN user and invoking RMAN commands to create the database objects for the recovery catalog, which uses the following:

```
C:\> rman catalog RMAN/RMAN MSGLOG=catalog.log
RMAN> create catalog tablespace rman_ts
Exit;
```

 In Oracle8i, the **LOG RMAN** command-line option enables RMAN to output messages and commands to a file. This helps in recording any errors that may occur during catalog creation so that corrective actions can be taken.

➤ Automating recovery catalog operations, such as backup and resynchronization

Control File Information

The *control file* contains information about the backup, restore, and recovery operations performed by the RMAN utility. The amount of information stored in the control file depends on the frequency of backups, the size of the target database, and the default or specified retention period. The init.ora parameter CONTROL_FILE_RECORD_KEEP_TIME is used to specify the number of days the RMAN information is stored in the control file before being overwritten. Setting a low value will cause the information to get overwritten more frequently and will minimize control file growth. The default is seven days and the maximum is 365 days. If a recovery catalog is being used, it is recommended that you specify a lower value.

 When you're using a recovery catalog, always ensure that the resynchronization process occurs more frequently than overwrites to the control file.

The control file will grow only when no free space is in the control file and overwrite space is not available for entries older than the time specified by CONTROL_FILE_RECORD_KEEP_TIME.

RMAN may create a snapshot control file when it needs a read-consistent image of the control file. A snapshot control file is needed when RMAN is querying the noncircular reuse records for data file, tablespace, online redo log file, and thread information. The default location in which the snapshot control file is created under Unix is $ORACLE_HOME/dbs/snapcf_<dbname>.f. You can specify a different location using the following command:

```
RMAN> set snapshot controlfile name to '<file specification>';
```

Because the recovery catalog contains information that is duplicated in the control file, the RMAN utility can use the recovery catalog to re-create control files in the event that they are lost.

Resynchronizing the Control File

Information in the recovery catalog is initially extracted from the target database control file. Any structural changes—such as adding tablespaces—will cause the control file and the recovery catalog to get out of synch because the control file updates are not automatically reflected in the recovery catalog. It is highly recommended that you automate the recovery catalog resynchronization process. The frequency of the resynchronization process depends on the following factors:

➤ How fast the archive log files are created

➤ How often the database structures change

➤ What the performance requirement of the resynchronization process is

Some RMAN commands—such as backup, copy, switch, and restore—will perform automatic resynchronization.

Practice Questions

Question 1

> What utility can be used to interact with RMAN in a GUI?
>
> ○ a. Software Manager
>
> ○ b. Backup and Recovery Wizards in OEM
>
> ○ c. Server Manager
>
> ○ d. SQL*Plus Worksheet
>
> ○ e. Enterprise Backup Utility

The correct answer is b. The Backup and Recovery Wizards are GUI client application programs that interface with the RMAN server processes in the target database. Answers a, c, d, and e are incorrect because they don't provide the capability to interact with RMAN.

Question 2

> What initialization parameter can be used to specify the number of days before RMAN information in the control file can be overwritten?
>
> ○ a. **CONTROL_FILE_RECORD_REUSE_TIME**
>
> ○ b. **CONTROL_FILE_RECORD_REUSE**
>
> ○ c. **CONTROL_FILE_RECORD_KEEP_TIME**
>
> ○ d. **CONTROL_FILE_RECORD_KEEP**
>
> ○ e. **CONTROL_FILE_EXPIRE_TIME**

The correct answer is c. The **CONTROL_FILE_RECORD_KEEP_TIME** initialization parameter can be used to specify the number of days that RMAN keeps backup, restore, and recovery information in the control file. Answers a, b, d, and e are incorrect because they are invalid initialization parameters.

Question 3

> Which of the following are characteristics of RMAN? [Choose two]
>
> ❑ a. It is the only backup option available for an Oracle8i database.
>
> ❑ b. It generates more redo information.
>
> ❑ c. It provides detection of corrupted blocks.
>
> ❑ d. It is compatible with EBU.
>
> ❑ e. It supports incremental block-level backups.

The correct answers are c and e. RMAN features include detection of corrupted blocks and support for incremental block-level backups. Answer a is incorrect because RMAN is not the only backup option for Oracle8i databases. Answer b is incorrect because RMAN generates less redo information. Answer d is incorrect because EBU is not compatible with RMAN and does not support Oracle8 or Oracle8i.

Question 4

> Which of the following RMAN components contains the metadata about the target databases?
>
> ○ a. Media Management Layer
>
> ○ b. Auxiliary database
>
> ○ c. Channel
>
> ○ d. Recovery catalog

The correct answer is d. The RMAN metadata is stored in the recovery catalog or in the target database's control file. The RMAN metadata is the information about the target databases that RMAN uses to perform backup and recovery operations. Answers a, b, and c are incorrect because they don't contain RMAN metadata.

Question 5

Under which of the following circumstances should you use RMAN with a recovery catalog?

○ a. When support for the execution of backup scripts is required

○ b. When you need to minimize the amount of required disk space

○ c. When the backup of archived redo log files requires the use of a recovery catalog

○ d. When historical information about backup, restore, and recovery actions is required

The correct answer is d. A recovery catalog should be used with RMAN to store and maintain historical information about backup, restore, and recovery actions. Answer a is incorrect because a recovery catalog only provides storage for the scripts. Answer b is incorrect because additional storage space is required for the recovery catalog. Answer c is incorrect because a recovery catalog is not required when you're performing backups of the archived redo log files.

Question 6

Which of the following needs to be created to support tablespace point-in-time recovery through RMAN?

○ a. An RMAN configuration file

○ b. A complete offline database backup using OS mechanisms

○ c. Backup scripts

○ d. A recovery catalog

The correct answer is d. A recovery catalog is required to perform tablespace point-in-time recovery. Answer a is incorrect because it is an invalid file. Answers b and c are incorrect because they don't need to be created to perform tablespace point-in-time recovery.

Question 7

Why would you issue the command **$ RMAN target scott/tiger nocatalog**?

○ a. To connect Scott to the RMAN utility locally without a recovery catalog, provided Scott has SYSDBA privileges

○ b. To connect Scott to the RMAN utility locally without a recovery catalog when Scott doesn't have SYSDBA privileges

○ c. To connect Scott to a recovery catalog residing on a remote system

○ d. To connect Scott to a local recovery catalog when Scott has SYSDBA privileges

○ e. To connect Scott to a local recovery catalog when Scott doesn't have SYSDBA privileges

---

The correct answer is a. The given command can be used to connect a user with SYSDBA privileges to the RMAN utility locally without a recovery catalog. Answer b is incorrect because Scott needs SYSDBA privileges to connect to the RMAN utility locally without a recovery catalog. Answers c, d, and e are incorrect because the given commands can't be used to connect to a recovery catalog.

Question 8

In a typical online transaction processing (OLTP) database environment, what would be the minimum frequency for the resynchronization of the recovery catalog and its target database?

- ○ a. Yearly
- ○ b. Quarterly
- ○ c. Monthly
- ○ d. Weekly
- ○ e. Daily

The correct answer is e. You should resynchronize the recovery catalog with its target database at least once a day because updates in the control file are not automatically applied to the recovery catalog. The frequency of the resynchronization process depends on the following factors:

➤ How fast the archive log files are created

➤ How often the database structures change

➤ What the performance requirement for the resynchronization process is

Answers a, b, c, and d are incorrect because they are inadequate for a typical OLTP database environment.

Question 9

Which database role contains privileges that enable the user with the granted role to query and maintain the recovery catalog?

- ○ a. **CONNECT**
- ○ b. **RESOURCE**
- ○ c. **DBA**
- ○ d. **SYSDBA**
- ○ e. **RECOVERY_CATALOG_OWNER**

The correct answer is e. The **RECOVERY_CATALOG_OWNER** role contains privileges that enable the user to query and maintain the recovery catalog. Answers a, b, c, and d are incorrect because these database roles don't contain privileges to query and maintain the recovery catalog.

Question 10

What RMAN command can be issued to configure the location for RMAN to create a temporary backup copy of the control file?

○ a. **RMAN> BACKUP CONTROLFILE NAME TO '/disk01/ RMAN_backup/prod_ctrl_1.snp';**

○ b. **RMAN> RESYNC CATALOG FROM CONTROLFILECOPY '/disk01/ RMAN_backup/prod_ctrl_1.snp';**

○ c. **RMAN> RESET DATABASE TO INCARNATION '/disk01/ RMAN_backup/prod_ctrl_1.snp';**

○ d. **RMAN> SET SNAPSHOT CONTROLFILE NAME TO '/disk01/ RMAN_backup/prod_ctrl_1.snp';**

The correct answer is d. The RMAN command **SET SNAPSHOT CONTROLFILE NAME TO** '*<file_specification>*' is used to define the location that RMAN will use to create a temporary backup of the control file. Answer a is incorrect because it is an invalid RMAN command. Answers b and c are incorrect because they perform other RMAN functions.

Need to Know More?

Loney, Kevin and Marlene Theriault. *Oracle8i DBA Handbook*. Oracle Press, Berkeley, CA, 1999. ISBN 0-07212-188-2. This comprehensive guide for DBAs includes general backup and recovery concepts. Chapter 10 discusses the details of how to implement RMAN.

Sharman, Peter. *Oracle8i DBA: Architecture and Administration Exam Cram*. The Coriolis Group, Scottsdale, AZ, 2001. ISBN 1-58880-036-9. See Chapter 3 for information on setting up and using the password file.

Velpuri, Rama. *Oracle8i Backup and Recovery Handbook*. Oracle Press, Berkeley, CA, 2000. ISBN 0-072-12717-1. This book provides guidance on data protection techniques and offers strategies for data storage, backup, and restore for Oracle8i. Chapter 7 provides good overview of RMAN concepts.

http://technet.oracle.com. This site provides the best information on Oracle's products and technologies. You can also purchase the following manuals online:

Baylis, Ruth. *Oracle8i Administrator's Guide Release 2*. Oracle Corporation, Redwood City, CA, 1999. Part No. A76956-01. This manual describes basic database administration, Oracle server configuration, database storage management, schema object management, and database security for Oracle8i. Chapter 1 discusses authentication password file administration.

Dialeris, Connie. *Oracle8i Recovery Manager User's Guide Release 2*. Oracle Corporation, Redwood City, CA, 1999. Part No. A76990-01. This manual provides guidance on how to administer the backup, restore, and recovery operations of an Oracle database system using the Recovery Manager utility. Chapters 1 and 2 discuss essential RMAN concepts and how to set up RMAN.

Lorentz, Diana. *Oracle8i Reference Release 2*. Oracle Corporation, Redwood City, CA, 1999. Part No. A76961-01. Chapters 1, 2, and 3 provide detailed information on database initialization parameters, static data dictionary views, and dynamic performance views.

www.revealnet.com. This site from RevealNet provides Oracle administration reference software.

Oracle Recovery Catalog Maintenance

. . . .

Terms you'll need to understand:

- ✓ **REGISTER DATABASE** command
- ✓ **RESYNC CATALOG** command
- ✓ **RESET DATABASE** command
- ✓ Backup piece
- ✓ Backup set
- ✓ Data file copy
- ✓ Channel
- ✓ **CHANGE** command
- ✓ **CATALOG** command

- ✓ **REPORT** command
- ✓ **LIST** command
- ✓ Stored scripts
- ✓ **RUN** command
- ✓ **RC_DATABASE**
- ✓ **RC_TABLESPACE**
- ✓ **RC_DATAFILE**
- ✓ **RC_STORED_SCRIPT**
- ✓ **RC_STORED_SCRIPT_LINE**

Techniques you'll need to master:

- ✓ Invoking Recovery Manager (RMAN) with a recovery catalog
- ✓ Registering a database
- ✓ Resynchronizing a database
- ✓ Resetting a database
- ✓ Understanding recovery catalog maintenance

- ✓ Recreating the recovery catalog
- ✓ Understanding report and list generation
- ✓ Using RMAN scripts for backup and recovery operations
- ✓ Understanding useful data dictionary views for the recovery catalog

This chapter provides information on using *Oracle Recovery Manager (RMAN)* with a recovery catalog. I'll focus on maintenance activities for the recovery catalog and will introduce you to commands for registering, resynchronizing, and resetting the database. You will learn how to use the **CHANGE** and **CATALOG** commands to maintain the recovery catalog and will learn how to rebuild a lost or damaged recovery catalog. You will also learn about RMAN's report generation, list generation, and stored scripts. Last of all, you will learn about useful data dictionary views for the recovery catalog.

Invoking Recovery Manager

Several methods invoke the RMAN tool, including the following:

➤ Without a recovery catalog. Refer to Chapter 5 for details.

➤ With a recovery catalog using the **RCVCAT** option.

➤ With an interactive mode interface.

➤ With a batch mode interface using the **CMDFILE** option.

➤ With a batch mode interface with a message log file using the **LOG** option for recording RMAN actions and results. The message log file can be appended or overwritten. The **APPEND** option can be used to continue writing to an existing message log file.

When you're starting RMAN, all command options are optional except one. You must connect to a target database.

Registering a Database

To use RMAN against a target database, you must set up the target database for remote SYSDBA access. To configure a database for remote SYSDBA access, perform the following steps:

1. Log in to your server as the Oracle user, and set the **ORACLE_HOME** and the **ORACLE_SID** environment variables.

2. Change to the dbs or database directory in your **ORACLE_HOME** directory.

3. Rename your password file if one exists. The password file name format is orapw concatenated with the **ORACLE_SID**. An example password file name is orapwORCL.

4. Run the ORAPWD executable to create a new password file, as illustrated by the following sample code:

```
Unix:
$ORACLE_HOME/bin/orapwd file=orapwORCL password=mypassword
entries=10

NT:
D:\ORANT\BIN> orapwd file=orapwORCL password=mypassword
entries=10
```

5. Shut down your database.

6. Edit the init<SID>.ora file. Add the following parameter statement to the file:

```
REMOTE_LOGIN_PASSWORDFILE = EXCLUSIVE
```

You can use the Instance Manager to modify initialization parameters.

7. Start your database using tools like the Server Manager or the Instance Manager.

8. Log in as internal or sys, and create a user that will have remote SYSDBA privileges. The following sample code creates a username of REMOTEUSER with password XXXXXXXX and the SYSDBA role:

```
SVRMGR> connect internal
Password:
Connected.
SVRMGR> create user REMOTEUSER identified by REMOTEPWD;
Statement processed.
SVRMGR> grant connect, resource to REMOTEUSER;
Statement processed.
SVRMGR> grant SYSDBA to REMOTEUSER;
Statement processed.
SVRMGR>
```

9. Download the init<SID>.ora file and the config<SID>.ora file from the server to the $ORACLE_HOME\sysman\ifiles directory on the client machine.

10. Edit the IFILE path in the init<SID>.ora file to match the location on the client machine.

11. Test the remote SYSDBA login account:

```
SQL> CONNECT REMOTEUSER/PASSWORD AS SYSDBA
```

where PASSWORD is the password created with the ORAPWD utility.

Before you can perform any backups against a target database using RMAN with a recovery catalog, you must register the target database in the recovery catalog. The target database must be in the mounted or open state because information about the target database is extracted from the control file to the recovery catalog. The following steps describe how to register a target database with the recovery catalog using the RMAN command-line interface:

1. Connect to the target database as SYSDBAUSER from the command line:

```
RMAN> RMAN Target SYSDBAUSER/PASSWORD@targetdb_loc RCVCAT
rman/rman@catalogdb_loc

Recovery Manager: Release 8.1.7.0.0 - Production

RMAN-06005: connected to target database: TARGETDB
RMAN-06008: connected to recovery catalog database

RMAN>
```

2. Issue the **REGISTER DATABASE** command. The **REGISTER DATABASE** command synchronizes the recovery catalog with the target database control file. The following sample code illustrates this command:

```
RMAN> register database;

RMAN-03022: compiling command: register
RMAN-03023: executing command: register
RMAN-08006: database registered in recovery catalog
RMAN-03023: executing command: full resync
RMAN-08029: snapshot controlfile name set to default value:
%ORACLE_HOME%\DATABASE\SNCF%ORACLE_SID%.ORASE\SN
RMAN-08002: starting full resync of recovery catalog
RMAN-08004: full resync complete
RMAN>
```

To register the target database using the Backup Management menu of *Oracle Enterprise Manager (OEM)*, perform the following steps:

1. Start the OEM console.

2. From the console navigator tree, select a database, tablespace, or datafile, and right-click to access the Backup Management menu.

3. Modify a backup configuration you are already using or select Create Backup Configuration so that you can create a backup configuration that uses a re-covery catalog. The Create Backup Configuration property window appears. Figure 6.1 illustrates the Backup Management|Create Backup Configuration option.

4. Fill out the General and Channels tabs. Figure 6.2 illustrates the General tab, and Figure 6.3 illustrates the Channels tab.

5. On the Recovery Catalog tab as illustrated in Figure 6.4, fill in the infor-mation regarding the recovery catalog where you want your backup information stored, the username, the password, and the service database where the recovery catalog resides.

6. Fill out the Preferred Credentials tab as illustrated in Figure 6.5.

7. Click Create. The database you selected will be registered automatically.

*Note: The **REGISTER DATABASE** command has to be executed for all new target databases.*

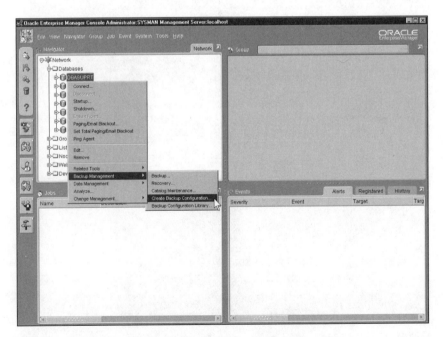

Figure 6.1 The Backup Management|Create Backup Configuration option.

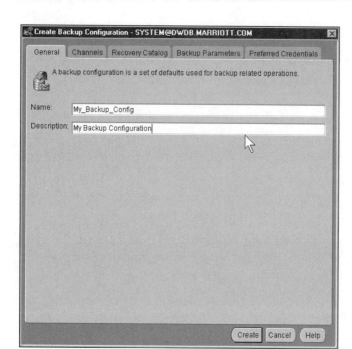

Figure 6.2 General tab.

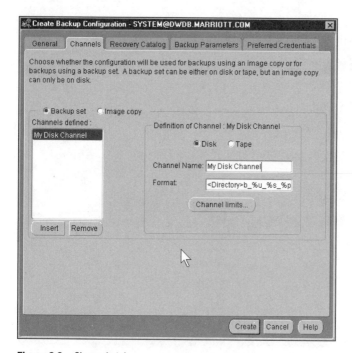

Figure 6.3 Channels tab.

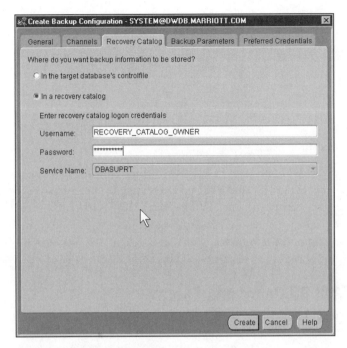

Figure 6.4   Recovery Catalog tab.

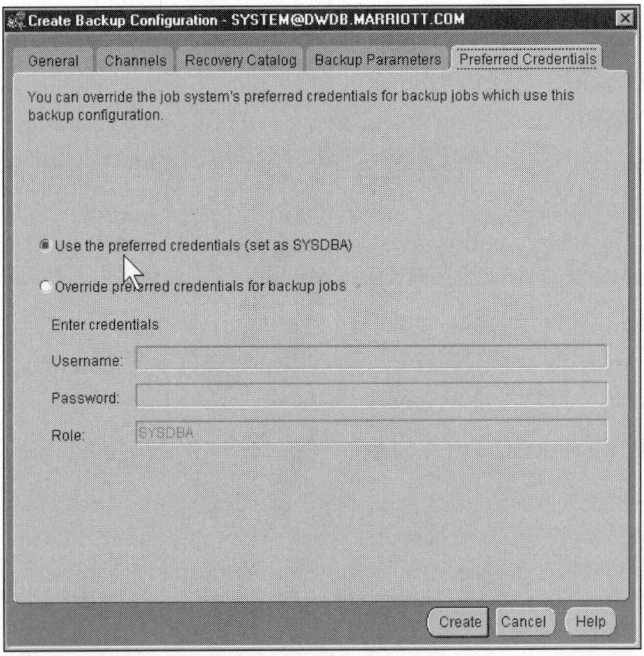

Figure 6.5   Preferred Credentials tab.

Resynchronizing a Database

The recovery catalog is not updated automatically when the following database events occur:

➤ A log switch takes place.

➤ A redo log file is archived.

➤ The database structure is changed.

The **RESYNC CATALOG** operation enables RMAN to compare the recovery catalog with the current control file of the target database and to update the recovery catalog with new or changed information. The **RESYNC CATALOG** operation should be performed frequently. For performance reasons, RMAN only resynchronizes the control file information that is inconsistent with the recovery catalog. The recovery catalog stores all pertinent information required for recovery.

RESYNC CATALOG Command Syntax

The command syntax for the **RESYNC CATALOG** command is as follows:

```
resync catalog [from controlfilecopy <control_file_name>];
```

Recovery Catalog Information Affected by the Resynchronization Process

When the **RESYNC CATALOG** command is issued to RMAN and the target database is in the mounted state, the following information in the recovery catalog may be updated:

➤ Structural database information that is associated with data files and tablespaces. If the target database is in the open state, the rollback segment information will also be updated.

➤ Log switch information. RMAN maintains log switch information so that it knows which archived redo log files are available.

➤ Archived log copy information that is associated with archived redo log files.

➤ Backup history information relating to backup sets, backup pieces, backup set members, and file copies. This update occurs only when the recovery catalog database is unavailable and when a backup or copy command is processed.

When to Perform the **RESYNC CATALOG** Operation

The database administrator (DBA) is responsible for issuing a **RESYNC CATA-LOG** command after making any structural database changes to the target database. A structural database change includes the following target database actions:

➤ Adding a rollback segment

➤ Dropping a rollback segment

➤ Adding a tablespace

➤ Dropping a tablespace

➤ Adding a data file to an existing tablespace

The DBA should be aware that, if the target database has mounted a noncurrent control file, such as a backup control file, a newly created control file, or an outdated control file, the structural database information in the recovery catalog will not be updated.

RMAN will perform automatic resynchronization before and after a backup, restore, or recovery command if a connection to the recovery catalog database has been established. If a connection to the recovery catalog database can't be established, the **RESYNC CATALOG** command needs to be issued manually after the backup and copy commands. The following code sample shows the results of the **RESYNC CATALOG** command, which, by default, is against the current target database control file:

```
RMAN> resync catalog;

RMAN-03022: compiling command: resync
RMAN-03023: executing command: resync
RMAN-08002: starting full resync of recovery catalog
RMAN-08004: full resync complete
RMAN>
```

To perform resynchronization against a backup control file, issue the following command:

```
RMAN> resync catalog from controlfilecopy
'<backup_control_file_specification>';
```

Resetting a Database

When an incomplete recovery has been performed for a target database, the target database will be opened with the **RESETLOGS** option, which resets the sequence number of the online redo log files to zero. Refer to Chapter 12 for detailed information on incomplete recovery.

The recovery catalog will not be accessible to RMAN until a **RESET DATABASE** command has been issued for that database. The **RESET DATABASE** command directs RMAN to create a new incarnation or version of the target database information in the recovery catalog. An incarnation of a database is a sequence number used to identify a version of the target database prior to the reset of the log sequence number to zero. RMAN maintains database incarnation information so that applicable backups and archived redo log files are associated with the right incarnation. This prevents you from incorrectly applying redo log files to the wrong version of the database.

RESET DATABASE Command Syntax

The command syntax for the **RESET DATABASE** command is as follows:

```
Reset database [to incarnation <incarnation key identifier>];
```

The following code sample illustrates the result you'll get if you try to reset your database when the incarnation is already registered:

```
RMAN> reset database;
RMAN-03022: compiling command: reset
RMAN-03023: executing command: reset
RMAN-03026: error recovery releasing channel resources
RMAN-00569: =======error message stack follows==========
RMAN-03006: non-retryable error occurred during execution
of command
RMAN-07004: unhandled exception during command execution
on channel
RMAN-10032: unhandled exception during execution of job step 1:
RMAN-20009: database incarnation already registered
```

The **RESET DATABASE TO INCARNATION** command is typically used to undo the **RESETLOGS** operation by restoring backups of prior incarnations or versions of the database. You can obtain the database incarnation key identifier by using the **LIST INCARNATION OF DATABASE** command, as illustrated by the following code sample:

```
RMAN> list incarnation of database;
RMAN-03022: compiling command: list
```

```
RMAN-06240: List of Database Incarnations
RMAN-06241: DB Key Inc Key DB Name DB ID  CUR Reset SCN Reset Time
RMAN-06242: -- --- --- --- -- ---- -- --  --- ----- --- ----- ----
RMAN-06243: 1      2        ORCO   115732 YES 1             26-DEC-99
RMAN-06244: 1      7        ORCO   115732 NO  1075          22-DEC-99
RMAN> reset database to incarnation 7;
```

Alternatively, you can perform the following steps when using the Catalog Maintenance Wizard of the Backup Management menu to reset the recovery catalog database:

1. Select the target database from the OEM console, and select the Backup Management menu.

2. Select Catalog Maintenance as illustrated in Figure 6.6.

3. The Catalog Maintenance Wizard Introduction window appears as illustrated in Figure 6.7.

4. Select the Reset Database radio button on the Operation Choice window as illustrated in Figure 6.8.

5. Select the backup configuration on the Configuration window as illustrated in Figure 6.9.

6. Click Finish to reset the recovery catalog database.

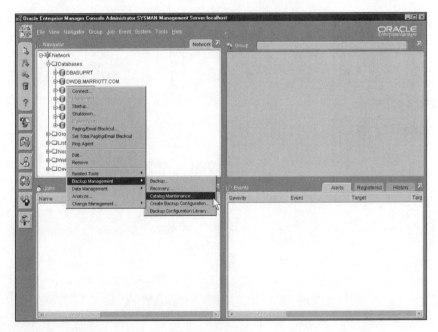

Figure 6.6   Catalog Maintenance pop-up menu option.

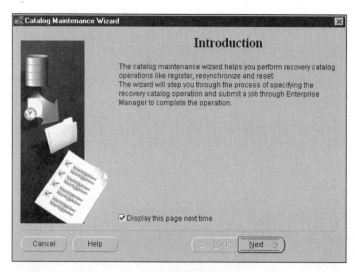

Figure 6.7 Catalog Maintenance Wizard Introduction window.

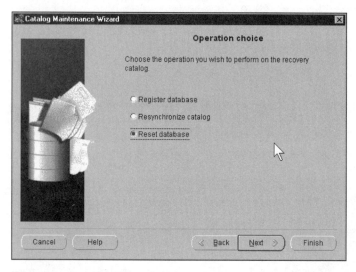

Figure 6.8 Operation Choice window.

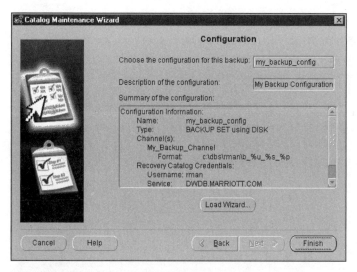

Figure 6.9   Configuration window.

Recovery Catalog Maintenance

To perform recovery catalog maintenance effectively, a DBA should have an understanding of the following terminology:

➤ *Backup piece*—A physical file on a disk or tape that contains one or more data files or archived redo log files in RMAN format

➤ *Backup set*—A logical structure that is comprised of backup pieces

➤ *Data file copy*—A physical copy of a data file or control file on disk

➤ *Archived logs*—Copies of redo log files for an archiving-enabled database

The commands for performing recovery catalog maintenance include the following:

➤ **ALLOCATE CHANNEL** and **RELEASE CHANNEL** commands

➤ **CHANGE** command

➤ **CATALOG** command

ALLOCATE CHANNEL and RELEASE CHANNEL Commands

A *channel* is an RMAN resource allocation. Each allocated channel starts a new Oracle server process that performs backup, restore, and recovery operations. The number of channels allocated affects the degree of parallelism for backup, restore, and recovery. The type of channel specified determines whether the Oracle server process reads and writes to disk or reads and writes through the Media Management Interface to a Media Manager. Any command that accesses the operating system must allocate a channel. Only one channel can be allocated at a time, so you should release the channel when all operating system (OS) commands have been completed. The following code sample illustrates the **ALLOCATE CHANNEL** and the **RELEASE CHANNEL** commands:

```
RMAN> allocate channel channel_a type disk;
RMAN> allocate channel for delete type 'SBT_TAPE';
RMAN> release channel channel_a;
```

The **FOR DELETE** option is used only for deleting files. It cannot be used as an input or output channel for a job. Refer to Chapter 8 for more information on the **ALLOCATE CHANNEL** command.

CHANGE Command

The **CHANGE** command is used on backup sets, backup pieces, data file copies, archive logs, and control files. It performs the following actions:

➤ It updates the recovery catalog to mark files as AVAILABLE or UNAVAILABLE for restore and recovery. The following code sample illustrates using the **CHANGE** command to mark an archived redo log file as unavailable:

```
RMAN> change archivelog '/u1/archive/arch_999.rdo' unavailable;
```

➤ It removes references to nonexistent physical files from the control file and the recovery catalog. The following code sample illustrates removing a reference to an archived redo log file that no longer exists in the file system:

```
RMAN> change archivelog '/u1/archive/arch_998.rdo' uncatalog;
```

➤ It determines files in the recovery catalog with corresponding physical files on storage devices and removes or deletes files from the recovery catalog without corresponding physical files. The following code sample illustrates using the Validate option to remove a batch of files from the recovery catalog when they have been deleted from the physical storage media:

```
RMAN> change archivelog all validate;
```

➤ It removes old files from the control file and recovery catalog and from the physical media. The following code sample illustrates deleting a data file backup:

```
RMAN> allocate channel for delete type disk;
RMAN> change datafilecopy '/u1/oradata/app1data.bak' delete;
RMAN> release channel;
```

CATALOG Command

The **CATALOG** command allows you to add data file copy information, archived redo log information, or control file copy information to the recovery catalog. The **CATALOG** command records information for any of the following types of files:

➤ Files created before the installation of RMAN

➤ Files created using OS backup mechanisms

➤ Files with the same database incarnation number

➤ Files that have an Oracle8 or later file format

➤ Files that belong to the target database

When mirrored disk drives are broken, you can use the **CATALOG** command to add the location of the file copies to the recovery catalog. When the disks are remirrored, you can use the **CHANGE...UNCATALOG** command to remove the file copies from the recovery catalog.

The following sample code illustrates adding data file copy and archived redo log files to the recovery catalog:

```
UNIX:
RMAN> catalog datafilecopy '/u1/backup/app1data.bak';
RMAN> catalog archivelog '/u1/archive/arch_102.log';

NT:
RMAN> catalog datafilecopy 'd:\orant\backup\app1data.bak';
RMAN> catalog archivelog 'd:\orant\archive\arch_102.log';
```

Recreating the Recovery Catalog

If the recovery catalog database is lost or damaged, follow these steps:

1. Extract information from a backup control file by issuing the **RESYNC CATALOG FROM BACKUP CONTROLFILE** *<FILE_NAME>* command, and rebuild the recovery catalog.

2. If an export dump file containing the data for the recovery catalog owner is available, import the data and use the **RESYNC** command to synchronize with the target database.

3. After rebuilding the catalog database, issue **CATALOG** commands to recatalog data file copies, control file copies, and archived redo log files.

You should be aware of the following issues when recreating the recovery catalog:

➤ The **CATALOG** command cannot be used to catalog backup sets or backup pieces. You must use the **RESYNC CATALOG FROM BACKUP CONTROLFILE** command to recreate information about backup sets.

➤ During resynchronization, RMAN may add records for files that no longer exist because no verification is performed. You can remove those records by using the **CHANGE...DELETE** command.

Report and List Generation

The recovery catalog reporting commands enable DBAs to analyze and list information contained in the recovery catalog. Oracle8i supports two reporting commands:

➤ REPORT command

➤ LIST command

REPORT Command

The REPORT command is used to facilitate analysis of the backup, copy, restore, and recovery operations. This command provides more detailed analysis than the **LIST** command. You can produce reports using the **REPORT** command to meet requirements such as:

➤ Determining what files need to be backed up. You can use the **REPORT NEED BACKUP...** command for this purpose.

➤ Determining which backups are no longer needed and can be deleted. You can use the **REPORT OBSOLETE** command for this purpose.

➤ Determining which files are not recoverable due to unrecoverable operations. You can use the **REPORT UNRECOVERABLE...** command for this purpose.

➤ Determining the physical structure of the database at a point-in-time in the past. You can use the **REPORT SCHEMA** command for this purpose.

The **REPORT NEED BACKUP** command is used to identify all data files needing a backup. This report assumes that the most recent backup would be used in the event of a restore. The options to the **REPORT NEED BACKUP** command are as follows:

➤ INCREMENTAL—An integer value that specifies the maximum number of incremental backups that should be restored during recovery. A full backup is needed for a data file if it needs at least this number of incremental backups for recovery. The following code sample illustrates producing a report of files needing four or more incremental backups for recovery:

```
RMAN> report need backup incremental 4 database;
```

➤ DAYS—An integer value that specifies the maximum number of days since the last full or incremental backup of a file. A file will need a backup if the most recent backup occurred at least this number of days in the past. The following code sample illustrates producing a report showing files for the appl1_data tablespace that have not been backed up for four days:

```
RMAN> report need backup days 4 tablespace appl_data;
```

➤ REDUNDANCY—An integer value that specifies the minimum level of redundancy needed. For example, a redundancy level of three requires a backup if at least three backups are not available. The following code sample illustrates producing a report showing a redundancy level of two:

```
RMAN> report need backup redundancy 2;
```

REPORT Command Syntax

The **REPORT** command syntax relevant to this chapter is as follows:

```
Report need backup <options> = integer <object> <name>;
Report unrecoverable <object> <name>;
Report obsolete redundancy = integer;
Report schema <atClause>;
```

Table 6.1 describes command elements and their associated values.

You cannot specify both **INCREMENTAL** and **DAYS** as options.

LIST Command

The **LIST** command is used to display information on the database elements from the recovery catalog. Specifically, the **LIST** command can provide information on the following recovery catalog elements:

➤ Backup sets that contain a backup of a specified list of data files

➤ Copies of specified data files

➤ Backup sets containing a backup of a data file for a specified tablespace

➤ Copies of any data file for a specified tablespace

➤ Backup sets that include a backup of archived redo logs for a specified range

➤ Copies of archived redo logs with a specified range or name

➤ Database incarnations

LIST Command Syntax

The **LIST** command syntax relevant to this chapter is as follows:

```
List <Options> of <Object List> <values>;
List incarnation of database of <values>;
```

Table 6.2 describes command elements and their associated values.

You cannot specify both **INCREMENTAL** and **DAYS**.

 You must connect to RMAN with a target database and a recovery catalog before using the **LIST** command.

The following code samples illustrate the use of the **LIST** command.

➤ List all file copies of data files in the **APP_DATA** tablespace:

```
RMAN> list copy of tablespace "APP_DATA";
```

➤ List incarnation for database **ORCL**:

```
RMAN> list incarnation of database ORCL;
```

➤ List all backup sets containing the data file ecs01.ora:

```
RMAN> list backupset of datafile "/u1/oradata/ecs01.ora";
```

Table 6.1	Elements of the REPORT command.
Element	**Value**
Options	Incremental; days; redundancy;
Object	Datafile; tablespace; database;
Name	Quoted_string;
AtClause	At time=*<quoted_string>*; at scn=integer; at logseq=integer;

Table 6.2	Elements of the LIST Command.
Element	**Value**
Options	Copy; backupset;
Object List	Datafile *<quoted_string>*; tablespace *<quoted_string>*; database; archivelog all;
Values	Tag=*<quoted_string>*; device type *<quoted_string>*; like *<quoted_string>*; from time=*<quoted_string>*; until time=*<quoted_string>*;

RMAN Scripts for Backup and Recovery Operations

An RMAN stored script is a set of RMAN commands that are stored in the recovery catalog. A RMAN stored script enables a DBA using RMAN on different platforms to access the scripts. A stored script can relate to a single database and can be executed only if you're using RMAN with the recovery catalog option. RMAN scripts enable DBAs to perform the following tasks:

➤ Plan, develop, and test backup, restore, and recovery command procedures.

➤ Specify and store frequently used backup, restore, and recovery operations in the recovery catalog database.

➤ Automate the backup, restore, and recovery process so user errors are minimized.

Script Commands

Four stored script commands enable DBAs to maintain scripts:

➤ CREATE—Creates a stored script in the recovery catalog:

```
Create script <quoted_string> {<commands-allocate, backup,
recover, sql> ; }
```

➤ REPLACE—Replaces and creates a stored script in the recovery catalog:

```
Replace script <quoted_string> {<commands-allocate, backup,
recover, sql> ; }
```

➤ DELETE—Deletes a stored script from the recovery catalog:

```
Delete script <quoted_string>;
```

➤ PRINT—Prints a stored script to the RMAN message log:

```
Print script <quoted_string>;
```

The following code samples illustrate the **CREATE SCRIPT, REPLACE SCRIPT,** and **DELETE SCRIPT** commands:

```
RMAN> create script DailyBackup {
        Allocate channel c1 type disk;
        Backup
        Incremental level 0
        Format 'df_%d_%s_%p'
        Fileperset 10
        (database include current controlfile);
        sql 'alter database archive log current';}

RMAN> replace script CtrlFileCopy {
        Allocate channel c1 type disk;
        Copy
        Current controlfile to '/u1/oradata/backup/cur_ctrl.ora';
        Release channel c1;
        }

RMAN> delete script CtrlFileCopy;
```

RUN Command

The **RUN** command can be used to execute a stored script. The **RUN** command can execute OS commands, *Structured Query Language (SQL)* scripts, backup commands, stored scripts, and so on. The basic syntax for the **RUN** command is as follows:

```
Run { <commands> ; }
```

Commands can be one of the following: **ALLOCATE, BACKUP, EXECUTE_ SCRIPT** *<NAME>*, **RECOVER, SQL, HOST,** and so forth.

The **RUN** command compiles the commands into PL/SQL code blocks called *steps*. The steps are not written to the recovery catalog, but are run immediately from memory after the compilation phase. The **RUN** commands can be stored in a script on the file system, or, alternatively, RMAN can be used to create scripts.

The following code samples illustrate the use of the **RUN** command:

➤ Run an OS command:

```
RMAN> run { host "ls -al"; }
```

➤ Run a SQL command:

```
RMAN> run { sql "alter system switch logfile"; }
```

➤ Run a stored script:

```
RMAN> run { execute script DailyBackup; }
```

Data Dictionary Views for the Recovery Catalog

Several data dictionary views for the recovery catalog were created as a result of running the **CREATE CATALOG** command. These data dictionary views include the following:

➤ **RC_DATABASE**—Provides information on currently registered databases and their current incarnations:

```
SQL> desc rc_database
 Name                                    Null?    Type
 ----                                    -----    ----
 DB_KEY                                  NOT NULL NUMBER
 DBINC_KEY                                        NUMBER
 DBID                                    NOT NULL NUMBER
 NAME                                    NOT NULL VARCHAR2(8)
 RESETLOGS_CHANGE#                       NOT NULL NUMBER
 RESETLOGS_TIME                          NOT NULL DATE
```

➤ **RC_TABLESPACE**—Provides information on the tablespaces from the target database that are currently stored in the recovery catalog. Information on dropped tablespaces and tablespaces that belong to older database incarnations are also provided:

```
SQL> desc rc_tablespace
 Name                                     Null?      Type
 ----                                     -----      ----
 DB_KEY                                   NOT NULL   NUMBER
 DBINC_KEY                                NOT NULL   NUMBER
 DB_NAME                                  NOT NULL   VARCHAR2(8)
 TS#                                      NOT NULL   NUMBER
 NAME                                     NOT NULL   VARCHAR2(30)
 CREATION_CHANGE#                         NOT NULL   NUMBER
 CREATION_TIME                                       DATE
 DROP_CHANGE#                                        NUMBER
 DROP_TIME                                           DATE
```

➤ **RC_DATAFILE**—Provides information on the data files from the target database that are currently registered in the recovery catalog:

```
SQL> desc rc_datafile
 Name                                     Null?      Type
 ----                                     -----      ----
 DB_KEY                                   NOT NULL   NUMBER
 DBINC_KEY                                NOT NULL   NUMBER
 DB_NAME                                  NOT NULL   VARCHAR2(8)
 TS#                                      NOT NULL   NUMBER
 TABLESPACE_NAME                          NOT NULL
VARCHAR2(30)
 FILE#                                    NOT NULL   NUMBER
 CREATION_CHANGE#                         NOT NULL   NUMBER
 CREATION_TIME                                       DATE
 DROP_CHANGE#                                        NUMBER
 DROP_TIME                                           DATE
 BYTES                                               NUMBER
 BLOCKS                                              NUMBER
 BLOCK_SIZE                               NOT NULL   NUMBER
 NAME
VARCHAR2(1024)
 STOP_CHANGE#                                        NUMBER
 READ_ONLY                                NOT NULL   NUMBER
```

➤ **RC_STORED_SCRIPT**—Provides information on scripts that are currently stored in the recovery catalog for a target database:

```
SQL> desc rc_stored_script
 Name                              Null?    Type
 ----                              -----    ----
 DB_KEY                            NOT NULL NUMBER
 DB_NAME                           NOT NULL VARCHAR2(8)
 SCRIPT_NAME                       NOT NULL VARCHAR2(100)
```

➤ **RC_STORED_SCRIPT_LINE**—Provides information on the commands that make up the stored scripts:

```
SQL> desc rc_stored_script_line
 Name                              Null?    Type
 ----                              -----    ----
 DB_KEY                            NOT NULL NUMBER
 SCRIPT_NAME                       NOT NULL VARCHAR2(100)
 LINE                              NOT NULL NUMBER
 TEXT                              NOT NULL
VARCHAR2(1024)
```

Practice Questions

Question 1

A new tablespace has been added to the production database. After you are connected to RMAN, which of the following commands should you issue to update the recovery catalog?

- ○ a. **CATALOG**
- ○ b. **CHANGE**
- ○ c. **REGISTER**
- ○ d. **RESYNC CATALOG**
- ○ e. **UPDATE CATALOG**

The correct answer is d. The **RESYNC CATALOG** command, when issued with the target database in the mounted or open state, will update the recovery catalog information for log switches, archived logs, backup history, and physical database structures. Answers a, b, and c are incorrect because they serve other purposes. Answer e is incorrect because it is an invalid command.

Question 2

Which of the following data dictionary views should be used to retrieve a list of tablespaces registered in the recovery catalog for the XYZ database?

- ○ a. **RC_DATAFILE**
- ○ b. **RC_TABLESPACE**
- ○ c. **RC_DATABASE**
- ○ d. **RC_TABLESPACES**
- ○ e. **DBA_TABLESPACES**

The correct answer is b. The **RC_TABLESPACE** data dictionary view provides information on tablespaces registered in the recovery catalog for the target database. Answers a and c are incorrect because these data dictionary views don't provide information on tablespaces registered in the recovery catalog. Answer d is incorrect because it is an invalid view. Answer e is incorrect because it provides information on the tablespaces for a database that may not be registered in the recovery catalog.

Question 3

> Evaluate this RMAN command:
>
> ```
> RMAN> delete script 'backup_c';
> ```
>
> What will this command accomplish if it is issued?
>
> ○ a. It will remove the backup_c script from the recovery catalog.
>
> ○ b. It will remove the script object from the backup_c file.
>
> ○ c. It will remove the script object from the backup_c recovery catalog.
>
> ○ d. It will remove the backup_c script from the target database.
>
> ○ e. It will drop the script object from the backup_c recovery catalog.

The correct answer is a. The **DELETE SCRIPT** command removes a script from the recovery catalog. Answers b, c, d, and e are incorrect because the sample command doesn't support these invalid tasks.

Question 4

> When connected to RMAN, which **RUN** command option enables you to execute an operating system command?
>
> ○ a. **ALLOCATE**
>
> ○ b. **BACKUP**
>
> ○ c. **SQL**
>
> ○ d. **HOST**
>
> ○ e. **EXECUTE SCRIPT**

The correct answer is d. The **HOST** option of the **RUN** command enables you to issue OS commands within RMAN. Answers a, b, c, and e are incorrect because these options serve other purposes.

Question 5

Which RMAN command should you use to identify all the data files that haven't been backed up in the last three days?

- ○ a. **RMAN> report need backup days 3**
- ○ b. **RMAN> list need backup days 3**
- ○ c. **RMAN> report need backup days 3 tablespace app_data**
- ○ d. **RMAN> list need backup days 3 tablespace app_data**
- ○ e. **RMAN> report need backup redundancy 3**
- ○ f. **RMAN> report need backup 3 days**

The correct answer is a. The **REPORT NEED BACKUP DAYS 3** command will list all the data files that have not been backed up in the last three days. Answers b and d are incorrect because they are invalid list commands. Answer c is incorrect because it will only show data files for the **app_data** tablespace that have not been backed up in the last three days. Answer e is incorrect because it will only list all data files that have less than three backups available. Answer f is incorrect because it is an invalid report command.

Question 6

What action is typically performed by the DBA after he or she creates a recovery catalog and starts RMAN for the first time?

- ○ a. Connecting to the target database
- ○ b. Creating the RMAN user
- ○ c. Registering the database
- ○ d. Updating the recovery catalog
- ○ e. Performing a backup against a target database

The correct answer is c. The DBA typically registers the target database after recovery catalog creation and initial invocation of RMAN. Answer a is incorrect because the connection to the target database has already been established upon starting RMAN. Answer b is incorrect because the RMAN user was created during recovery catalog initialization. Answers d and e are incorrect because, before a backup can be performed against a target database or updates can be applied to the recovery catalog, the target database must be registered in the recovery catalog.

Question 7

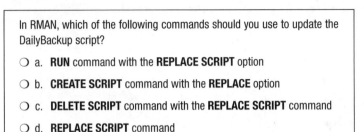

In RMAN, which of the following commands should you use to update the DailyBackup script?

○ a. **RUN** command with the **REPLACE SCRIPT** option

○ b. **CREATE SCRIPT** command with the **REPLACE** option

○ c. **DELETE SCRIPT** command with the **REPLACE SCRIPT** command

○ d. **REPLACE SCRIPT** command

The correct answer is d. The **REPLACE SCRIPT** command overwrites a stored script in the recovery catalog. Answers a, b, and c are incorrect because they are invalid command specifications.

Question 8

The XYZ database is registered in a recovery catalog. Which of the following RMAN commands should be issued after a point-in-time recovery has been performed for the XYZ database?

○ a. **RESTORE DATABASE**

○ b. **RECOVER CATALOG**

○ c. **RESTORE CATALOG**

○ d. **RESET CATALOG**

○ e. **RESET DATABASE**

The correct answer is e. After the XYZ database has been restored, recovered, and opened with the **RESETLOGS** option, the DBA needs to register the new version of the database in the recovery catalog using the **RESET DATABASE** command. Answers a, b, c, and d are incorrect because they are invalid commands.

Question 9

> Which RMAN command enables you to list the commands in the DailyBackup script?
>
> ○ a. **print DailyBackup**
>
> ○ b. **run print DailyBackup**
>
> ○ c. **execute print DailyBackup**
>
> ○ d. **print script DailyBackup**

The correct answer is d. The **PRINT SCRIPT** command sends the script to the RMAN message log, which lists the commands in the script. Answers a, b, and c are invalid command specifications.

Question 10

> Evaluate this command:
>
> ```
> RMAN> list backupset of datafile
> '/ul/oradata/app103.ora';
> ```
>
> What task is accomplished after this command is issued?
>
> ○ a. A list of all the data files in the same backup set as app103.ora is displayed.
>
> ○ b. A list of all backups sets containing app103.ora is displayed.
>
> ○ c. The location of the backup for app103.ora is displayed.
>
> ○ d. The app103.ora file is added to the backup set.

The correct answer is b. The **LIST** command with the **BACKUPSET** option displays all the backup sets that contain the user-specified data file, tablespace, or all the archived redo logs. Answers a, c, and d are incorrect because the sample command doesn't accomplish these tasks.

Need to Know More?

 Loney, Kevin and Marlene Theriault. *Oracle8i DBA Handbook*. Oracle Press, Berkeley, CA, 1999. ISBN 0-07212-188-2. This comprehensive guide for DBAs includes general backup and recovery concepts. Chapter 10 discusses the details of how to implement RMAN.

 Velpuri, Rama. *Oracle8i Backup and Recovery Handbook*. Oracle Press, Berkeley, CA, 2000. ISBN 0-072-12717-1. This book provides information on how to maximize uptime and recover data without compromising mission critical systems. Actual corporate scenarios and case studies are included. Chapter 7 discusses how to create, maintain, and query the recovery catalog.

 http://technet.oracle.com. This site provides the best information on Oracle's products and technologies. You can also purchase the following manuals online:

Dialeris, Connie. *Oracle8i Recovery Manager User's Guide Release 2*. Oracle Corporation, Redwood City, CA, 1999. Part No. A76990-01. This manual provides guidance on how to administer the backup, restore, and recovery operations of an Oracle database system using the Recovery Manager utility. Chapters 1 and 2 discuss essential RMAN concepts and how to set up RMAN. Chapter 3 discusses recovery catalog management and Chapter 4 is a good resource to learn about generating lists and reports from RMAN.

Lorentz, Diana. *Oracle8i Reference Release 2*. Oracle Corporation, Redwood City, CA, 1999. Part No. A76961-01. This manual describes the architecture, processes, structures, and other concepts of Oracle8i and provides detailed information on static and dynamic data dictionary views. Chapters 1, 2, and 3 provide detailed information on database initialization parameters, static data dictionary views, and dynamic performance views.

 www.revealnet.com. This site from RevealNet provides Oracle administration reference software.

7

Physical Backups without Oracle Recovery Manager

Terms you'll need to understand:

✓ Physical database backup
✓ Closed (offline) database backup
✓ Open (online) database backup
✓ Backup mode
✓ Logging mode
✓ Nologging mode
✓ Read-only tablespace

✓ **V$DATAFILE**
✓ **V$CONTROLFILE**
✓ **V$LOGFILE**
✓ **V$TABLESPACE**
✓ **V$BACKUP**
✓ **V$DATAFILE_HEADER**

Techniques you'll need to master:

✓ Understanding physical backup methods
✓ Understanding recovery implications of closed and open database backups
✓ Understanding backup implications of Logging and Nologging modes

✓ Backing up control files
✓ Backing up read-only tablespaces
✓ Understanding useful data dictionary views for database backups

Oracle provides a variety of backup methods that help protect an Oracle database. There are three standard methods of backing up an Oracle database: exports, open (online) database backups, and closed (offline) database backups. An export is a logical backup of the database and is described in Chapter 13. A logical backup involves making a copy of the logical database structures with or without the associated business data. A logical backup does not involve the physical database files. The other two backup methods are physical backups of the database files. This chapter describes how to perform physical backups without using the Oracle Recovery Manager (RMAN) utility. Refer to Chapters 5, 6, and 8 for detailed information on the RMAN utility.

Physical Backup Methods

A physical database backup is a backup of the database files that is performed using operating system facilities while the database is *open* or *closed*. There are two types of physical backups:

➤ Closed (offline or cold) database backup

➤ Open (online or hot) database backup

Each physical backup method provides a different level of data recoverability. Selecting the most effective backup method for your database environment will help to minimize data loss from media failures and to maximize data recovery.

You also may use third-party products for your database backups. If you do use a third-party product, you will need to understand how it works, standalone or with Oracle. For some third-party backup products, such as Legato, Oracle offers interfaces between the RMAN utility and the third-party backup product.

Closed Database Backups

A *closed* or *cold* database backup is an operating system backup of the database files that is made after the database has been shut down cleanly using **SHUTDOWN NORMAL, SHUTDOWN IMMEDIATE,** or **SHUTDOWN TRANSACTIONAL.** This backup method provides a complete snapshot of the database at the time of the database shutdown.

Closed database backups performed using **SHUTDOWN ABORT** are not reliable. DBAs typically restart the database and perform a normal shutdown prior to starting a closed database backup.

Typically, the files in a closed database backup include the following:

➤ Data files

➤ Control files

➤ Online redo log files

➤ Parameter files

➤ Password file

If the database has been shut down cleanly, it is not necessary to include the online redo log files as part of a closed full database backup. However, having the backup online redo log files does help in full database restore situations.

Use the closed database backup method to recover to the point of the last backup after a media failure.

Full pathnames of database files should be maintained and used in backups, though this can cause problems if the same file systems are not available to restore the data files. In multiple database environments, you should give special consideration to setting up standard naming conventions so that the appropriate database files are associated with the corresponding databases.

Taking a Closed (or Cold) Database Backup

Performing a full *closed (or cold)* database backup when the Oracle server instance is shut down involves the following steps:

1. Generate an up-to-date listing of all pertinent files to back up.

2. Cleanly shut down the Oracle instance using the **SHUTDOWN NORMAL, SHUTDOWN IMMEDIATE,** or **SHUTDOWN TRANSACTIONAL** command.

3. Copy all data files, control files, redo log files, parameter files, and the password file to the designated backup location using the applicable operating system backup utility.

4. Restart the Oracle instance, and open the database for general use.

You should consider the following when taking a closed database backup:

➤ If users might still be accessing the database at the time of database shutdown, the **SHUTDOWN IMMEDIATE** or the **SHUTDOWN TRANSACTIONAL** command is more appropriate than the default **SHUTDOWN NORMAL** command.

➤ Consider fully automating the closed database backup process to minimize operator errors and to ensure that pertinent files are consistently backed up.

➤ Files associated with read-only tablespaces don't need to be included in the full database backups.

➤ The parameter file and the password file should be included in the full database backup even though they are not physically part of the database.

Open (or Hot) Database Backups

Organizations that operate 24 hours a day and seven days a week have special needs for backup and recovery. If the business cannot afford to shut down the database to perform backups, it should have the option to perform backups while the database is open and in use. An *open (or hot)* database backup is a physical file backup of the database while the database is open and running in ARCHIVELOG mode. The online redo log files are archived manually by using the **ALTER SYSTEM ARCHIVE LOG SEQUENCE** command or by using automatic archiving (ARCH background process), if it has been enabled. DBAs can take backups of one or more tablespaces on a tablespace-by-tablespace basis, or they can take backups of individual data files while the database is open and available for use.

 Use the open database backup method to recover to the point of failure after a media failure.

Taking an Open Database Backup

Performing an open database backup when the Oracle server instance is online and in use involves the following steps:

1. Issue the **ALTER TABLESPACE BEGIN BACKUP** command. This command will freeze the sequence number in the data file header so that, if subsequent recovery is needed, the redo log files can be applied from the backup start time. See the following code sample:

```
SVRMGR> alter tablespace appl_data begin backup;
```

2. Use an operating system backup utility to copy all the data files that make up the tablespace to the designated backup storage location. When the tablespaces are sequentially backed up, the log sequence numbers in the file headers of the backup files may not be the same. See the following code sample:

```
For Unix:
$ cp /u01/oradata/app1TEST.ora /u04/backup/oradata/
app1TEST.ora

For NT:
C:> copy d:\orant\database\app1TEST.ora
f:\backup\oradata\app1TEST.ora
```

3. Issue the **ALTER TABLESPACE END BACKUP** command to set the data files, which make up the tablespace backed up in the previous step, into normal mode. See the following code sample:

```
SVRMGR> alter tablespace app1_data end backup;
```

4. Issue the **ALTER SYSTEM SWITCH LOGFILE** command to trigger a log switch. The log switch will in turn trigger a database checkpoint that will synchronize all the file headers. See the following code sample:

```
SVRMGR> alter system switch logfile;
```

The above steps should be repeated for all tablespaces, including the **SYSTEM** tablespace, rollback segment tablespace, temporary tablespace, and so on. These tablespaces can be backed up concurrently or sequentially.

Automated scripts that have passed testing are highly recommended for performing open database backups.

You should consider the following when taking an open database backup:

➤ When a tablespace of data files has been put into Backup mode, more redo log information is generated because the LGWR process will write the entire Oracle block in which the changed transaction record resides to the redo log files, versus just the row information. This may affect the size of the redo log files and may therefore increase storage space requirements. The performance of the LGWR process will be affected because more writing will be performed.

➤ DBAs should try to minimize the time the data files for a tablespace are in Backup mode because more redo information is written while in Backup mode. It is highly recommended that you take open database backups on a tablespace-by-tablespace basis.

Recovery Implications of Closed and Open Database Backups

Closed and open database backups provide different levels of data recoverability. DBAs should consider the advantages and disadvantages of each backup method to derive an effective backup strategy.

Advantages and Disadvantages of Closed Database Backups

Advantages of closed database backups include the following:

➤ A closed database backup is easy to understand and manage because it involves only three simple steps:

1. Shutting down the database cleanly

2. Copying all pertinent database files to the designated backup location

3. Starting up and opening the database

➤ Closed database backups require minimal operator intervention. DBAs typically automate the closed database backup process by running scripts that perform the three simple steps.

Closed database backups require less disk space because there are no archived redo logs for a database in NOARCHIVELOG mode.

➤ A closed database backup may be an especially reliable backup method because all database files are closed before the copy operation and they are consistent to a point-in-time.

Disadvantages of closed database backups include the following:

➤ They are unacceptable to organizations that require 24×7 continuous database availability because the database is unavailable during the backup operation.

➤ Several factors (such as the database size, the number of data files, and the speed of the operating system copy process) affect the amount of downtime needed for taking closed database backups. The amount of downtime required may not meet site-specific operational needs.

➤ The closed database backup method supports recovery to the point of the last full closed database backup after a media failure when archiving is not enabled. Business users may experience lost transactions and may need to reenter data if their database transactions occurred after the last full closed database backup.

Advantages and Disadvantages of Open Database Backups

Advantages of open database backups include the following:

➤ The database is available for normal use during the backup.

➤ Backups can be performed at a more granular level—tablespace or data file level.

➤ They meet backup requirements of 24×7 organizations.

➤ They support recovery to the point of failure after a media failure.

Disadvantages of open database backups include the following:

➤ They are conceptually more complex to understand and manage. The complexity increases the number of potential failure points.

➤ For database environments with high transaction volume, the free storage space on disk may run out quickly due to the accelerated rate at which redo log files are archived.

➤ They increase the level of effort from DBAs.

➤ They require additional DBA training.

Backup Implications of Logging and Nologging Modes

Oracle provides two logging modes—Logging and Nologging—to support direct-load and some *Data Definition Language (DDL)* operations that can be performed with or without logging of redo or undo information.

Logging Mode

In the *Logging* mode, full redo or undo data logging is performed for instance and media recovery. Full recovery is supported from the last backup. Logging mode is the default mode.

Nologging Mode

In the *Nologging* mode, full redo or undo data logging is bypassed. Some minimal logging is performed for data dictionary changes and new extent invalidations. During media recovery, the extent invalidations mark a range of data blocks as logically corrupt because the redo data is not available. The Nologging mode can be specified for the table, index, or partition into which data will be inserted by using commands, such as **ALTER TABLE, ALTER INDEX,** or **ALTER TABLESPACE.**

The Nologging mode improves the performance of direct-load operations because the amount of redo or undo logging has been reduced significantly. Upon completion of the operation in Nologging mode, the pertinent database object should be reset to Logging mode so that subsequent modifications will be logged. A backup should be taken of the data after a Nologging operation so that media recovery can be performed when the need arises.

The following code samples show how to set the Nologging attribute for a table, index, partition, or tablespace:

```
ALTER TABLE mytab NOLOGGING;

ALTER INDEX myindex NOLOGGING;

ALTER TABLE myparttab MODIFY PARTITION parta NOLOGGING;

ALTER TABLESPACE appl_ts NOLOGGING;
```

When the Nologging attribute is set for a table, partition, tablespace, or index, only selective operations performed on the schema object will make use of the Nologging mode. The Nologging attribute of the schema object will have no effect on operations, such as **UPDATE, DELETE,** or conventional path **INSERT.** The Nologging mode is only applicable for the following operations:

➤ SQL

➤ Loader direct path load

➤ Direct-load insert

➤ CREATE TABLE AS SELECT

➤ CREATE INDEX

➤ ALTER TABLE MOVE/SPLIT PARTITION

➤ ALTER INDEX SPLIT/REBUILD PARTITION

➤ ALTER INDEX REBUILD

Backing Up Control Files

Every Oracle database has at least one control file. A control file is the most important database file. It contains information on the physical structure of the database, database consistency, database synchronization, and database backup (when using the RMAN utility).

Every time that an instance of an Oracle database is mounted, its control file is used to identify the data files and redo log files that must be opened for database operation to proceed. If the physical makeup of the database is altered (for example, a new data file or redo log file is created), the database's control file is automatically modified by Oracle to reflect the change. You should back up the control file any time structural changes are made to the database. Commands that make structural changes to the database configuration include the following:

- ALTER DATABASE ADD LOGFILE

- ALTER DATABASE DROP LOGFILE

- ALTER DATABASE ADD LOGFILE MEMBER

- ALTER DATABASE DROP LOGFILE MEMBER

- ALTER DATABASE ADD LOGFILE GROUP

- ALTER DATABASE DROP LOGFILE GROUP

- ALTER DATABASE NOARCHIVELOG

- ALTER DATABASE ARCHIVELOG

- ALTER DATABASE RENAME FILE

- CREATE TABLESPACE

- ALTER TABLESPACE ADD DATAFILE

- ALTER TABLESPACE RENAME DATAFILE

- ALTER TABLESPACE READ WRITE

- ALTER TABLESPACE READ ONLY

- DROP TABLESPACE

When backing up a control file, you can create a binary copy of the control file or a text script trace file that can be modified and subsequently run to create the copy. The **ALTER DATABASE BACKUP CONTROLFILE TO TRACE** command can be used to provide a text script trace file. The following code sample shows the content of a text script trace file:

CONTENT OF TEXT SCRIPT TRACE FILE:

```
Dump file C:\ORANT817\admin\DWDB\udump\ORA00179.TRC
Tue May 29 01:28:37 2001
ORACLE V8.1.7.0.0 - Production vsnsta=0
vsnsql=e vsnxtr=3
Windows NT Version 4.0 Service Pack 6, CPU type 586
Oracle8i Enterprise Edition Release 8.1.7.0.0 - Production
With the Partitioning option
JServer Release 8.1.7.0.0 - Production
Windows NT Version 4.0 Service Pack 6, CPU type 586
Instance name: dwdb

Redo thread mounted by this instance: 1

Oracle process number: 14

Windows thread id: 179, image: ORACLE.EXE
*** SESSION ID:(11.1) 2001-05-29 01:28:37.189
*** 2001-05-29 01:28:37.189
# The following commands will create a new control file
# and use it to open the database.
# Data used by the recovery manager will be lost.
# Additional logs may be required for media recovery
# of offline data files. Use this
# only if the current version
# of all online logs is available.
STARTUP NOMOUNT
CREATE CONTROLFILE REUSE DATABASE "DWDB" NORESETLOGS ARCHIVELOG
    MAXLOGFILES 32
    MAXLOGMEMBERS 2
    MAXDATAFILES 254
    MAXINSTANCES 1
    MAXLOGHISTORY 1815
LOGFILE
  GROUP 1 'C:\ORANT817\ORADATA\DWDB\RED001.LOG'  SIZE 1M,
  GROUP 2 'C:\ORANT817\ORADATA\DWDB\RED002.LOG'  SIZE 1M,
  GROUP 3 'C:\ORANT817\ORADATA\DWDB\RED003.LOG'  SIZE 1M
DATAFILE
  'C:\ORANT817\ORADATA\DWDB\SYSTEM01.DBF',
  'C:\ORANT817\ORADATA\DWDB\RBS01.DBF',
  'C:\ORANT817\ORADATA\DWDB\USERS01.DBF',
  'C:\ORANT817\ORADATA\DWDB\TEMP01.DBF',
  'C:\ORANT817\ORADATA\DWDB\TOOLS01.DBF',
  'C:\ORANT817\ORADATA\DWDB\INDX01.DBF',
  'C:\ORANT817\ORADATA\DWDB\DR01.DBF',
  'C:\ORANT817\ORADATA\DWDB\OEM_REPOSITORY.ORA'
```

```
CHARACTER SET WE8IS08859P1
;
# Recovery is required if any of the datafiles
# are restored backups,
# or if the last shutdown was not normal or immediate.
RECOVER DATABASE
# All logs need archiving and a log switch is needed.
ALTER SYSTEM ARCHIVE LOG ALL;
# Database can now be opened normally.
ALTER DATABASE OPEN;
# No tempfile entries found to add.
```

The **ALTER DATABASE BACKUP CONTROLFILE TO** filespec command will create a binary copy of the control file. Similar to the redo log files, Oracle supports mirroring and multiplexing of the control file to protect the control file from media failures. The init.ora parameter **CONTROL_FILES** can be used for multiplexing and naming the control files. The control files should be copied to the designated backup location during full backups.

Backing Up Read-Only Tablespaces

Read-only tablespaces are designed to hold infrequently changed database objects, such as lookup tables. Data in read-only tablespaces requires minimal backup and maintenance. When the status of a tablespace has been changed to read-only, the DBA needs to back up the read-only tablespace only once while the tablespace is in read-only status. The operations of read-only tablespaces include the following:

➤ The status of a tablespace is changed from read-write to read-only using the **ALTER TABLESPACE** command, as illustrated by the following code sample:

```
SVRMGR> ALTER TABLESPACE lookup_data READ ONLY;
```

➤ Upon issuance of the **ALTER TABLESPACE** command, a database checkpoint is triggered for all the data files associated with the tablespace. The data file headers are set with the current *System Change Number (SCN)* and will not change while the status of the tablespace is read-only.

➤ Upon specifying a tablespace as read-only, you should take a backup of all data files for the tablespace to support subsequent recovery operations if needed. A new control file backup should also be taken.

➤ The DBWR background process will not perform any operations on the data files that comprise the read-only tablespaces. The DBWR background process will write only to data files whose tablespaces are in a read-write state. Normal checkpoints will occur for data files whose tablespaces are in a read-write state.

Things to Remember about Read-Only Tablespaces

When the database supports read-only tablespaces, the DBA should consider the following issues:

➤ Because writes are not performed on the data files for a read-only tablespace, the data files need to be recovered only when they are damaged.

➤ When the tablespace status has been changed from read-only to read-write, the DBWR background process will resume writing to the data files for the tablespace, and normal checkpoints will occur. The DBA should resume the normal backup schedule for all data files for this tablespace.

➤ The **ALTER TABLESPACE READ ONLY** command updates the control file. During recovery operations, the control file must accurately identify read-only tablespaces to avoid the recovery of the control file.

➤ It is possible to remove database objects from a read-only tablespace.

Useful Data Dictionary Views for Database Backups

You can use the following data dictionary views to obtain information about the database files that could be incorporated into the backup plan. You will need to be familiar with the data dictionary views associated with the different aspects of backup and recovery. As the views, such as the following, are introduced throughout this book, you should familiarize yourself with these views by querying the data they contain:

➤ **V$DATAFILE**—Provides the names and statuses of all data files:

```
SQL> desc V$DATAFILE
 Name                            Null?    Type
 ----                            -----    ----
 FILE#                                    NUMBER
 CREATION_CHANGE#                         NUMBER
 CREATION_TIME                            DATE
 TS#                                      NUMBER
 RFILE#                                   NUMBER
 STATUS                                   VARCHAR2(7)
 ENABLED                                  VARCHAR2(10)
 CHECKPOINT_CHANGE#                       NUMBER
 CHECKPOINT_TIME                          DATE
 UNRECOVERABLE_CHANGE#                    NUMBER
```

```
UNRECOVERABLE_TIME                          DATE
LAST_CHANGE#                                NUMBER
LAST_TIME                                   DATE
OFFLINE_CHANGE#                             NUMBER
ONLINE_CHANGE#                              NUMBER
ONLINE_TIME                                 DATE
BYTES                                       NUMBER
BLOCKS                                      NUMBER
CREATE_BYTES                                NUMBER
BLOCK_SIZE                                  NUMBER
NAME                                        VARCHAR2(513)


SQL> select name datafile_name, status from v$datafile;

DATAFILE_NAME                                     STATUS
-------------                                     ------

D:\ORANT\DATABASE\SYS1ORCL.ORA                    SYSTEM
D:\ORANT\DATABASE\USR1ORCL.ORA                    ONLINE
D:\ORANT\DATABASE\RBS1ORCL.ORA                    ONLINE
D:\ORANT\DATABASE\TMP1ORCL.ORA                    ONLINE
```

➤ **V$CONTROLFILE**—Provides the names of all control files:

```
SQL> desc V$CONTROLFILE
 Name                          Null?     Type
 ----                          -----     ----
 STATUS                                  VARCHAR2(7)
 NAME                                    VARCHAR2(513)


SQL> select name controlfile_name from v$controlfile;

CONTROLFILE_NAME
----------------

D:\ORANT\DATABASE\CTL1ORCL.ORA
D:\ORANT\DATABASE\CTL2ORCL.ORA
```

➤ **V$LOGFILE**—Provides the names of all redo log files:

```
SQL> desc v$logfile
 Name                          Null?     Type
 ----                          -----     ----
 GROUP#                                  NUMBER
 STATUS                                  VARCHAR2 (7)
 MEMBER                                  VARCHAR2 (513)


SQL> select member log_member from v$logfile;
```

```
LOG_MEMBER
----------
D:\ORANT\DATABASE\LOG4ORCL.ORA
D:\ORANT\DATABASE\LOG3ORCL.ORA
D:\ORANT\DATABASE\LOG2ORCL.ORA
D:\ORANT\DATABASE\LOG1ORCL.ORA
```

➤ **V$TABLESPACE**—Provides the names of all tablespaces:

```
SQL> desc v$tablespace;
 Name                            Null?    Type
 ----                            -----    ----
 TS#                                      NUMBER
 NAME                                     VARCHAR2(30)

SQL> select name tablespace_name from v$tablespace;

TABLESPACE_NAME
---------------
SYSTEM
TEMPORARY_DATA
ROLLBACK_DATA
USER_DATA
```

When you're setting up scripts to perform open database backups, it is helpful to obtain the listing of all data files with their respective tablespaces to ensure that all pertinent files are included in the operating system copy procedure. As shown in the following code sample, the **V$TABLESPACE** and the **V$DATAFILE** data dictionary views can be used together to obtain the listing of all data files with their respective tablespaces:

```
SQL> select t.name TABLESPACE_NAME,
  2         d.name FILENAME
  3    from v$tablespace t, v$datafile d
  4    where t.ts# = d.ts#
  5    order by 1;

TABLESPACE_NAME                  FILENAME
---------------                  --------
ROLLBACK_DATA                    D:\ORANT\DATABASE\RBS1ORCL.ORA
SYSTEM                           D:\ORANT\DATABASE\SYS1ORCL.ORA
TEMPORARY_DATA                   D:\ORANT\DATABASE\TMP1ORCL.ORA
USER_DATA                        D:\ORANT\DATABASE\USR1ORCL.ORA
```

You can use the following data dictionary views to obtain information about the status of data files during open database backups:

➤ **V$BACKUP**—Provides information as to which data files are in Backup mode. The status column value changes from **NOT ACTIVE** to **ACTIVE** when the **ALTER TABLESPACE BEGIN BACKUP** command is issued. The status column value changes to **NOT ACTIVE** when the file is backed up. The following code sample shows the column descriptions for the **V$BACKUP** data dictionary view and the changes to the status column values:

```
SQL> desc v$backup;
 Name                           Null?    Type
 ----                           -----    ----
 FILE#                                   NUMBER
 STATUS                                  VARCHAR2(18)
 CHANGE#                                 NUMBER
 TIME                                    DATE

SQL> alter tablespace user_data begin backup;

Tablespace altered.

SQL> select * from v$backup;

 FILE#   STATUS              CHANGE# TIME
 ----    ------              ------- ----
 1       NOT ACTIVE               0
 2       ACTIVE             1748313 17-DEC-99
 3       NOT ACTIVE               0
 4       NOT ACTIVE               0

SQL> alter tablespace user_data end backup;

Tablespace altered.

SQL> select * from v$backup;

 FILE#   STATUS              CHANGE# TIME
 ----    ------              ------- ----
 1       NOT ACTIVE               0
 2       NOT ACTIVE         1748313 17-DEC-99
 3       NOT ACTIVE               0
 4       NOT ACTIVE               0
```

➤ **V$DATAFILE_HEADER**—Provides information about data files that are in Backup mode. As shown by the following code sample, the **FUZZY** column value for the tablespace's data files changes to **YES** when the files are in Backup mode, and the **FUZZY** column value changes to **NULL** when the files are out of Backup mode:

```
SQL> desc v$datafile_header;
 Name                         Null?     Type
 ----                         -----     ----
 FILE#                                  NUMBER
 STATUS                                 VARCHAR2(7)
 ERROR                                  VARCHAR2(18)
 FORMAT                                 NUMBER
 RECOVER                                VARCHAR2(3)
 FUZZY                                  VARCHAR2(3)
 CREATION_CHANGE#                       NUMBER
 CREATION_TIME                          DATE
 TABLESPACE_NAME                        VARCHAR2(30)
 TS#                                    NUMBER
 RFILE#                                 NUMBER
 RESETLOGS_CHANGE#                      NUMBER
 RESETLOGS_TIME                         DATE
 CHECKPOINT_CHANGE#                     NUMBER
 CHECKPOINT_TIME                        DATE
 CHECKPOINT_COUNT                       NUMBER
 BYTES                                  NUMBER
 BLOCKS                                 NUMBER
 NAME                                   VARCHAR2(513)

SQL> alter tablespace user_data begin backup;

Tablespace altered.

SQL> select name, status, fuzzy from v$datafile_header;

NAME                                    STATUS  FUZ
----                                    -----   ---
D:\ORANT\DATABASE\SYS1ORCL.ORA          ONLINE
D:\ORANT\DATABASE\USR1ORCL.ORA          ONLINE  YES
D:\ORANT\DATABASE\RBS1ORCL.ORA          ONLINE
D:\ORANT\DATABASE\TMP1ORCL.ORA          ONLINE

SQL> alter tablespace user_data end backup;

Tablespace altered.
```

```
SQL> select name, status, fuzzy from v$datafile_header;

NAME                                STATUS  FUZ
----                                -----   ---
D:\ORANT\DATABASE\SYS1ORCL.ORA      ONLINE
D:\ORANT\DATABASE\USR1ORCL.ORA      ONLINE
D:\ORANT\DATABASE\RBS1ORCL.ORA      ONLINE
D:\ORANT\DATABASE\TMP1ORCL.ORA      ONLINE

SQL>
```

Practice Questions

Question 1

Which of the following sequence of steps is correct for performing an online backup of a tablespace without using the Recovery Manager utility?

○ a. Shut down the database, copy the data files for the tablespace using operating system commands, start up the instance, and force a checkpoint.

○ b. Place the tablespace in Backup mode, copy the data files for the tablespace using operating system commands, place the tablespace in Normal mode, and force a checkpoint.

○ c. Place the tablespace in Backup mode, copy the data files for the tablespace using operating system commands, and force a checkpoint.

○ d. Copy the data files for the tablespace using operating system commands, place the tablespace in Backup mode, force a checkpoint, and place the tablespace in Normal mode.

The correct answer is b. The steps for performing an online backup are as follows:

1. Place the database in Backup mode using the **ALTER TABLESPACE BEGIN BACKUP** command.

2. Use operating system commands to copy all the data files for the tablespace.

3. Use **ALTER TABLESPACE END BACKUP** command to place the tablespace in Normal mode.

4. Force a checkpoint to ensure file headers are synchronized.

Answer a is incorrect because the database remains online when you're performing online backups. Answer c is incorrect because the step to return the tablespace to Normal mode has been omitted. Answer d is incorrect because the sequence of steps is not in the correct order.

Question 2

Which of the following commands should cause you to back up the control file? [Choose two]

- ❑ a. **CREATE INDEX**
- ❑ b. **CREATE TABLE**
- ❑ c. **ALTER DATABASE RENAME FILE**
- ❑ d. **CREATE SNAPSHOT**
- ❑ e. **ALTER TABLESPACE ADD DATAFILE**

The correct answers are c and e. The control file should be backed up when structural changes are made to the database. Answers c and e add and rename data files, causing structural changes to the database. Answers a, b, and d are incorrect because those commands do not cause structural changes to the database.

Question 3

Which files are not part of the physical database structure, but should be backed up when you're performing a closed database backup? [Choose two]

- ❑ a. Archived log files
- ❑ b. Database parameter file
- ❑ c. Password file
- ❑ d. Control files
- ❑ e. Online redo log files

The correct answers are b and c. A closed database backup should include database files, such as control files, data files, and online redo log files. It is advisable to back up auxiliary files, such as the database parameter file and the password file. Answer a is incorrect because archived log files are not relevant for performing a closed database backup. Answers d and e are incorrect because they are part of the physical database files that are included in a closed database backup.

Question 4

> Which of the following views can be used to ensure that all the data files for
> a tablespace are in Backup mode?
>
> ○ a. **V$CONTROLFILE**
>
> ○ b. **V$TABLESPACE**
>
> ○ c. **V$DATABASE**
>
> ○ d. **V$DATAFILE**
>
> ○ e. **V$LOGFILE**
>
> ○ f. **V$BACKUP**

The correct answer is f. The **V$BACKUP** view provides information on data
files that are in Backup mode. Answers a, b, c, d, and e are incorrect because they
don't contain information on the Backup mode of data files.

Question 5

> When you're performing online backups, the database must be in which mode?
>
> ○ a. MOUNT EXCLUSIVE
>
> ○ b. NOARCHIVELOG
>
> ○ c. NOMOUNT
>
> ○ d. ARCHIVELOG

The correct answer is d. The database must be in ARCHIVELOG mode to
perform online backups. Answers a, b, and c are incorrect because online backups
require a database to be in ARCHIVELOG mode.

Question 6

Which data dictionary view can you use to get a listing of all the data files in the database for preparing an online backup procedure?

○ a. **DBA_DATAFILES**

○ b. **DBA_TABLESPACES**

○ c. **DBA_TABLES**

○ d. **DBA_DATA_FILES**

The correct answer is d. The **DBA_DATA_FILES** data dictionary view provides information on all the data files for a database. Answer a is incorrect because it is an invalid view. Answers b and c are incorrect because they don't contain information about the data files in a database.

Question 7

Which backup strategy is appropriate for a 24×7 organization?

○ a. Perform frequent online backups in NOARCHIVELOG mode.

○ b. Perform frequent offline backups in NOARCHIVELOG mode.

○ c. Perform frequent offline backups in ARCHIVELOG mode.

○ d. Perform frequent online backups in ARCHIVELOG mode.

The correct answer is d. If continuous database availability is required, the online backup method should be selected, and the database should always be in ARCHIVELOG mode when you're performing online backups. Answer a is incorrect because online backups require ARCHIVELOG mode. Answers b and c are incorrect because a 24×7 organization requires continuous database availability and cannot tolerate the downtime associated with offline backups.

Question 8

Why should a backup of a table be performed after the data is loaded using a direct load operation with the Nologging mode?

- ○ a. The table needs to be included in the incremental backup set.
- ○ b. The table needs to be included in the current backup set.
- ○ c. The table structure has changed.
- ○ d. The **insert** statements were not recorded in the redo log files.

The correct answer is d. When data is loaded using a direct load operation with the Nologging mode, the insertions are not recorded in the redo log files; therefore, the table should be backed up after the data load to ensure the recoverability of the inserted data. Answers a and b are incorrect because a backup of a table is required due to the unavailability of the full redo or undo logging information. Answer c is incorrect because a direct load operation in Nologging mode does not cause the table structure to change.

Question 9

What is the recommended action after a tablespace has been placed in read-only mode?

- ○ a. Force a checkpoint.
- ○ b. Force a log switch.
- ○ c. Resync the control file.
- ○ d. Perform a backup of the tablespace.

The correct answer is d. You need to back up the tablespace immediately after it has been placed in read-only mode. It is a good idea to take a control file backup also. Answers a, b, and c are incorrect because they are neither required nor recommended.

Question 10

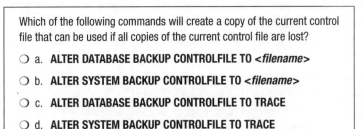

Which of the following commands will create a copy of the current control file that can be used if all copies of the current control file are lost?

- ○ a. **ALTER DATABASE BACKUP CONTROLFILE TO** *<filename>*
- ○ b. **ALTER SYSTEM BACKUP CONTROLFILE TO** *<filename>*
- ○ c. **ALTER DATABASE BACKUP CONTROLFILE TO TRACE**
- ○ d. **ALTER SYSTEM BACKUP CONTROLFILE TO TRACE**
- ○ e. **ALTER SESSION BACKUP CONTROLFILE TO** *<filename>*

The correct answer is a. The **ALTER DATABASE BACKUP CONTROLFILE TO** *<filename>* command is used to take an online backup of the control file. Answer c is incorrect because it only creates a text script trace file that may subsequently be modified and executed to create the binary control file. Answers b, d, and e are incorrect because they are invalid commands.

Need to Know More?

 Loney, Kevin and Marlene Theriault. *Oracle8i DBA Handbook*. Oracle Press, Berkeley, CA, 1999. ISBN 0-07212-188-2. This comprehensive guide for DBAs includes general backup and recovery concepts.

 Velpuri, Rama. *Oracle8i Backup and Recovery Handbook*. Oracle Press, Berkeley, CA, 2000. ISBN 0-072-12717-1. This book provides information on how to maximize uptime and recover data without compromising mission-critical systems. Actual corporate scenarios and case studies are included.

 http://technet.oracle.com. This site provides the best information on Oracle's products and technologies. You can also purchase the following manuals online:

Dialeris, Connie. *Oracle8i Backup and Recovery Guide Release 2*. Oracle Corporation, Redwood City, CA, 1999. Part No. A76993-01. This manual provides guidance on data protection techniques and offers strategies for data storage, backup, and restore for Oracle 8i.

Leverenz, Lefty. *Oracle8i Concepts Release 2*. Oracle Corporation, Redwood City, CA, 1999. Part No. A76965-01. This manual describes all features of the Oracle8i server running on all operating systems.

Lorentz, Diana. *Oracle8i Reference Release 2*. Oracle Corporation, Redwood City, CA, 1999. Part No. A76961-01. This manual describes the architecture, processes, structures, and other concepts of Oracle8i and provides detailed information on static and dynamic data dictionary views.

 www.revealnet.com. This site from RevealNet provides Oracle administration reference software.

Physical Backups Using Oracle Recovery Manager

Terms you'll need to understand:

✓ Whole backup

✓ Full backup

✓ Incremental backup

✓ Operating system backup

✓ Open database backup

✓ Closed database backup

✓ **ALLOCATE CHANNEL** command

✓ Image copy

✓ Backup set

✓ Tag

✓ **COPY** command

✓ **BACKUP** command

✓ Backup piece

✓ **V$ARCHIVED_LOG**

✓ **V$COPY_CORRUPTION**

✓ **V$BACKUP_CORRUPTION**

✓ **V$BACKUP_SET**

✓ **V$BACKUP_PIECE**

✓ **V$BACKUP_DATAFILE**

✓ **V$BACKUP_REDOLOG**

Techniques you'll need to master:

✓ Understanding Recovery Manager (RMAN) backup terms and concepts

✓ Using the **ALLOCATE CHANNEL** command

✓ Understanding the types of RMAN backups

✓ Using the **COPY** command

✓ Using the **BACKUP** command

✓ Using scripts to create backup sets

✓ Performing incremental and cumulative backups

✓ Troubleshooting backup problems

✓ Understanding RMAN-centric data dictionary views

Oracle database administrators (DBAs) have two options when performing physical backups. They can take backups with or without the Oracle Recovery Manager (RMAN). This chapter focuses on performing physical backups using RMAN. Refer to Chapter 7 for detailed information on taking physical backups without using RMAN.

 Oracle recommends a flexible backup strategy that includes RMAN backups and operating system backups.

RMAN Backup Terms and Concepts

When using RMAN as part of a backup strategy, it is important for the DBA to gain an understanding of key RMAN terms and backup concepts, including the following:

➤ *Whole backup*—A backup comprised of the control file and all data files.

➤ *Full backup*—A backup of one or more user-specified files. Only blocks that contain data are backed up.

➤ *Incremental backup*—A backup of data files that contain blocks that have changed since the last incremental backup. Incremental backups require a base-level or incremental level 0 backup. A base-level backup backs up all blocks containing data for the specified files.

 Although incremental level 0 backups and full backups copy all blocks containing data in the specified data files, full backups can't be used in an incremental backup strategy.

➤ *Operating system (OS) backup*—A backup of database files, such as a data file using OS utilities, rather than RMAN mechanisms.

➤ *Open database backup*—A backup of all or a portion of the database while it is open (online). This is also known as hot backup. DBAs should not put tablespaces in hot backup mode using the **ALTER TABLESPACE BEGIN BACKUP** command because RMAN uses a different mechanism that significantly reduces the amount of redo required.

➤ *Closed database backup*—A backup of all or a portion of the database while it is closed (offline). The target database must be mounted, but not open, during a closed database backup. When you're using a recovery catalog, the recovery catalog database must be in the open state.

RMAN supports backups of the following database components:

➤ The entire database

➤ The control file

➤ All data files in a tablespace

➤ A single data file

➤ All archived redo log files

➤ User-specified archived log files

> When RMAN is being used, the online redo log files are not backed up.

Channel Allocation

A *channel* is an RMAN resource allocation. It is the method RMAN uses to interface with the Oracle server and the OS of the target database. A channel has the following characteristics:

➤ Every RMAN **BACKUP**, **RESTORE**, or **RECOVER** command requires at least one channel.

➤ Each allocated channel starts a new Oracle server process for the target database, which performs backup, restore, and recovery procedures.

➤ The number of channels allocated affects the degree of parallelism for backup, restore, and recovery. This number determines the maximum degree of parallelization.

➤ The specified channel type determines whether the Oracle server process will read and write to disk or use the media management interface. If the channel is of type disk, the Oracle server process will read and write backups to disk. If the channel is of type **SBT_TAPE**, the Oracle server process will read and write backups through a media manager. You can use the **V$BACKUP_DEVICE** view to determine supported device types for your OS or media manager.

Channel Control Commands

There are three channel control commands that specify limits on input/output (I/O) bandwidth, the size of the backup pieces, and the number of concurrently opened files:

➤ **READ RATE**—Limits the number of buffers read per second per file. It reduces online performance through excessive disk I/O. The syntax for this parameter is as follows:

```
SET LIMIT CHANNEL <channel name> READ RATE = <integer>
```

➤ **KBYTES**—Places a limit on the backup piece file size. This parameter is useful when an OS or device type has a restriction on the maximum file size. The syntax is as follows:

```
SET LIMIT CHANNEL <channel name> KBYTES = <integer>
```

➤ **MAXOPENFILES**—Limits the number of concurrently open files for a large backup. The default value is 32. The parameter is useful in preventing the "too many files open" OS error. The syntax is as follows:

```
SET LIMIT CHANNEL <channel name> MAXOPENFILES = <integer>
```

ALLOCATE CHANNEL Syntax

The **ALLOCATE CHANNEL** command can be issued in a script or through the **RUN** command. Each allocated channel creates four output buffers. Each output buffer has a size of **DB_BLOCK_SIZE*DB_FILE_DIRECT_IO_COUNT**. The syntax for the **CHANGE...DELETE** command is as follows:

```
ALLOCATE CHANNEL FOR DELETE <device type> <options>;
```

The syntax for backup, restore, and recovery is as follows:

```
ALLOCATE CHANNEL <channel name> <device type> <options>;
```

The device type can be specified as **type=disk** for reading and writing from disk, **type=<*quoted_string*>** for identifying a type of sequential I/O device that is platform specific, or **name=<*quoted_string*>** for identifying a port-specific I/O device.

The options for the **ALLOCATE CHANNEL** command are **PARMS**, **CONNECT**, and **FORMAT**. The **parms** option is a port-specific string and is not applicable when **type=disk**. The **connect** option specifies a connect string for the target database and is applicable for the Oracle Parallel Server. The **FORMAT** option specifies the default naming convention for backup pieces.

Examples Using ALLOCATE CHANNEL

The following code sample in which a file is removed from the operating system shows channel allocation for the **CHANGE...DELETE** command:

```
RMAN> allocate channel for delete type disk;
RMAN> change datafilecopy
   2> '/u1/oradata/appl1.bak' delete;
RMAN> release channel;
```

The following code sample shows the creation of a channel named **ctest1** of type disk. The files created through this channel will have the format **/u1/oradata/ backup/df1.app**. The channel can open only one file at a time, which is not suitable for tape streaming. The code is as follows:

```
RMAN> run {
   2> allocate channel ctest1 type disk
   3> format = '/u1/oradata/backup/df1.app';
   4> set limit channel ctest1 maxopenfiles = 1;
   5> backup datafile 'appl.ora', 'applx.ora';}
```

Types of RMAN Backups

RMAN supports two types of backups:

➤ Image copies

➤ Backup sets

Each backup type can be used independently or together. DBAs typically determine the optimal combination of these backups to incorporate into their backup and recovery strategy.

Using Tags

RMAN enables the DBA to assign a descriptive name to a backup set or image copy. This descriptive name is called a *tag*. A tag is subject to the same naming restrictions as other database objects. Tags offer numerous benefits, including:

➤ They provide a meaningful way for DBAs to reference a group of file copies or a backup set.

➤ They enable DBAs to query backed up files easily by incorporating them with the **LIST** command.

➤ They can be used in the **RESTORE** and **SWITCH** commands.

➤ They enable DBAs to use the same tag for multiple file copies or backup sets.

When a tag resolves to multiple data files, backup sets, or image copies, RMAN uses the most recent data file that is available.

Image Copies

An *image copy* is a copy of a single file on disk (data file, archived redo log file, or control file) produced by an Oracle server process similar to an OS-produced file copy. The syntax for the image copy is as follows:

```
Copy <input file> to <location> <options>;
```

The input file can be specified as **datafile, datafilecopy [tag], backuppiece [tag], archivelog, controlfilecopy [tag],** or **current controlfile.** The options can be specified as **tag=<*name*>, level 0, check logical,** or **nochecksum.**

The COPY Command

The **COPY** command is used as part of the **RUN** command to create an image copy of a file. The following code sample illustrates using the **RUN** command to make image copies for two data files:

```
RMAN> run{
    2> allocate channel ctest2 type disk;
    3> copy level 0
    4> datafile 2 to '/u1/oradata/backup/app2.ora',
    5> datafile 1 to '/u1/oradata/backup/app1.ora';
    6> release channel ctest2;}
```

The **ALLOCATE CHANNEL** command is required to write data to an output device. The **COPY** command performs the image copy. The **LEVEL 0** in line 3 indicates that the image copy will be part of an incremental backup set. Lines 4 and 5 specify the data files that need image copies and the target locations. A **RELEASE CHANNEL** should be issued to release the process if not needed. If not, RMAN will automatically perform this function.

The **RUN** command works only when the target database is mounted or when the target database is open and in ARCHIVELOG mode.

Image Copy Process

RMAN uses the following steps when it copies a file:

1. A server process (channel) works on one file at a time.

2. All blocks are copied.

3. A block corruption check is performed.

4. Checksum is calculated for verifying the integrity of the image copy.

5. The file header of the image copy is updated.

6. The control file is updated with the image copy information. It is highly recommended that the DBA query the **V$COPY_CORRUPTION** view for corruption information after performing each image copy operation.

RMAN executes each copy command sequentially by default. To take advantage of parallel operations for the execution of one command at a time, you can do the following:

➤ Use one copy command for multiple files.

➤ Allocate multiple channels.

The following example code creates three channels (two channels will be active and one channel will be idle). Two files (1 and 3) will be copied in parallel, and the second **COPY** command will execute after the first **COPY** command has completed:

```
RMAN> run {
    2>      allocate channel c1 type disk;
    3>      allocate channel c2 type disk;
    4>      allocate channel c3 type disk;
    5>      copy
    6>          datafile 1 to '/u1/oradata/backup/app1.ora',
    7>          datafile 3 to '/u1/oradata/backup/app3.ora',
    8>      copy
    9>          datafile 2 to '/u1/oradata/backup/app2.ora';}
```

Note: Parallelism requires more system resources, but it results in improved backup and recovery performance.

An OS file copy made outside of RMAN is a valid image copy, but it cannot be used by RMAN until a **CATALOG** command is issued. RMAN supports both open and closed OS backup files. The following sample code shows an OS file copy used by RMAN:

```
...
SVRMGR> alter tablespace app_data begin backup;
SVRMGR> !cp app01.ora app01.bak
SVRMGR> alter tablespace app_data end backup;
...
$ rman target dbauser/dbapwd@target_db rcvcat
dbauser/dbapwd@catalog_db
RMAN> catalog datafilecopy 'app01.bak'
...
```

Image copies also support data files that are stored on mirrored disk systems. When a mirror disk fails, you can break the mirror to temporarily suspend restore operations. When mirroring has been resumed, you can use the **CHANGE...DELETE** command to remove the image copies and then use the **CATALOG** command to add the new image copies to the recovery catalog.

Things to Remember about Image Copy

You should be aware of the following image copy characteristics:

➤ An image copy can only be written to disk. When files are stored on disk, you can use them immediately without having to perform a restore from other offline storage media.

➤ An image copy is a physical copy of a single data file, archived log file, or control file.

➤ An image copy, like the OS backups, will copy all blocks, including unused blocks. Image copies differ from OS backups because the Oracle server process performs the physical copy operation, checks for block corruptions, and registers the copy in the control file. The **NOCHECKSUM** option can be used to speed up the copy process. The **CHECK LOGICAL** option can be used to test data and index blocks that pass physical checks for logical corruption.

➤ An image copy can be part of a full or incremental level 0 backup because a file copy always includes all blocks. A level 0 backup is typically used with an incremental backup set.

Backup Sets

A *backup set* is a backup of one or more data files, archived log files, or control files stored in an Oracle proprietary format. There are two types of backup sets:

➤ *Data file backup set*—This backup set is created when you back up a control file or one or more data files. This type of backup contains only used data file blocks because of the compression mechanism.

➤ *Archived log backup set*—This backup set is created when you back up archived log files.

Unlike image copies, which are typically available on disks, backup sets may require that you perform RMAN restore operations before performing recovery operations.

Each file in a backup set must have the same Oracle block size. Control files and data files have the same block size, but the block size for archived log files are platform dependent. You can include a control file in a backup set by using the **INCLUDE CONTROL FILE** syntax or by backing up file number 1, which is the system data file. The control file is written to the last data file backup set.

BACKUP Command

The **BACKUP** command is used to create backup sets. It is typically issued through the **RUN** command or in a script. The syntax is as follows:

```
BACKUP <level> ( <backup type> <options> );
```

Table 8.1 describes command elements and their associated values.

The **FORMAT** option specifies a location and a unique name for each backup set. The valid format specifiers include the following:

➤ **%p**—Indicates the backup piece number within the backup set. This value starts with one for each backup set and is incremented when each backup piece is created.

➤ **%s**—Indicates the backup set number, which is a counter in the control file. This counter starts at one and is incremented for each backup set.

➤ **%d**—Indicates the target database name.

➤ **%t**—Indicates the backup set timestamp as the number of seconds since a fixed reference date and time. This is a 4-byte value.

➤ **%u**—Indicates an eight-character name that represents the backup set number and the backup set creation time.

The **DELETE INPUT** option specifies that the archived log files are deleted from the OS, control file, and recovery catalog after they have been backed up. The **SKIP** option specifies file types to exclude from the backup set.

Table 8.1	Elements of the BACKUP command.
ELEMENT	**VALUE**
Level	Full, Incremental=0, Incremental=1, Incremental=2, and Incremental=3
Backup type	Datafile *<quoted_string>*, datafilecopy *<tag>* *<quoted_string>*, tablespace *<quoted_string>*, database, archivelog all, current controlfile, controlfilecopy *<quoted_string>*, or backupset *<key>*
Options	Include tag=*<quoted_string>*, format=*<quoted_string>*, include current controlfile, filesperset=*<integer>*, channel *<name>*, delete input, skip offline, skip readonly, and skip inaccessible

Multiplexing Files into Backup Sets

When multiple files are written to the same backup set or backup piece, RMAN automatically:

➤ Allocates files to available channels

➤ Multiplexes the files

➤ Bypasses empty blocks

When RMAN multiplexes multiple data files into one physical file (set) and stores it on tape, RMAN writes a number of blocks from the first file, then the second file, then the third file, and so on until all data files are backed up. The following example code shows four data files that will be multiplexed together via the **FILESPERSET** option:

```
RMAN> run {
  2>      allocate channel mychannel type 'SBT_TAPE';
  3>      backup
  4>      (database filesperset = 4);}
```

Data File Backup Set Process

RMAN follows these steps when creating a data file backup set:

1. Four memory buffers are allocated for each file in the backup set. The size of each buffer can be calculated as **DB_BLOCK_SIZE*DB_ FILE_ DIRECT_IO_COUNT**.

2. For each channel, files are sorted in descending size order.

3. A checkpoint is triggered for each file in the backup set.

4. Each file header block is copied.

5. The files are multiplexed if there are multiple files per set.

6. For incremental backups, the System Change Number (SCN) in the buffer block is checked to determine whether it should be processed. For full or level 0 backups, RMAN checks whether the buffer block has ever been used.

7. When corrupt blocks are encountered, they are stored in the control file. You can query the **V$BACKUP_CORRUPTION** view for the corrupted block information after the backup operation.

8. The checksum is calculated.

9. Filled output buffers are sent to the output device.

Archived Log Backup Sets

An archived log backup set can have only archived log files. It is always a full backup. Incremental backups are not supported because the DBA can specify the range of archived log files to back up. The archived log file backup process is as follows:

1. Archived log files for the backup set are ordered by channel and size.

2. Blocks are read and copied similar to the data file backup process. No blocks are bypassed.

3. Sequence and thread numbers are replaced with the block offset in the backup piece.

4. The backup set process is terminated if any corruptions are encountered.

The following code sample shows archived log sequence numbers 200 to 205 backed up to a backup set, where each backup piece contains six archived logs; the archived logs are deleted from disk:

```
RMAN> run {
  2>    allocate channel tc1 type 'SBT_TAPE';
  3>    backup filesperset 6
  4>       format '/u1/oradata/backup/ar_%t_%s_%p'
  5>       (archivelog from logseq=200 until logseq=205
  6>       thread=1 delete input); }
```

Using Scripts to Create Backup Sets

The **CREATE SCRIPT** command allows you to create a set of RMAN commands that can be stored in the recovery catalog. This script can be called into action on demand via the **RUN** command whenever it is needed. The script syntax is as follows:

```
CREATE SCRIPT <script name> { <commands> ; }
```

The valid commands include **ALLOCATE, BACKUP, COPY, RECOVER, SQL,** and **HOST**.

The following code sample shows the contents of a script file that creates three sets in parallel for a database with eight files. Each set contains three multiplexed files:

```
create script BackupTest {
allocate channel ct1 type 'SBT_TAPE';
allocate channel ct2 type 'SBT_TAPE';
backup
     filesperset 3
     format '/u1/oradata/backup/df_%d_%s_%p'
     tag=mytag
     (database include current controlfile);}
```

After this script is stored in the recovery catalog, you can run it by issuing the following **RUN** command:

```
RMAN> run { execute script BackupTest; }
```

You can use the **LIST** command to list all files in the backup set, as shown in the following example code:

```
RMAN> list backupset of database tag=mytag;
RMAN-03022: compiling command: list
RMAN-06230: List of Datafile Backups
RMAN-06231: Key  File Type          LV …
RMAN-06232: ---  ---- ----          ---
RMAN-06233: 1132   1 Incremental    0 …
RMAN-06233: 1132   2 Incremental    0 …
...
```

The following code sample checks for any block corruptions:

```
SQL> select * from v$backup_corruption where file# in (1,2,3,...);
```

Backup Piece

A *backup piece* is a physical file made up of one or more Oracle data files or archived log files. A backup piece can belong to only one backup set. A backup set is comprised of a group of backup pieces. The **SET LIMIT CHANNEL ... KBYTES** command creates multiple pieces for a backup set. In the Backup Manager, you need to set the backup piece size when creating or altering a channel. The following code sample shows the **APP_DATA** tablespace backed up to one tape drive where the maximum file size for the tape is 4 gigabytes (GB):

```
RMAN> run {
  2> allocate channel ctest type 'SBT_TAPE';
  3> set limit channel ctest kbytes 4194304;
  4> backup
  5> format 'df_%t_%s_%p' filesperset 3
  6> (tablespace app_data); }
```

The number of backup pieces written depends on the size of the output file. If the output file is greater than 4GB, multiple backup pieces are written. Each backup piece contains blocks from up to three data files.

Things to Remember about Backup Sets

You should be aware of the following backup set characteristics:

➤ A backup set is a logical structure.

➤ A backup set may contain one or more physical files (backup pieces).

➤ Backup sets are created by the **BACKUP** command.

➤ Backup sets support tape streaming. The **FILESPERSET** option specifies the number of data files in a backup set.

➤ Backup sets support writing to disk or tape. The default tape output device is **SBT_TAPE**, which writes to a tape device when using a media manager.

➤ Before performing recovery operations, you need to extract files from the restored backup set.

➤ Archived log backup sets are full backups by default; incremental backups are not supported for them.

➤ Blocks that don't contain data are not written in the backup sets because compression is performed.

➤ You can set maximum size limits for each backup set piece to support backup sets that exceed the maximum size for an OS file, disk, or tape.

➤ To take advantage of parallel operations for creating backup sets, you can do the following:

> Back up multiple files.

> Allocate multiple channels.

> Use the **FILESPERSET** option in the **BACKUP** command. When the **FILESPERSET** option is not explicitly specified, only one channel will be used to create one backup piece for all the files.

> Parallel operations are only available within each **BACKUP** or **COPY** command.

When working with backup sets, you should consider the following factors:

➤ The number of files in the target database

➤ The number of available storage devices

➤ The number of files per set needed for tape streaming

➤ The number of backup sets needed

➤ The number of files multiplexed per set

➤ The number of channels needed

Performing Incremental and Cumulative Backups

A data file backup set may be full, cumulative, or incremental. A full backup consists of one of the following file types: one or more data files, one or more image copies, one or more archived log files, or a control file that contains all blocks. An incremental backup (**level >= 0**) consists of one or more data files or a control file that contains blocks modified after the previous incremental backup. A cumulative incremental backup (**level >= 0**) contains all blocks modified after the previous backup at a lower level than the current backup level.

Incremental Backups

The characteristics of incremental backups are as follows:

➤ The default is set to noncumulative.

➤ An incremental level n backup contains all blocks modified after the previous incremental backup at the same or lower level.

➤ An incremental backup requires an existing level 0 backup set or image copy because it is based on changes made to the level 0 backups.

➤ An incremental backup normally contains fewer blocks than level 0 backups.

➤ Backup performance is better than level 0 backups.

➤ There are five levels of incremental backup—level 0 through level 4. When using multilevel incremental backups, only incremental backups from any level since the last base level (level 0) backup need to be restored.

➤ A level 0 backup should be performed if many blocks are modified frequently. If the updates are concentrated on a few blocks, higher level backups (level > 0) are more appropriate.

A sample backup scheme may consist of a level 0 incremental backup performed every Saturday, and a level 1 incremental backup performed Sunday through Friday. If a failure occurs on Tuesday, Sunday and Monday incremental backups need to be restored. The following code sample sets the incremental level to 1:

```
RMAN> run {
  2> allocate channel xyz type disk
  3>       format = '/u1/oradata/backup/inc_%s_%p.ora';
  4> backup incremental level = 1 (database); }
```

Cumulative Incremental Backups

A *cumulative incremental backup* copies all modified blocks since the previous incremental backup at a level lower than the current incremental level. A cumulative incremental backup copies all blocks previously backed up at the same level. This backup process is more time intensive and results in larger backup files than normal incremental backups. Performing cumulative incremental backups improves recovery speed because fewer backups at each level are needed during recovery.

Things to Consider When Performing Backups Using RMAN

You should consider the following issues when using RMAN to create backups:

➤ RMAN must be able to connect to the target database. When a recovery catalog is not used, the target database must be either mounted or open to perform either closed or open backups, respectively.

➤ RMAN does not support backing up online redo log files. RMAN does support backing up archived redo log files when the target database is in ARCHIVELOG mode.

➤ If the target database is in NOARCHIVELOG mode, RMAN supports clean database, tablespace, and data file backups.

➤ RMAN does not back up password files, parameter files, or other configuration files.

➤ When using a recovery catalog, the recovery catalog database must be open.

➤ When an RMAN job terminates abnormally, you need to manually delete incomplete files (backup pieces) from the operating system. You can terminate an RMAN job by using the Ctrl+C key combination in the Interactive mode or by killing the RMAN process in the Batch mode.

➤ It is a good practice to back up the control file frequently, along with any data file backup and database backup.

➤ When Oracle8i detects corrupt data blocks during a backup, it writes information in the control file and in the alert log. The corrupt blocks are still included in the backup. You can query information about corrupt blocks from the control file using the **V$BACKUP_CORRUPTION** view for backup sets or **V$COPY_CORRUPTION** for image copies. You can use the **SET MAXCORRUPT** command to limit the number of new block corruptions allowed for a data file backup.

➤ Whenever RMAN performs a copy or backup set, it allocates input and output buffers. If I/O slaves are not used, memory is allocated from the large pool. You may need to configure the **LARGE_POOL_SIZE** parameter.

➤ When asynchronous I/O is supported by the OS, I/O slaves can be configured using three parameters: **DISK_ASYNCH_IO = TRUE, TAPE_ASYNCH_IO = TRUE**, and **BACKUP_TAPE_IO_SLAVES = TRUE**.

➤ When asynchronous I/O is not available from the OS, you can set up more disk I/O slaves for each channel using two parameters: **BACKUP_TAPE_IO_SLAVES = TRUE** and **BACKUP_DISK_IO_SLAVES = n**. Having additional I/O slaves requires more sessions.

➤ You can query the **V$SGASTAT** view where **name = 'KSFQ buffers'** to get information on memory usage by RMAN.

Troubleshooting Backup Problems

In the course of creating backups using RMAN, you may encounter problems along the way. The following are representative problems:

➤ When RMAN returns Remote Procedure Call (RPC) error messages, such as "RPC call failed to start on channel," ignore them; these harmless messages simply indicate that the target database is running slowly. Subsequent "RPC call OK" messages indicate that the target database is running at a normal speed.

➤ When RMAN returns error number "7004 unhandled exception…on channel..," this translates to "No tape device is available for RMAN to use." Check that the tape device is working properly.

➤ You can query the **V$SESSION_LONGOPS** view to check the status of a backup. The following sample code can be used to calculate the percentage of work completed:

```
SVRMGR> select round(sofar/totalwork*100,2) PCT_COMP
     2> from v$session_longops
     3> where compnam = 'dbms_backup_restore';
```

➤ If the percent completion value has not changed for a while, query the **V$SESSION_WAIT** view for any outstanding wait events:

```
SVRMGR> select event, pltext, seconds_in_wait
     2> from v$session_wait
     3> where wait_time = 0;
```

➤ When you suspect that the backup appears to be hung because RMAN progress has stopped and the **V$SESSION_WAIT** view does not return any information for the criteria **compnam ='dbms_backup_restore'**, you need to check the media manager to make sure the backup is still running smoothly. You also need to check the sbtio.log file located in the $ORACLE_HOME/rdbms/ log directory, because media managers write information to this file.

Useful Data Dictionary Views

The following RMAN-centric data dictionary views can be used to query information about the control file:

➤ **V$ARCHIVED_LOG**—Provides information on archived redo log files, including backup status:

```
SQL> desc v$archived_log
 Name                          Null?    Type
 ----                          -----    ----
 RECID                                  NUMBER
 STAMP                                  NUMBER
 NAME                                   VARCHAR2(513)
 THREAD#                                NUMBER
 SEQUENCE#                              NUMBER
 RESETLOGS_CHANGE#              .        NUMBER
 RESETLOGS_TIME                         DATE
 FIRST_CHANGE#                          NUMBER
 FIRST_TIME                             DATE
 NEXT_CHANGE#                           NUMBER
 NEXT_TIME                              DATE
 BLOCKS                                 NUMBER
 BLOCK_SIZE                             NUMBER
 ARCHIVED                               VARCHAR2(3)
 DELETED                                VARCHAR2(3)
 COMPLETION_TIME                        DATE
```

➤ **V$COPY_CORRUPTION**—Provides information on corrupted blocks for image copies:

```
SQL> desc v$copy_corruption
 Name                            Null?     Type
 - - - -                         - - - - - - - - -
 RECID                                     NUMBER
 STAMP                                     NUMBER
 COPY_RECID                                NUMBER
 COPY_STAMP                                NUMBER
 FILE#                                     NUMBER
 BLOCK#                                    NUMBER
 BLOCKS                                    NUMBER
 CORRUPTION_CHANGE#                        NUMBER
 MARKED_CORRUPT                            VARCHAR2(3)
```

➤ **V$BACKUP_CORRUPTION**—Provides information on corrupted blocks for backup sets:

```
SQL> desc v$backup_corruption
 Name                            Null?     Type
 - - - -                         - - - - - - - - -
 RECID                                     NUMBER
 STAMP                                     NUMBER
 SET_STAMP                                 NUMBER
 SET_COUNT                                 NUMBER
 PIECE#                                    NUMBER
 FILE#                                     NUMBER
 BLOCK#                                    NUMBER
 BLOCKS                                    NUMBER
 CORRUPTION_CHANGE#                        NUMBER
 MARKED_CORRUPT                            VARCHAR2(3)
```

➤ **V$BACKUP_SET**—Provides information on all backup sets:

```
SQL> desc v$backup_set
 Name                            Null?     Type
 - - - -                         - - - - - - - - -
 RECID                                     NUMBER
 STAMP                                     NUMBER
 SET_STAMP                                 NUMBER
 SET_COUNT                                 NUMBER
 BACKUP_TYPE                               VARCHAR2(1)
```

```
CONTROLFILE_INCLUDED                    VARCHAR2(3)
INCREMENTAL_LEVEL                       NUMBER
PIECES                                  NUMBER
START_TIME                              DATE
COMPLETION_TIME                         DATE
ELAPSED_SECONDS                         NUMBER
BLOCK_SIZE                              NUMBER
```

➤ **V$BACKUP_PIECE**—Provides information on all backup pieces in all backup sets:

```
SQL> desc v$backup_piece
Name                         Null?      Type
----                         -----      ----
RECID                                   NUMBER
STAMP                                   NUMBER
SET_STAMP                               NUMBER
SET_COUNT                               NUMBER
PIECE#                                  NUMBER
DEVICE_TYPE                             VARCHAR2(17)
HANDLE                                  VARCHAR2(513)
COMMENTS                                VARCHAR2(81)
MEDIA                                   VARCHAR2(65)
CONCUR                                  VARCHAR2(3)
TAG                                     VARCHAR2(32)
DELETED                                 VARCHAR2(3)
START_TIME                              DATE
COMPLETION_TIME                         DATE
ELAPSED_SECONDS                         NUMBER
```

➤ **V$BACKUP_DATAFILE**—Provides information on data files, including the number of corrupt blocks and the total number of blocks in each data file. This is useful when you need to create equal-sized backup sets:

```
SQL> desc v$backup_datafile
Name                         Null?      Type
----                         -----      ----
RECID                                   NUMBER
STAMP                                   NUMBER
SET_STAMP                               NUMBER
SET_COUNT                               NUMBER
FILE#                                   NUMBER
CREATION_CHANGE#                        NUMBER
CREATION_TIME                           DATE
RESETLOGS_CHANGE#                       NUMBER
```

```
RESETLOGS_TIME                     DATE
INCREMENTAL_LEVEL                  NUMBER
INCREMENTAL_CHANGE#                NUMBER
CHECKPOINT_CHANGE#                 NUMBER
CHECKPOINT_TIME                    DATE
ABSOLUTE_FUZZY_CHANGE#             NUMBER
MARKED_CORRUPT                     NUMBER
MEDIA_CORRUPT                      NUMBER
LOGICALLY_CORRUPT                  NUMBER
DATAFILE_BLOCKS                    NUMBER
BLOCKS                             NUMBER
BLOCK_SIZE                         NUMBER
OLDEST_OFFLINE_RANGE               NUMBER
COMPLETION_TIME                    DATE
```

➤ **V$BACKUP_REDOLOG**—Provides information on archived redo logs in backup sets:

```
SQL> desc v$backup_redolog
Name                          Null?    Type
----                          -----    ----
RECID                                  NUMBER
STAMP                                  NUMBER
SET_STAMP                              NUMBER
SET_COUNT                              NUMBER
THREAD#                                NUMBER
SEQUENCE#                              NUMBER
RESETLOGS_CHANGE#                      NUMBER
RESETLOGS_TIME                         DATE
FIRST_CHANGE#                          NUMBER
FIRST_TIME                             DATE
NEXT_CHANGE#                           NUMBER
NEXT_TIME                              DATE
BLOCKS                                 NUMBER
BLOCK_SIZE                             NUMBER
```

Practice Questions

Question 1

> What backup-related information in the **V$SESSION_LONGOPS** view would be of interest to DBAs?
>
> ○ a. Information about archives that have been backed up
>
> ○ b. Block corruption information
>
> ○ c. Database events that are in wait state
>
> ○ d. Percentage completion of backups in progress

The correct answer is d. The **V$SESSION_LONGOPS** view provides information on the progress of a backup. Answers a, b, and c are incorrect because the **V$SESSION_LONGOPS** view does not provide these types of information.

Question 2

> Your production database has eight data files stored across two disk drives. You have a requirement to perform a full database backup with two files in each backup set. How many channels should be allocated to take advantage of parallel backup operation?
>
> ○ a. 5
>
> ○ b. 4
>
> ○ c. 3
>
> ○ d. 2
>
> ○ e. 1

The correct answer is d. To take advantage of parallel backup operation, you should allocate two channels of type disk to read concurrently from the two disk drives where the eight data files needing backup reside. You should always allocate one type of disk channel per disk drive. Allocating multiple channels for spreading a backup set across multiple physical disk drives will balance the I/Os across the disk drives. Answers a, b, and c are incorrect because you only have two disk drives. You should always allocate one type of disk channel per disk drive. Answer e is incorrect because a single channel can open one file at a time, so parallel operations do not apply.

Question 3

Which three types of files are not included in RMAN backups? [Choose three]

❑ a. Archived log file

❑ b. Parameter file

❑ c. Password file

❑ d. Data file

❑ e. Control file

❑ f. OS file

The correct answers are b, c, and f. RMAN doesn't back up parameter files, password files, or operating system files. Answers a, d, and e are incorrect because RMAN does back up archived log files, data files, and control files.

Question 4

Evaluate the following RMAN command:

```
RMAN> run {
    2> allocate channel c1 type disk;
    3> format = '/u1/backup/app1_%s_%p.bak';
    4> backup
    5> incremental level = 0
    6> (database); }
```

What does this command accomplish?

○ a. It backs up blocks changed since the last full backup.

○ b. It takes advantage of parallel backup operation.

○ c. It creates an image copy of the database.

○ d. It initiates an incremental backup plan.

The correct answer is d. This sample RMAN command allocates a single channel for the backup set, specifies the name and location of the backup set, and creates a level 0 backup set. A level 0 backup is the basis for incremental backups. Answer a is incorrect because a level 0 (base level) backup copies all blocks in the data files. Answer b is incorrect because parallel backup operation is not applicable when only one channel is allocated. Answer c is incorrect because image copies are created by the **COPY** command.

Question 5

What is an RMAN backup set?

○ a. One or more files stored in proprietary RMAN format

○ b. A single file stored in proprietary RMAN format

○ c. Only one or more data files

○ d. One or more operating system files

○ e. Only one or more archived redo log files

The correct answer is a. A backup set is a backup of one or more Oracle files and is created by the RMAN **BACKUP** command. There are two types of backup sets: data file backup sets and archived log backup sets. Answer b is incorrect because a backup set could contain multiple files. Answer c is incorrect because it applies to the data file backup set. Answer d is incorrect because it applies to image copy backups. Answer e is incorrect because it applies to archived log backup sets.

Question 6

When using RMAN to back up the target database, what are the two supported states for the target database? [Choose two]

❑ a. OPEN

❑ b. CLOSED

❑ c. MOUNT

❑ d. NOMOUNT

The correct answers are a and c. When you're performing offline backups using RMAN, the target database should be mounted, but not open. When performing online backups using RMAN, the target database should be open. If a recovery catalog is being used, the recovery catalog database should be open. Answer b is incorrect because it is applicable to taking offline database backups when not using RMAN. Answer d is incorrect because the control file is not available to RMAN when the target database is in the NOMOUNT state.

Question 7

> What types of backups does RMAN create? [Choose two]
>
> ❑ a. Image copy
>
> ❑ b. Export file
>
> ❑ c. OS file copy
>
> ❑ d. Image log
>
> ❑ e. Backup set
>
> ❑ f. Backup log

The correct answers are a and e. RMAN supports image copy backups and backup sets. Answer b is incorrect because export files are created by the EXPORT utility. Answer c is incorrect because OS backups are not created by RMAN, but are supported. Answers d and f are incorrect because they are invalid backup types.

Question 8

> Which format specifier would enable you to include the target database name in the backup file name?
>
> ○ a. **%u**
>
> ○ b. **%n**
>
> ○ c. **%p**
>
> ○ d. **%s**
>
> ○ e. **%t**
>
> ○ f. **%d**

The correct answer is f. The valid format specifiers for the **FORMAT** option of the RMAN **BACKUP** command are as follows: **%d**—target database name, **%t**—backup set timestamp, **%s**—backup set number, **%p**—backup piece number, **%n**—padded target database name, and **%u**—encoded backup set number and the backup set create time. Answers a, b, c, d, and e are incorrect because they specify other attributes.

Question 9

> What RMAN command should you use to copy a single control file?
>
> ○ a. **CATALOG**
>
> ○ b. **BACKUP**
>
> ○ c. **CHANGE**
>
> ○ d. **COPY**

The correct answer is d. The RMAN **COPY** command creates an image copy of a file similar to an OS file copy. It can be used to copy a control file, data file, or archived redo log file. Answers a, b, and c are incorrect because they serve other purposes.

Question 10

> Which of the following data dictionary views should you use to list corrupt blocks found during an image copy?
>
> ○ a. **V$BACKUP_CORRUPTION**
>
> ○ b. **V$COPY_CORRUPTION**
>
> ○ c. **V$BACKUP_DATA_FILE**
>
> ○ d. **V$BLOCK_CORRUPTION**

The correct answer is b. The **V$COPY_CORRUPTION** view provides information on the number of corrupt blocks encountered during an image copy backup. Answer a is incorrect because it provides information on the number of corrupt blocks encountered for a backup set. Answers c and d are incorrect because they are invalid views.

Need to Know More?

Loney, Kevin and Marlene Theriault. *Oracle8i DBA Handbook*. Oracle Press, Berkeley, CA, 1999. ISBN 0-07212-188-2. This comprehensive guide for DBAs includes general backup and recovery concepts.

Velpuri, Rama. *Oracle8i Backup and Recovery Handbook*. Oracle Press, Berkeley, CA, 2000. ISBN 0-072-12717-1. This book provides information on how to maximize uptime and recover data without compromising mission critical systems. Actual corporate scenarios and case studies are included. Chapter 7 provides a good discussion of taking backups using RMAN.

http://technet.oracle.com. This site provides the best information on Oracle's products and technologies. You can also purchase the following manuals online:

Dialeris, Connie et al. *Oracle8i Recovery Manager User's Guide and Reference Release 2*. Oracle Corporation, Redwood City, CA, 1999. Part No. A76990-01. This manual provides guidance on how to administer the backup, restore, and recovery operations of an Oracle database system using the RMAN utility. Chapter 5 describes how to use RMAN to manage backup and copy operations.

Lorentz, Diana. *Oracle8i Reference Release 2*. Oracle Corporation, Redwood City, CA, 1999. Part No. A76961-01. This manual describes the architecture, processes, structures, and other concepts of Oracle8i and provides detailed information on static and dynamic data dictionary views.

www.revealnet.com. This site from RevealNet provides Oracle administration reference software.

Types of Failures and Troubleshooting

Terms you'll need to understand:

- ✓ Statement failure
- ✓ User process failure
- ✓ User error failure
- ✓ Instance failure
- ✓ Media failure
- ✓ DBVERIFY

- ✓ **DB_BLOCK_CHECKSUM**
- ✓ **LOG_BLOCK_CHECKSUM**
- ✓ **DB_BLOCK_CHECKING**
- ✓ **ANALYZE VALIDATE STRUCTURE**
- ✓ Alert.log
- ✓ **BACKGROUND_DUMP_DEST**

Techniques you'll need to master:

- ✓ Understanding the types of failures
- ✓ Using the DBVERIFY utility
- ✓ Using the **DBMS_REPAIR** package
- ✓ Using the LogMiner utility
- ✓ Configuring data file checksums

- ✓ Configuring redo log checksums
- ✓ Using the **ANALYZE VALIDATE STRUCTURE** command
- ✓ Using the alert.log file to trouble-shoot backup and recovery problems
- ✓ Using the trace files to diagnose backup and recovery problems

An understanding of the common types of failures in an Oracle database environment will enable the Oracle database administrator (DBA) to choose and perform appropriate recovery operations. It's important to understand the significance of database synchronization for instance and media recovery because an Oracle database cannot be opened if any data files, redo log files, and control files are out of sync. To help maintain high recoverability and to prevent data corruption, the DBA should perform the following recommended actions based on site-specific needs:

➤ Use the DBVERIFY utility to verify the validity of a backup and to identify data corruptions in data files.

➤ Use the **DBMS_REPAIR** package to identify logical block corruptions in tables, partitions, or indexes.

➤ Use the LogMiner utility to identify and undo logical corruptions.

➤ Configure checksum operations to ensure that data block corruptions don't exist in archived redo log files.

➤ Use the **ANALYZE VALIDATE STRUCTURE** command to validate the structural integrity and consistency of tables and indexes.

When backup and recovery problems are encountered, the DBA can use available log files and trace files to help troubleshoot the problems and find effective resolutions.

Types of Failures in an Oracle Database

Every database system is susceptible to failure. Typical failures include the following:

➤ Statement failure

➤ User process failure

➤ User error failure

➤ Instance failure

➤ Media failure

Each type of failure requires a different level of effort from the DBA. Recovery methods depend on the type of failure, the affected parts of the database, and the site-specific backup strategy.

Statement Failure

Statement failure occurs when a *Structured Query Language (SQL)* statement fails. Representative statement failures include the following:

➤ A logical error exists in the user application. The user application attempts to insert a child record before creating the parent record.

➤ The user issues a **SELECT** statement against a nonexistent database table.

➤ The user enters bad data, which violates integrity constraints, into the database table.

➤ The user does not have the proper privileges to perform a database operation. For example, the user tries to insert a row into a database table with only **SELECT** privileges.

➤ The user attempts to create a database table that exceeds the allotted database space usage limit.

➤ The user performs an **INSERT** or **UPDATE** on a database table, causing Oracle to perform dynamic extension, but the tablespace contains insufficient free space.

The Oracle server or the operating system will typically return an error code and a message when a statement failure has been encountered. An automatic rollback operation is performed by the Oracle server for the failed SQL statement. Program control is returned to the user application.

Note: The Oracle error code and error message can be used to troubleshoot and to help resolve the failure.

To resolve statement failures, the following activities are typically performed by the DBA and/or the application developer:

➤ Fix the user application to reflect correct logical flow. This activity is typically performed by the application developer.

➤ Ensure the database table exists and is user accessible. Verify that the table reference is specified properly and then reissue the SQL statement. The DBA and the application developer typically perform this activity.

➤ Reconstruct and reissue the SQL statement with good data. This activity is typically performed by the application developer.

➤ Provide the required database privileges for the user to issue the statement successfully. The DBA typically performs this activity.

➤ Issue the **ALTER USER** command to change the user's quota limit. This activity is typically performed by the DBA.

➤ Issue the **ALTER TABLESPACE** command to add file space to the tablespace as shown by the code example that follows. Alternatively, the DBA can issue the **ALTER DATABASE DATAFILE** command with the **RESIZE** and the **AUTOEXTEND** options as shown by the following code example:

```
ALTER TABLESPACE test_ts ADD DATAFILE
'd:\oradata\test02.ora' SIZE 100M;
ALTER DATABASE DATAFILE 'd:\oradata\test02.ora' RESIZE 200M;
ALTER DATABASE DATAFILE 'd:\oradata\test02.ora' AUTOEXTEND ON NEXT
50M MAXSIZE 200M;
```

Note: The Storage Manager of the DBA Studio administrative tool is part of the Oracle Enterprise Manager (OEM) that can be used to add new data files to tablespaces and to enable automatic extension of data files.

User Process Failure

User process failure occurs when a user process that is connected to the Oracle instance ends abnormally. Typical causes of user process failures include the following:

➤ A user requests an abnormal disconnect. For example, a user pressed Ctrl+Break in the text version of SQL*Plus while connected to an Oracle database in a client/server environment.

➤ The user's session was abnormally ended when the user rebooted the client workstation while connected to an Oracle database in a client/server environment.

➤ A memory exception was raised by the user's application program that terminated the session. The user's application program omitted critical exceptions handling.

The DBA will rarely need to be involved in resolving user process failures. User process failure is recovered automatically by the Process Monitor (PMON) background process, which wakes up periodically to clean up after an abnormally terminated user process. The PMON process performs the following actions in the cleanup of failed user processes:

➤ Detects abnormally terminated server processes

➤ Rolls back database transactions of abnormally terminated processes

➤ Releases system resources and locks held by the failed user processes

User Error Failure

User error failure occurs when a user makes a mistake. Typical user error failures include the following:

➤ The user accidentally drops a database table as shown by the following example:

```
SQL>  DROP TABLE app_info_tab;
```

➤ The user deletes data from a database table in error as shown by the following example:

```
SQL>  DELETE from app_info_tab;
SQL>  Commit;
```

➤ The user accidentally truncates a database table as shown by the following example:

```
SQL>  TRUNCATE TABLE app_info_tab;
```

➤ The user found an error in his or her committed data as shown by the following example:

```
SQL>  UPDATE app_info_tab SET status_code = '10';
SQL>  Commit;
```

To resolve user error failures, the following activities are typically performed by the DBA:

➤ Properly train the database users so that they are aware of the ramifications of their database actions on database integrity and availability.

➤ Understand the business and application operations that may lead to data loss caused by user errors.

➤ Understand and implement recovery procedures, such as recovery using a valid backup for data loss caused by user errors.

➤ Understand and implement point-in-time recovery, which can recover the database to the point in time just before the error occurred.

Instance Failure

Instance failure occurs when an Oracle instance fails. Types of instance failures include the following:

➤ Power outages that cause the database server to become unavailable

➤ Operating system crashes that make the database instance inoperative

➤ Hardware problems, such as central processing unit (CPU) failure or memory corruption, that cause the database server to become unavailable

➤ Failure of one or more of the Oracle background processes: Database Writer (DBWR), Log Writer (LGWR), PMON, or System Monitor (SMON)

To resolve instance failures, the following activities should typically be performed by the DBA:

➤ Use the **STARTUP** command to start the instance, as shown by the code example that follows. Instance recovery restores a database to its transaction-consistent state immediately before the instance failure. The Oracle server will automatically perform instance recovery that includes the roll-forward and rollback phases when the database is opened, if it is necessary:

```
SVRMGR> connect / as SYSDBA;
Connected.
SVRMGR> startup;
. . .
Database opened.
SVRMGR>
```

➤ Inform database users that uncommitted data will need to be reentered.

➤ Use available trace files and the instance alert.log file to help diagnose the cause of the failure.

Instance recovery is composed of six phases:

➤ Unsynchronized data files

➤ Roll-forward process

➤ Committed and uncommitted data in data files

➤ Rollback process

➤ Committed data in data files

➤ Synchronized data files

Unsynchronized Data Files

Instance failure can lead to unsynchronized files. An example is when a **SHUTDOWN ABORT** action is performed by the DBA. In this scenario, uncommitted data is lost because modified data in memory has not been written to disk and because files are not synchronized before the shutdown.

Roll–Forward Process

The DBWR background process writes both committed and uncommitted data to the data files. In the *roll-forward phase*, all changes recorded in the log files are applied to the data blocks. Because the redo log files contain both before and after images of data, rollback segment entries may get created if one or more uncommitted data blocks are in the data file and if no rollback entry exists. The recovery process uses redo log buffers when applying changes in the redo log files. With respect to read-only data files, the changes in the redo log files are applied only if the status in the file header does not match the status in the control file.

Commited and Uncommitted Data in Data Files

Upon roll-forward phase completion, the data files will reflect all committed data, although some uncommitted data may still exist. The database is opened for normal operations.

Rollback Process

In the *rollback phase*, uncommitted data from the data files is eliminated using the rollback segment entries created during the roll-forward phase. Data blocks are rolled back when the Oracle server or the user submits data block requests. For more information on the rollback process, refer to the "Deferred Transaction Recovery" section in Chapter 3.

Committed Data in Data Files

Upon completion of the roll-forward and the rollback phases, the data files will contain only committed data.

Synchronized Data Files

At this phase, data file synchronization is achieved.

Media Failure

Media failure occurs when files needed by the database can no longer be accessed. This is the most serious type of failure and typically requires active DBA involvement. Typical causes of media failures include the following:

➤ Disk drive controller malfunction

➤ Disk drive head crash

➤ Physical problem in performing database file read or write operations

➤ Accidental erasure of a database file

The key to resolving media failures is a tested backup strategy. The extent to which a DBA can minimize data loss and downtime resulting from a media failure is dependent upon the availability of backups. An effective recovery strategy is dependent upon the following factors:

➤ The backup method chosen

➤ The files affected

If archiving has been enabled, archived redo log files can be used to recover data committed since the last backup.

 You need to be familiar with the types of failures in an Oracle database because each failure type requires a different level of effort from the DBA to achieve effective recovery.

Database Synchronization

The Oracle server will not open a database unless all data files, redo log files, and control files are synchronized. The exception is when the data files are offline or are part of a read-only tablespace. The types of failures affect the state of database synchronization. For statement or user error failures, the state of database synchronization remains unchanged. For instance failures, the database files may not be synchronized, and recovery is performed automatically by the Oracle server. For media failures, the database files are not synchronized, and recovery will require significant DBA involvement.

Synchronization of all data files, redo log files, and control files is based on the current checkpoint number. Archived and online redo log files are used to recover committed transactions, roll back uncommitted transactions, and synchronize the database files. During the recovery phase, Oracle automatically requests and applies the pertinent archived redo log files. Subsequently, Oracle automatically applies the online redo log files if necessary. The DBA should ensure that the redo log files exist in the currently set storage location to enable redo log application by the recovery process.

Using the DBVERIFY Utility

The DBVERIFY utility enables DBAs to perform physical data structure integrity checks on the data files. The DBVERIFY utility can be used to perform the following functions:

➤ Verify online data files

➤ Verify a portion of a data file

➤ Verify offline data files

➤ Specify an error log to receive the output from the DBVERIFY utility

DBVERIFY's impact on database activities is minimal because the utility is external to the database. The DBVERIFY utility is invoked using a command-line interface. It is typically used to verify that backed up data files are valid before the files are used to restore a database or are used as a diagnostic aid for resolving data corruption errors.

The executable name of DBVERIFY is dbv. The executable can be found in the Bin directory of the applicable Oracle Home directory. Refer to your Oracle documentation for using DBVERIFY on your system.

Parameters used with the DBVERIFY utility include the following:

➤ FILE—The name of the database file to verify.

➤ START—The block at which DBVERIFY will start. The block specification is in Oracle blocks. The default is to start with the first block in the file.

➤ END—The last block address to verify. The default is the last block in the file.

➤ BLOCKSIZE—The Oracle block size; the default is 2 kilobytes (KB).

➤ LOGFILE—The name of the log file to receive screen output. The default is to send output to the terminal screen.

➤ FEEDBACK—Causes DBVERIFY to display a single period (.) for every n pages verified. The default is no feedback.

➤ HELP—Lists onscreen usage help.

➤ PARFILE—The name of the parameter file to use.

The following example code shows how to get online help:

```
D:\ORANT>dbv help=y
DBVERIFY: Release 8.1.7.0.0 -
Production on Mon May 28 21:33:43 2001
(c) Copyright 2000 Oracle Corporation. All rights reserved.
Keyword    Description          (Default)
-------    -----------          ---------
FILE       File to Verify       (NONE)
START      Start Block          (First Block of File)
END        End Block            (Last Block of File)
BLOCKSIZE  Logical Block Size   (2048)
LOGFILE    Output Log           (NONE)
FEEDBACK   Display Progress     (0)
```

To verify the integrity of a data file named users01.ora, starting with block 1 and ending with block 100, invoke the DBVERIFY utility (for Unix) with the following specifications:

```
$ dbv /oradata/test01.ora start=1 end=100
```

For Windows NT, invoke the DBVERIFY utility with the following specifications:

```
C:\ORANT817>dbv file=c:\orant817\oradata\dwdb\users01.dbf
blocksize=8192 start=1 end=100
```

The following is a sample output from the DBVERIFY utility:

```
DBVERIFY: Release 8.1.7.0.0 -
Production on Mon May 28 21:47:56 2001

(c) Copyright 2000 Oracle Corporation. All rights reserved.

DBVERIFY - Verification starting :
FILE = c:\orant817\oradata\dwdb\users01.dbf
DBVERIFY - Verification complete

Total Pages Examined        : 100
Total Pages Processed (Data) : 0
Total Pages Failing   (Data) : 0
Total Pages Processed (Index): 0
Total Pages Failing   (Index): 0
Total Pages Processed (Other): 1
Total Pages Empty           : 99
```

```
Total Pages Marked Corrupt    : 0
Total Pages Influx            : 0
```

The following sample output illustrates blocksize mismatch:

```
C:\ORANT817>dbv file=test99.ora
DBVERIFY: Release 8.1.7.0.0 -
Production on Mon May 28 21:57:15 2001

(c) Copyright 2000 Oracle Corporation. All rights reserved.

DBV-00103: Specified BLOCKSIZE (2048) differs from actual (8192)
```

The following sample output illustrates corruptions found in the user-specified file:

```
DBVERIFY: Release 8.1.7.0.0 -
Production on Mon May 28 22:02:34 2001

(c) Copyright 2000 Oracle Corporation. All rights reserved.

DBVERIFY - Verification starting : FILE =
c:\orant817\oradata\dwdb\redo01.log
Page 1 is marked corrupt
***
Corrupt block relative dba: 0x00000001 (file 0, block 1)
Bad header found during dbv:
Data in bad block -
 type: 58 format: 6 rdba: 0x00000001
 last change scn: 0x0000.19afda5e seq: 0x68 flg: 0x40
 consistency value in tail: 0x00000000
 check value in block header: 0x0, block checksum disabled
 spare1: 0x0, spare2: 0x0, spare3: 0x810
***


. . . ..
Page 3 is marked corrupt
***
Corrupt block relative dba: 0x00000003 (file 0, block 3)
Bad header found during dbv:
Data in bad block -
 type: 58 format: 6 rdba: 0x00000003
 last change scn: 0x0034.19933929 seq: 0x0 flg: 0x00
 consistency value in tail: 0x2d31474e
 check value in block header: 0x3538, block checksum disabled
 spare1: 0x0, spare2: 0x0, spare3: 0x3332
***
```

```
DBVERIFY - Verification complete

Total Pages Examined        : 3
Total Pages Processed (Data) : 0
Total Pages Failing   (Data) : 0
Total Pages Processed (Index): 0
Total Pages Failing   (Index): 0
Total Pages Processed (Other): 0
Total Pages Empty           : 0
Total Pages Marked Corrupt  : 3
Total Pages Influx          : 0
```

The page in the output from the DBVERIFY utility is the number of the Oracle blocks processed.

Using the **DBMS_REPAIR** Package

The sys-owned **DBMS_REPAIR** package can be used to identify logical (software) block corruptions in tables, partitions, or indexes. This package normally does not report physical block corruptions. The procedure to detect block corruptions using **DBMS_REPAIR** is as follows:

1. Create a repair table using the **DBMS_REPAIR.ADMIN_TABLES** procedure. The following code illustrates a representative procedure call syntax:

   ```
   dbms_repair.admin_tables('MY_REPAIR_TABLE',
   DBMS_REPAIR.REPAIR_TABLE,
   DBMS_REPAIR.CREATE_ACTION, 'MY_TABLESPACE');
   ```

2. Check for object corruptions by executing the **DBMS_REPAIR. CHECK_OBJECT** procedure. The block addresses of the corrupted blocks will be stored in the repair table created by the previous step. The following code illustrates a representative procedure call syntax:

   ```
   dbms_repair.check_object('SCHEMA_OWNER',
   'MY_OBJECT_NAME',
   corrupt_count=> :my_variable);
   ```

3. Mark corrupted blocks. Oracle8i marks the corrupted blocks but does not fix them. The following code illustrates a representative procedure call syntax:

   ```
   dbms_repair.fix_corrupt_blocks('SCHEMA_OWNER',
   'MY_OBJECT_NAME',fix_count=> :my_fix_count_variable);
   ```

4. Skip corrupted blocks by executing the **DBMS_REPAIR.SKIP_ CORRUPT_ BLOCKS** procedure. This enables reading of noncorrupted blocks. The following code illustrates a representative procedure call syntax:

```
dbms_repair.skip_corrupt_blocks('SCHEMA_OWNER',
'MY_OBJECT_NAME');
```

Things to Know When Using the DBMS_REPAIR Package

The DBA should be aware of the following when using the **DBMS_REPAIR** package:

➤ When skipping of corrupted blocks is enabled, indexes may point to blocks marked as corrupt. Use the **DBMS_REPAIR.ADMIN_TABLES** procedure to create a table to hold the results of index checking. Use the **DBMS_REPAIR.DUMP_ORPHAN_KEYS** procedure to identify inconsistent index entries and then to rebuild the applicable indexes.

➤ Referential integrity constraints may be violated when corrupted blocks are skipped. The DBA can disable and then reenable constraints to identify violations.

➤ When the freelist head is corrupt and an error is returned, use **REBUILD_ FREELISTS** to repair this condition.

➤ The **DBMS_REPAIR** package ignores out-of-line columns for tables with Large Objects (LOBS), nested tables, and **VARRAYS**.

➤ The **DBMS_REPAIR** package will not work for index-organized tables and LOB indexes.

➤ The **DBMS_REPAIR.DUMP_ORPHAN_KEYS** procedure does not support bitmap and function-based indexes. The limit on key length is 3,950 bytes.

Using the LogMiner Utility

Oracle8i's LogMiner utility enables the DBA to analyze the redo log files to identify and undo logical corruptions. When processing the redo log files, LogMiner translates information into SQL statements that represent the logical transactions issued against the database. Specifically, LogMiner pinpoints the time or the System Change Number (SCN) to which incomplete recovery needs to be performed. It also enables the DBA to perform granular logical recovery by undoing changes made by one or more database transactions.

Steps to Analyze Redo Log Files

The following steps can be taken to analyze redo log files:

1. Specify the dictionary file location by enabling the init.ora parameter **UTL_FILE_DIR** to point to the directory where the dictionary file will be created.

2. Execute the **DBMS_LOGMNR_D.BUILD** procedure to create the dictionary file. The dictionary file is used to resolve object names and must contain all the objects found in the redo log files. The following code illustrates a representative procedure call:

```
dbms_logmnr_d.build('mydict.ora',
'/oradata/DWDB/wkdir/logminer');
```

 In Oracle 8.1.5, the dbmslogmnrd.sql script is automatically run as part of the catproc.sql script to create the **DBMS_LOGMNR_D** package for analyzing an Oracle8i database. For Oracle 8.1.6 and 8.1.7, the script file name is dbmslmd.sql.

3. Supply the list of online or archived redo log files by invoking the **DBMS_LOGMNR.ADD_LOGFILE** procedure. The following code illustrates representative procedure calls to create a new list, to specify the first file, and then to specify additional files to be analyzed:

```
dbms_logmnr.add_logfile('/oradata/MYDB/logmydb1.ora',
dbms_logmnr.NEW);)
dbms_logmnr.add_logfile('/oradata/MYDB/logmydb2.ora',
dbms_logmnr.ADDFILE);
```

4. Invoke the **DBMS_LOGMNR.START_LOGMNR** procedure to start log analysis. This operation will extract transaction details that occurred between the specified timeframes. SCN ranges are also supported. The following code illustrates log file analysis initiation and the releasing of resources:

```
dbms_logmnr.start_logmnr(dicfilename=>
'/oracle/DWDB/wkdir/logminer/mydict.ora',)
starttime=>to_date('01/05/2001:10AM', 'DD/MM/YYYY:HHSM'),
endtime=>to_date('01/05/2001:12AM', 'DD/MM/YYYY:HHSM'));
dbms_logmnr.end_logmnr;
```

5. Query the **V$LOGMNR_CONTENTS** view to view the log analysis data. The **SQL_REDO** column contains user-issued Data Manipulation Language (DML) statements that were executed against the database. The **SQL_UNDO** column contains DML statements that will undo or reverse the DML actions executed in the **SQL_REDO** column. The following code illustrates a sample query against the **V$LOGMNR_CONTENTS** view:

```
SELECT timestamp, username, sql_redo
FROM v$logmnr_contents
WHERE seg_name = 'ORGANIZATIONS';


TIMESTAMP    USER   SQL_REDO
---------    ----   --------
01-MAY-2001  TEST   insert into ORGANIZATION(…);
01-MAY-2001  TEST   update ORGANIZATION set discount= … WHERE …
03-MAY-2001  TEST   delete from ORGANIZATION where rowid = …
```

Things to Consider When Using LogMiner

The following need to be considered when using LogMiner:

➤ The view **V$LOGMNR_CONTENTS** is visible only to the analyzing session. This view is not available after the analyzing session signs out.

➤ Each redo log record translates to one row in the **V$LOGMNR_CONTENTS** view.

➤ SQL on chained data rows is not supported.

➤ DML statements issued against scalar data and transaction control statements are supported.

➤ Undoing Data Definition Language (DDL) operations, such as **TRUNCATE** and **DROP**, are not supported.

➤ **HEX** values for segment names will be shown if the object definition is not in the dictionary file or if modifications are made to clustered tables.

➤ The analyzing session can query **V$LOGMNR_DICTIONARY**, **V$LOGMNR_LOGS**, and **V$LOGMNR_PARAMETERS** views to verify the dictionary files, log files, and user-supplied analysis arguments.

Configuring Checksum Operations

When the DBA suspects that data files or online redo log files may be corrupt, he or she can use checksums to detect the corruptions. Different procedures are used to configure Oracle to use checksum to verify blocks in the data files and the online redo log files.

Data File Checksum

To configure Oracle to perform data file block checking, set the
DB_BLOCK_CHECKSUM initialization parameter to **TRUE**. The default
value is **FALSE**. When data file block checking is enabled, Oracle computes a
checksum for each data file block and writes that checksum in the header of the
data file block. Oracle uses the checksum to detect corruption in the block and
will try to verify the data block each time that it reads the data block from disk.
When Oracle detects a corruption, it will return error code ORA-01578 and will
include information about the corrupted block in a trace file. The DBA should
be aware that performance overhead is associated with the activation of data file
checksum operations. Oracle recommends setting **DB_BLOCK_CHECKSUM**
to **TRUE** to troubleshoot data corruption errors only when directed by the Oracle
support personnel.

 Because of the performance overhead implications, DBAs should set
initialization parameters prudently.

Log File Checksum

If an online redo log file has an undiscovered corruption before the archiver creates
the archive copy, the corruption has been propagated to the archived log file. This
corrupted archived log file is unusable for subsequent data file recovery operations.
To configure Oracle to perform redo log block checking, set the **LOG_BLOCK_
CHECKSUM** initialization parameter to **TRUE**. The default value is **FALSE**.
When redo log block checking is enabled, Oracle computes a checksum for each
redo log block written to the current log and writes that checksum in the header of
the redo log block. Oracle uses the checksum to detect corruption in the redo log
block. Oracle attempts to verify the redo log block when it writes the block to an
archive log file and when the block is read from an archived log file during recovery.

If a redo log block is corrupted while trying to write the archive log, Oracle will
try to read the block from another member of the log file group. If all members
have the corrupted block, archiving will stop, and the database may hang because
redo generation is no longer possible. If the database hangs because of an irrecov-
erable checksum error, the DBA can issue the **ALTER DATABASE CLEAR
LOGFILE** command to initialize the log files. This will be addressed in Chapter 14. If all members have the corrupted block, the redo log file cannot be used
for recovery operations. A backup should be performed at this time. The DBA
should be aware that some performance overhead is associated with the activation of redo log file checksum operations. Checksums should be used only when
corruption is suspected as a result of host input/output (I/O) subsystem failure.

Using the **DB_BLOCK_CHECKING** Parameter

This parameter is used to perform a logical block check on data and index blocks when they have been modified. The Oracle server will generate the ORA-01578 error and write it to the alert.log file if the server encounters a corrupted block. This is a dynamic parameter that incurs minimal performance impact while reading because no block checks are performed. Enabling this parameter will incur a performance hit for update operations.

Using **ANALYZE VALIDATE STRUCTURE** Command to Detect Block Corruption

The **ANALYZE VALIDATE STRUCTURE** command can be used to validate the structural integrity of tables and indexes. For a table, Oracle verifies the integrity of data blocks and data rows. For a temporary table, Oracle validates the structure of the table and the associated indexes for the current session. For a cluster, Oracle validates the structure of the clustered tables. For a partitioned table, Oracle verifies that data rows belong to the proper partition. For an index, Oracle verifies the integrity of each data block in the index and checks for block corruption. By using the **CASCADE** clause, you will be able to confirm that each row in the table has a corresponding index entry and that each index entry points to a row in the table. The following code samples illustrate using the **ANALYZE VALIDATE STRUCTURE** command:

Validate the structure of the **my_index** index:

```
ANALYZE INDEX my_index VALIDATE STRUCTURE;
```

Validate the structure of the table and the associated indexes:

```
ANALYZE TABLE customer VALIDATE STRUCTURE CASCADE;
```

Using Log and Trace Files to Diagnose Problems

The alert log (alert<SID>.log) is a file written by the Oracle server that contains informational, warning, and error messages relating to the status of the instance and the database. The initialization parameter **BACKGROUND_ DUMP_ DEST** controls where the alert log is placed. Information in the alert log includes the following:

➤ Database instance startups

➤ Database instance shutdowns

➤ A history of any physical changes that have been made to the database, such as the addition or change in status of data files, redo logs, and rollback segments

➤ Optional information concerning checkpoints

➤ Database errors, such as a corrupted member of a mirrored redo log or the filling of the archive log destination

➤ Informational messages helpful for tuning, such as excessive archive waits for a checkpoint or waits that occur while redo logs are being written to archive

➤ Database events

The alert log is usually the first item that the DBA examines for information when a serious system problem has been discovered. The alert log is continuously appended to by the Oracle server, so the DBA should periodically copy it to an alternate storage location for historical purposes and should purge it to minimize unnecessary disk usage.

 Oracle recommends checking the alert log on a regular basis to determine whether problems exist.

The following sample code shows the partial contents of an Oracle alert log file:

```
Dump file C:\ORANT817\admin\DWDB\bdump\dwdbALRT.LOG
Mon May 28 21:44:40 2001
ORACLE V8.1.7.0.0 - Production vsnsta=0
vsnsql=e vsnxtr=3
Windows NT Version 4.0 Service Pack 6, CPU type 586
Starting up ORACLE RDBMS Version: 8.1.7.0.0.
System parameters with non-default values:
  processes               = 150
  shared_pool_size        = 31457280
  large_pool_size         = 614400
  java_pool_size          = 20971520
  control_files           =
C:\ORANT817\oradata\DWDB\control01.ctl,
C:\ORANT817\oradata\DWDB\control02.ctl,
C:\ORANT817\oradata\DWDB\control03.ctl
```

```
db_block_buffers            = 2048
db_block_size               = 8192
compatible                  = 8.1.0
log_buffer                  = 32768
log_checkpoint_interval     = 10000
log_checkpoint_timeout      = 1800
db_files                    = 1024
db_file_multiblock_read_count= 8
max_enabled_roles           = 30
remote_login_passwordfile= EXCLUSIVE
db_domain                   = MARRIOTT.COM
global_names                = TRUE
distributed_transactions  = 10
instance_name               = DWDB
service_names               = DWDB.MARRIOTT.COM
mts_dispatchers             =
(PROTOCOL=TCP)(PRE=oracle.aurora.server.SGiopServer)
open_links                  = 4
sort_area_size              = 65536
sort_area_retained_size   = 65536
db_name                     = DWDB
open_cursors                = 300
os_authent_prefix           =
job_queue_processes         = 4
job_queue_interval          = 60
parallel_max_servers        = 5
background_dump_dest        = C:\ORANT817\admin\DWDB\bdump
user_dump_dest              = C:\ORANT817\admin\DWDB\udump
max_dump_file_size          = 10240
oracle_trace_collection_name=
PMON started with pid=2
DBWO started with pid=3
LGWR started with pid=4
CKPT started with pid=5
SMON started with pid=6
RECO started with pid=7
SNPO started with pid=8
SNP1 started with pid=9
SNP2 started with pid=10
SNP3 started with pid=11
Mon May 28 21:44:43 2001
starting up 1 shared server(s) ...
starting up 1 dispatcher(s) for network address
'(ADDRESS=(PARTIAL=YES)(PROTOCOL=TCP))'
...
Mon May 28 21:44:45 2001
alter database mount exclusive
```

```
Mon May 28 21:44:50 2001
Successful mount of redo thread 1, with mount id 2176294610.
Mon May 28 21:44:50 2001
Database mounted in Exclusive Mode.
Completed: alter database mount exclusive
Mon May 28 21:44:50 2001
alter database open
Beginning crash recovery of 1 threads
Mon May 28 21:44:52 2001
Thread recovery: start rolling forward thread 1
Recovery of Online Redo Log: Thread 1 Group 2 Seq 1595
Reading mem 0
  Mem# 0 errs 0: C:\ORANT817\ORADATA\DWDB\REDO02.LOG
Mon May 28 21:45:01 2001
Thread recovery: finish rolling forward thread 1
Thread recovery: 0 data blocks read, 0 data blocks written,
0 redo blocks read
Crash recovery completed successfully
Mon May 28 21:45:03 2001
Thread 1 advanced to log sequence 1596
Thread 1 opened at log sequence 1596
  Current log# 3 seq# 1596 mem# 0:
C:\ORANT817\ORADATA\DWDB\REDO03.LOG
Successful open of redo thread 1.
Mon May 28 21:45:03 2001
SMON: enabling cache recovery
SMON: enabling tx recovery
Mon May 28 21:46:51 2001
Completed: alter database open
```

In addition to the alert log file, the DBA can use trace files to help troubleshoot system problems because they contain information about the error. The Oracle trace files are created by the Oracle background processes when errors are encountered or for informational purposes and are written to the location specified by the initialization parameter **BACKGROUND_DUMP_DEST**. The name of the background process that created the trace file is included in the trace file name. The following sample illustrates trace file names for a Windows NT system:

```
orclARCH.trc
orclSMON.trc
orclDBWR.trc
orclPMON.trc
```

The following sample output from a trace file created by LGWR shows a missing online redo log file:

```
. . .
ORA-00313: open failed for members of log group 2 of thread 1
ORA-00312: online log 2 thread 1: '/oradata/log2b.ora'
ORA-27037: unable to obtain file status
SVR4 Error: 2: No such file or directory
Additional information: 3
ORA-00321: log 2 of thread 1, cannot update log file header
ORA-00312: online log 2 thread 1: 'oradata/log2b.ora'
ORA-00313: open failed for members of log group 2 of thread 1
. . .
```

The DBA should monitor trace files on a regular basis to help detect database problems. Periodically purging trace files will also reduce unnecessary disk usage.

Practice Questions

Question 1

> Your database files are spread across six disks. Which type of failure occurs when one of the disks suffers a head crash?
>
> ○ a. Instance failure
>
> ○ b. Statement failure
>
> ○ c. User process failure
>
> ○ d. Media failure

The correct answer is d. One of the causes of media failure is a disk drive head crash. Answers a, b, and c are not correct because a disk drive head crash will not cause these types of failures.

Question 2

> The Oracle server automatically handles which of the following recovery operations? [Choose two]
>
> ❏ a. Backup file restorations
>
> ❏ b. Roll-forward operations
>
> ❏ c. Rollback operations
>
> ❏ d. Control file creation

The correct answers are b and c. The Oracle server automatically performs instance recovery at instance start when required. The recovery process involves two stages: the roll-forward phase and the rollback phase. In the roll-forward phase, the Oracle server applies changes in the redo log files to the data files. During the rollback phase, the Oracle server removes any uncommitted data from the data files. Answer a is not correct because backup file restorations are typically handled by the DBA. Answer d is not correct because control file creation is performed by the DBA.

Question 3

> Which type of failure occurs when a user accidentally deletes all the rows from the **DEPT** table?
>
> ○ a. User process failure
>
> ○ b. Statement failure
>
> ○ c. Instance failure
>
> ○ d. Media failure
>
> ○ e. User error failure

The correct answer is e. User errors are caused by database users and typically require DBA involvement. User education and training will help minimize user error failures. Typical user error failures include committing data in error, accidentally deleting all rows in a table, and dropping a table that is still needed. Answers a, b, c, and d are not correct because accidentally deleting all rows in a table will not cause these kinds of failures.

Question 4

> Which type of failure occurs when a power outage causes the database server to become unavailable?
>
> ○ a. User error failure
>
> ○ b. Instance failure
>
> ○ c. Media failure
>
> ○ d. User process failure
>
> ○ e. Statement failure

The correct answer is b. An instance failure can be caused by a power outage. Recovery from an instance failure is automatic at database startup. Answers a, c, d, and e are incorrect because a power outage doesn't cause these types of failures.

Question 5

> Which files must be synchronized for recovery? [Choose three]
>
> ❑ a. Redo log files
>
> ❑ b. Export files
>
> ❑ c. Trace files
>
> ❑ d. Control files
>
> ❑ e. Data files
>
> ❑ f. Rollback files

The correct answers are a, d, and e. The Oracle server will not open a database when the redo log files, control files, and data files are not synchronized. Database recovery is required to achieve database synchronization. Answer b is incorrect because export files do not require synchronization. Answer c is incorrect because trace files are not used in recovery. Answer f is incorrect because rollback files don't exist.

Question 6

> Which file do DBAs typically examine first when a problem has been encountered by a database instance?
>
> ⭕ a. Configuration file
>
> ⭕ b. Trace file
>
> ⭕ c. Alert log file
>
> ⭕ d. SGA file

The correct answer is c. DBAs typically look in the alert log file first when there is a serious database problem. The alert log file is a historical view of what has happened to the database, and it records all background process errors and structural changes made to the database. Answer a is incorrect because the configuration file doesn't contain any error information. Answer b is incorrect because a trace file is typically examined after the alert log file. Answer d is incorrect because there is no such thing as an SGA file.

Question 7

If the DBWR process fails and the database shuts down, which file will contain information about the error that caused the DBWR process to fail?

○ a. Initialization file

○ b. DBWR trace file

○ c. listener log file

○ d. Control file

The correct answer is b. When a background process fails, it will generate a trace log file to record the information about the error. The name of the trace file will typically include the process name and have a .trc file extension. Answers a and d are incorrect because they don't contain information on DBWR errors. Answer c is incorrect because the listener log file contains networking connectivity errors.

Question 8

Which initialization parameter should be set to detect redo log file block corruptions before they are archived?

○ a. **BACKGROUND_DUMP_DEST**

○ b. **LOG_BLOCK_CHECKSUM**

○ c. **DB_BLOCK_CHECKSUM**

○ d. **CHECKSUM**

The correct answer is b. **LOG_BLOCK_CHCKSUM** checks redo log files for corruptions. Answer c is incorrect because **DB_BLOCK_CHECKSUM** pertains to detection of data file corruptions, not redo log file corruptions. Answer a is incorrect because it sets the location where trace files written by the Oracle background processes will be placed. Answer d is incorrect because it is an invalid initialization parameter.

Question 9

A database batch update process modified 10,000 rows early this morning. How can you use LogMiner to undo these changes?

- O a. Execute a script file containing all of the SQL statements in the **SQL_REDO** column of the **V$LOGMNR_CONTENTS** view.
- O b. Execute a script file containing all of the SQL statements in the **SQL_UNDO** column of the **V$LOGMNR_CONTENTS** view.
- O c. Execute a script file containing all of the SQL statements in the **SQL_REDO** column of the **V$LOGMNR_DICTIONARY** view.
- O d. Execute a script file containing all of the SQL statements in the **SQL_UNDO** column of the **V$LOGMNR_CONTENT** view.

The correct answer is b. The **SQL_UNDO** column of the **V$LOGMNR_CONTENTS** view contains the SQL statements required to reverse the original SQL statement. Answer a is incorrect because the **SQL_REDO** column contains the original SQL statement issued against the database. Answers c and d are incorrect because the specified view names are invalid.

Question 10

The **DBMS_REPAIR** package enables the DBA to identify corrupt logical blocks in tables, partitions, and indexes. Which database object should you query to get information about the corrupted blocks after you invoked the **DBMS_REPAIR.FIX_CORRUPT_BLOCKS** procedure?

- O a. **V$LOGMNR_CORRUPTED_BLOCKS**
- O b. **DBA_CORRUPTED_BLOCKS**
- O c. **DBA_TABLES**
- O d. **REPAIR_TABLE**

The correct answer is d. The **DBMS_REPAIR.FIX_CORRUPT_BLOCKS** procedure only marks the corrupted blocks and does not repair corrupt blocks. Information about the corrupted blocks are stored in the **REPAIR_TABLE**. Answers a and b are incorrect because they are invalid database objects. Answer c is incorrect because it does not contain information about corrupted blocks.

Need to Know More?

 Loney, Kevin and Marlene Theriault. *Oracle8i DBA Handbook*. Oracle Press, Berkeley, CA, 1999. ISBN 0-07212-188-2. This comprehensive guide for DBAs includes general backup and recovery concepts.

 Velpuri, Rama. *Oracle8i Backup and Recovery Handbook*. Oracle Press, Berkeley, CA, 2000. ISBN 0-072-12717-1. This book provides information on how to maximize uptime and recover data without compromising mission critical systems. Actual corporate scenarios and case studies are included.

 http://technet.oracle.com. This site provides the best information on Oracle's products and technologies. You can also purchase the following manuals online:

Dialeris, Connie. *Oracle8i Backup and Recovery Guide Release 2*. Oracle Corporation, Redwood City, CA, 1999. Part No. A76993-01. This manual provides guidance for data protection techniques and offers strategies for data storage, backup, and restore for Oracle 8i.

Leverenz, Lefty. *Oracle8i Concepts Release 2*. Oracle Corporation, Redwood City, CA, 1999. Part No. A76965-01. This manual describes all features of the Oracle8i server running on all operating systems.

Lorentz, Diana. *Oracle8i Reference Release 2*. Oracle Corporation, Redwood City, CA, 1999. Part No. A76961-01. This manual describes the architecture, processes, structures, and other concepts of Oracle8i and provides detailed information on static and dynamic data dictionary views.

 www.revealnet.com. This site from RevealNet provides Oracle administration reference software.

Oracle Recovery without Archiving

....

Terms you'll need to understand:

✓ Restore

✓ Recover

✓ **ALTER DATABASE RENAME FILE** command

✓ **RESTORE** command

Techniques you'll need to master:

✓ Understanding restoring and recovering data

✓ Understanding typical steps to recover a database system

✓ Understanding the implications of media failure in NOARCHIVELOG mode

✓ Recovering NOARCHIVELOG databases after media failure

✓ Restoring files to alternate locations

✓ Using Recovery Manager (RMAN) to recover a NOARCHIVELOG database

✓ Using the **RESTORE** command

One of the critical tasks of an Oracle database administrator (DBA) is to understand database recovery in order to derive an effective recovery strategy that meets site-specific needs. Recovery operations differ depending on the archiving mode of the database. This chapter focuses on database recovery topics relating to databases running in NOARCHIVELOG mode. You will learn about the implications of media failure under NOARCHIVELOG mode, recovering NOARCHIVELOG mode databases, restoring database files to different locations, and using Oracle Recovery Manager (RMAN) to recover a NOARCHIVELOG mode database. Refer to Chapters 11 and 12 for recovery operations with ARCHIVELOG mode databases.

Restoring and Recovering Data

Before performing recovery operations, a DBA should understand the following concepts:

➤ When a file is restored, an original copy of the file is retrieved from a backup.

➤ When a file is recovered, a restored file is brought current up to the required point in time. The recover process is also known as *rolling forward* and is only possible when the database is in ARCHIVELOG mode.

Typical steps to recovering a database system include the following:

1. Detect the failure. Is the database responding to the application? Has the system displayed explicit error messages? Problems such as a corrupt control file might not be detected while the database is online.

2. Analyze the failure. The recovery procedure depends on the analysis of the type and extent of the failure. The analysis time spent can be significant for large databases.

3. Determine the database components requiring recovery and the inter-component dependencies. When a component such as a database table is lost, you need to determine whether you need to recover the tablespace, a data file, or the database. When a table needs recovery, you'll have to re-create the associated indexes.

4. Determine the location of the backup. Is the backup on disk or tape? Is the backup on-site or off-site? Are mirrored copies available? Is an RMAN recovery catalog available?

5. Perform the restore. You need to restore the physical files from disk or tape to a location where the database can access it for recovery purposes. If RMAN is part of the backup and recovery strategy, it can be used to perform the restore operation. The amount of time required to restore is affected by the type of restore operation, file size, file format, file location, and the parallelization of the restore operation.

6. For archiving databases, apply redo log files and resynchronize the database. RMAN automates this recovery process.

Implications of Media Failure in NOARCHIVELOG Mode

NOARCHIVELOG mode is the default mode used by an Oracle database instance. In this mode, the filled groups of online redo log files are not archived, and, therefore, no redo history is maintained. No additional administrative overhead or disk space is required because no archival of the redo log is made. Due to the recycling of the online redo log files, all the work done after the most recent backup is lost because older redo log files needed for recovery are no longer available.

When the database is operating in NOARCHIVELOG mode, recovery from media failure is limited to the most recent full database backup. You need to restore all data files, redo log files, and control files from your backup even if only one file is lost. Your database is unrecoverable if no offline consistent backup is available. Typically, the only databases that run in NOARCHIVELOG mode are those that have a low volume of transactions, such as decision support databases that contain only summarized information from other high activity external databases or a training database that needs to start with a clean slate for each training session.

 The only time that you don't need to restore all the database files when recovering a NOARCHIVELOG mode database after a media failure is when no online redo log files have been overwritten by LGWR since the most recent backup.

Recovering NOARCHIVELOG Databases after Media Failure

In the event of a media failure for a database running in NOARCHIVELOG mode, you must recover from the most recent full database backup. The database is unavailable during the recovery process.

Follow these steps to perform the recovery process:

1. Shut down the database with the **SHUTDOWN ABORT** statement, as shown here:

```
SVRMGR> SHUTDOWN ABORT;
```

2. Resolve any hardware problems.

3. Restore all data files, redo log files, and control files from applicable off-line database backups using operating system copy commands or third-party media management mechanisms. All files must be restored, not just the damaged ones.

4. Open the database using the code shown here:

```
SVRMGR> STARTUP OPEN PFILE=init_SID.ora;
```

Restoring Files to Alternate Locations

If the disk cannot be replaced after a media failure, the DBA needs to move the database files to other disks and to update the control file accordingly. The following steps restore the database files to alternate locations:

1. Shut down the database if it is open.

2. Restore data files, redo log files, and control files from applicable offline backups using operating system (OS) copy commands or third-party media managers. All files must be restored, not just the ones that were lost.

3. Update the control file specification in the **CONTROL_FILES** parameter of the initSID.ora file. The path and file names need to be changed to reflect a new location for the control file of the Oracle database if the control file was lost in the disk failure.

4. Start up and mount the database, but don't open it, as in the code shown here:

```
SVRMGR> STARTUP MOUNT pfile=init_ecsprod.ora
```

5. Update the control file to reflect new locations of data files or redo log files. The DBA typically issues the **ALTER DATABASE** statement with the **RENAME FILE** option from Server Manager. Full path names for the data file at old and new locations should be specified. The following sample code illustrates this operation:

```
SVRMGR> ALTER DATABASE ecs_prod
    2> RENAME FILE '/u1/oradata/ecs_prod/ecs_data.ora'
    3> TO '/u2/oradata/ecs_prod/ecs_data.ora';
```

6. Mimic incomplete recovery, as illustrated by the following code:

```
SVRMGR> ALTER DATABASE RECOVER DATABASE UNTIL CANCEL;
```

7. Cancel the incomplete recovery without applying any redo logs.

8. Open the database, as illustrated by the following code:

```
SVRMGR> ALTER DATABASE OPEN RESETLOGS;
```

9. Shut down the database using the **NORMAL** or **IMMEDIATE** option, and take a backup.

Using RMAN to Recover a NOARCHIVELOG Mode Database

When performing the restore operation for a NOARCHIVELOG mode database, RMAN uses the recovery catalog or the target database control file to determine which full and incremental backups or image copies it will use. The **RESTORE** command is used in the restore operation.

RESTORE Command

The **RESTORE** command enables RMAN to restore files from backup sets or from image copies on disk to the specified location. Files with the same name are overwritten. The **RESTORE** command syntax applicable to the exam objectives and to this chapter is as follows:

```
RESTORE <restore_object> <options>;
```

Table 10.1 describes the **RESTORE** command elements and associated values.

The following code sample illustrates using the **RESTORE** command to restore a NOARCHIVELOG target database in NOMOUNT mode:

```
RMAN> Run {
  2> Allocate channel c1 type disk;
  3> Restore controlfile to 'u1/oradata/controlappl.ora';
  4> Sql "alter database mount";
  5> Restore database;
  6> Sql "alter database open resetlogs";}
```

You should consider the following when using the **RESTORE** command:

➤ The **RESTORE** command needs to be specified within the **RUN** command.

➤ At least one channel needs to be allocated preceding the **RESTORE** command.

➤ The target database must be mounted to perform full database restores.

Table 10.1	Elements of the RESTORE command.
ELEMENT	**VALUE**
Restore_object	Controlfile to <location>; database; datafile <*file_spec*>; tablespace <*ts_spec*>; archivelog all
Options	Channel <*channel id*>; from tag = <*tag_name*>; parms = <*parameters*>; from <*backupset or datafilecopy*>

➤ RMAN only restores backups that were created on the same type of channels that are allocated for the **RESTORE** command.

➤ You need to open the database with the **RESETLOGS** option after restoring using a backup control file.

The following steps demonstrate the use of RMAN to recover a NOARCHIVELOG database:

1. Shut down the target database.

2. Start the target database in MOUNT or NOMOUNT mode.

Note: If the target database is open when you're recovering a NOARCHIVELOG database, RMAN will return an error.

3. Make sure the recovery catalog database is open.

4. Start RMAN by connecting to both the target database and the recovery catalog.

5. Execute a run script that allocates applicable channels, restores control files and data files from offline database backups, opens the database, and releases the applicable channels. You should be aware that both the **RESTORE CONTROLFILE** and the **RESTORE DATABASE** commands are required when you're performing database restores. The **RESTORE DATABASE** command alone will restore only the data files. To bypass the **RECOVER** command, you should make sure the backups for the control file and the data files were taken at the same time so that they are synchronized. The following code sample illustrates an RMAN run script for Windows NT that can be used to restore all your database files when your database runs in NOARCHIVELOG mode:

```
E:\ORANT\BIN> rman80 target username/passwd@target_db rcvcat
username/passwd@catalog_db
```

```
RMAN> run{
allocate channel c1 type disk;
restore controlfile to 'e:\orant\database\control1.ora';
restore database;
sql 'alter database open resetlogs';
release channel c1; }
```

6. Shut down the database and take a full off-line database backup. This action
   is required when you're restoring your database with RMAN because the
   RESETLOGS task has been performed. Using RMAN to restore a
   NOARCHIVELOG mode database requires more effort than using OS
   mechanisms.

7. Open the database for normal use. Inform business users to reenter data that
   was lost after the most recent backup.

Practice Questions

Question 1

> When a media failure occurs for a test database running in NOARCHIVELOG mode, what is the first step the DBA should perform to recover this database after the hardware problem that caused the media failure has been resolved?
>
> O a. Issue the **RECOVER DATABASE** command.
>
> O b. Restore all database files from the most recent full offline backup.
>
> O c. Shut down the database.
>
> O d. Start the database.

The correct answer is c. DBAs typically perform the following steps to recover from a media failure when the database is running in NOARCHIVELOG mode:

1. Issue the **SHUTDOWN ABORT** command.

2. Restore all the database files from the most recent full offline backup.

3. Restart the database.

Answer a is incorrect because this command is not required for this sample scenario. Answers b and d are incorrect because they are not the first step performed by the DBA under the sample scenario.

Question 2

> When a data file has been restored to a new location and you need to issue the **ALTER DATABASE RENAME FILE** command to update the control file, in which state should the database be?
>
> O a. OPEN
>
> O b. MOUNT
>
> O c. NOMOUNT
>
> O d. Shut down

The correct answer is b. The database should be mounted and should not be open when the control file is being updated with the **ALTER DATABASE RENAME FILE** command. Answers a, c, and d are incorrect because these database states don't support the **ALTER DATABASE RENAME FILE** command.

Question 3

> If RMAN is part of your backup and recovery strategy and the target data-
> base is in NOARCHIVELOG mode, the target database should be in what
> state when you're restoring data files? [Choose two]
>
> ❑ a. Shut down
>
> ❑ b. NOMOUNT
>
> ❑ c. MOUNT
>
> ❑ d. OPEN

The correct answers are b and c. When you're using RMAN to restore data files
for a NOARCHIVELOG database, the database must be in NOMOUNT or
MOUNT state. Answers a and d are incorrect because the database must be
started and not opened.

Question 4

> What files are required to perform incomplete recovery when a media fail-
> ure occurs in a NOARCHIVELOG mode database?
>
> ○ a. All the data files
>
> ○ b. All the data files and the redo log files
>
> ○ c. All the data files and the archived redo log files
>
> ○ d. All the data files, redo log files, and archived log files
>
> ○ e. Valid offline database backup

The correct answer is e. All the database files—data files, control files, and redo
log files—must be restored when a media failure has occurred for a
NOARCHIVELOG mode database. Answers a and b are incorrect because they
are only a subset of the database files needed. Answers c and d are incorrect
because archived redo log files are not maintained for a NOARCHIVELOG
mode database.

Question 5

Which of the following files needs to be updated if you've restored the control file to a new location after a media failure?

○ a. Alert log file

○ b. Database initialization file

○ c. Trace file

○ d. Password file

○ e. Data files

The correct answer is b. If the location of the control file has changed, the database initialization file (initSID.ora) needs to be updated with the new location. Answers a, c, and e are incorrect because DBAs don't update these files. Answer d is incorrect because the password file does not contain information about control file locations.

Question 6

The disk on which the control file resides has crashed, and you need to restore it to a new location. What two steps must you perform before opening the NOARCHIVELOG database for general use? [Choose two]

❑ a. Restore the control file to the new location, and restore all data files and all redo log files from the most recent offline backup.

❑ b. Rename the data files in the init.ora file.

❑ c. Reenter the lost transactions.

❑ d. Edit the init.ora file to reflect the new control file location.

❑ e. Issue the **ALTER DATABASE RENAME FILE** command.

The correct answers are a and d. Answer b is incorrect because it is an invalid action. Answer c is incorrect because it is performed after the database is opened for general use. Answer e is incorrect because the **ALTER DATABASE RENAME FILE** command is used to update the control file with the new location of a data file.

Question 7

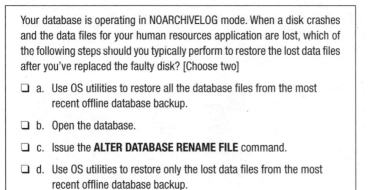

Your database is operating in NOARCHIVELOG mode. When a disk crashes and the data files for your human resources application are lost, which of the following steps should you typically perform to restore the lost data files after you've replaced the faulty disk? [Choose two]

❏ a. Use OS utilities to restore all the database files from the most recent offline database backup.

❏ b. Open the database.

❏ c. Issue the **ALTER DATABASE RENAME FILE** command.

❏ d. Use OS utilities to restore only the lost data files from the most recent offline database backup.

❏ e. Modify the database initialization file.

The correct answers are a and b. When recovering a NOARCHIVELOG mode database, you need to restore all the database files using the most recent offline database backup and then open the database for general use. Answer c is incorrect because the **ALTER DATABASE RENAME FILE** command is only needed when a data file relocation has taken place. Answer d is incorrect because, when performing recovery for a NOARCHIVELOG database, you need to restore all the database files from the most recent offline database backup. Answer e is incorrect because modifications to the database initialization file are needed when a control file relocation has taken place.

Question 8

> You are the DBA for a reporting database that is changed infrequently. This database is refreshed monthly, and a full offline backup is performed after each refresh operation. To minimize disk space usage, in what database mode could you operate this database?
>
> ○ a. ARCHIVELOG mode with monthly full offline backups
>
> ○ b. ARCHIVELOG mode with daily online backups
>
> ○ c. ARCHIVELOG mode with daily full offline backups
>
> ○ d. NOARCHIVELOG mode with daily online backups
>
> ○ e. NOARCHIVELOG mode with monthly full offline backups
>
> ○ f. NOARCHIVELOG mode with monthly online backups

The correct answer is e. A database running in NOARCHIVELOG mode conserves disk space because no storage space is required for the archived redo log files. Answers a, b, and c are incorrect because ARCHIVELOG mode databases require additional disk space for the archived redo log files. Answers d and f are incorrect because online backups are applicable to databases operating in ARCHIVELOG mode.

Question 9

> What does the following Server Manager command accomplish?
>
> ```
> SVRMGR> alter database rename file
>      2> '/disk3/oradata/appl.ora'
>      3> to '/disk4/oradata/appl.ora';
> ```
>
> ○ a. Moves a data file in the operating system.
>
> ○ b. Updates the control file with the new location of a data file.
>
> ○ c. Renames a data file in the operating system at the same location.
>
> ○ d. Updates the database initialization file with the new location of a data file.

The correct answer is b. The **ALTER DATABASE RENAME FILE** command is used to update the control file with the new location of a data file after it has been restored. Answer a is incorrect because the sample command does not physically move the data file in the OS. Answer c is incorrect because the sample command does not perform the OS rename operation. Answer d is incorrect because the database initialization file does not contain information about the location of the data files.

Question 10

> A media failure occurred for your training database running in NOARCHIVELOG mode. You've moved the data files to another drive because the original drive containing the original data files can't be replaced immediately. What command should you issue to update the database with this location change?
>
> ○ a. **ALTER TABLESPACE RENAME FILE**
>
> ○ b. **ALTER DATAFILE RENAME**
>
> ○ c. **ALTER SYSTEM RENAME FILE**
>
> ○ d. **ALTER DATABASE RENAME FILE**

The correct answer is d. When a media failure occurs and you've moved a data file to a new location, the **ALTER DATABASE RENAME FILE** command needs to be issued to update the control file. Answers a, b, and c are incorrect because they are invalid commands.

Question 11

Evaluate the following RMAN command:

```
RMAN> run{
allocate channel c1 type disk;
restore database;
sql 'alter database open resetlogs';
release channel c1; }
```

What command is missing if you need to perform a full database restore for a NOARCHIVELOG database?

○ a. **RESTORE CONTROLFILE TO** command

○ b. **RESTORE DATAFILE** command

○ c. **RESTORE TABLESPACE** command

○ d. **RESTORE ARCHIVELOG ALL** command

The correct answer is a. When you're performing full database restores using RMAN for a NOARCHIVELOG database, you must include the **RESTORE CONTROLFILE** and the **RESTORE DATABASE** commands. Answers b, c, and d are not correct because they serve other purposes.

Need to Know More?

 Loney, Kevin and Marlene Theriault. *Oracle8i DBA Handbook*. Oracle Press, Berkeley, CA, 1999. ISBN 0-07212-188-2. This comprehensive guide for DBAs includes general backup and recovery concepts. Chapter 10 describes backup and recovery procedures and provides example recovery scenarios.

 Velpuri, Rama. *Oracle8i Backup and Recovery Handbook*. Oracle Press, Berkeley, CA, 2000. ISBN 0-072-12717-1. This book provides information on how to maximize uptime and recover data without compromising mission critical systems. Actual corporate scenarios and case studies are included. Chapter 6 describes recovery principles and implementation.

 http://technet.oracle.com. This site provides the best information on Oracle's products and technologies. You can also purchase the following manuals online:

Dialeris, Connie. *Oracle8i Backup and Recovery Guide Release 2*. Oracle Corporation, Redwood City, CA, 1999. Part No. A76993-01. Chapter 5 describes how to restore and recover a database.

Lorentz, Diana. *Oracle8i SQL Reference Release 2*. Oracle Corporation, Redwood City, CA, 1999. Part No. A76989-01. This manual contains a complete description of the Structured Query Language (SQL) used to manage information in an Oracle database.

Lorentz, Diana. *Oracle8i Reference Release 2*. Oracle Corporation, Redwood City, CA, 1999. Part No. A76961-01. Chapters 1, 2, and 3 provide detailed information on database initialization parameters, static data dictionary views, and dynamic performance views.

 www.revealnet.com. This site from RevealNet provides Oracle administration reference software.

Complete Oracle Recovery with Archiving

Terms you'll need to understand:

✓ Complete recovery

✓ Incomplete recovery

✓ **RECOVER** command

✓ **ALTER DATABASE RECOVER** command

✓ **V$RECOVER_FILE**

✓ **ALTER DATABASE CLEAR UNARCHIVED LOGFILE** command

✓ **V$RECOVERY_STATUS**

✓ **V$RECOVERY_FILE_STATUS**

✓ **SET AUTORECOVERY ON** command

✓ **V$LOG_HISTORY**

✓ **V$RECOVERY_LOG**

✓ **SET NEWNAME** command

✓ **SWITCH** command

Techniques you'll need to master:

✓ Understanding the implications of instance failure with an ARCHIVELOG database

✓ Understanding the pros and cons of recovering an ARCHIVELOG database

✓ Understanding complete recovery operations

✓ Using the **RECOVER** command

✓ Performing recovery for an ARCHIVELOG database after a media failure

✓ Understanding pertinent data dictionary views for database recovery

✓ Using Recovery Manager (RMAN) to perform complete recovery for an ARCHIVELOG database

When an Oracle database is operating in ARCHIVELOG mode, the Oracle database administrator (DBA) has two recovery options—complete or incomplete recovery. In *complete recovery*, the database is restored and recovered through the application of all redo information generated (in the online and archived redo log files) since the last available backup. This recovery option is typically performed when one or more data files or control files is damaged or lost due to a media failure. The damaged or lost files are fully recovered using all redo information generated since the restored backup.

In *incomplete recovery*, the database is restored and recovered through the application of only some of the redo information generated since the last available backup. Incomplete recovery is typically performed when the online redo log files are lost due to hardware problems or due to a user error requiring recovery to the point in time before the error occurred or when an archived redo log file essential for recovery is not available.

This chapter focuses on complete recovery concepts and procedures. Specifically, you will learn about the implications of instance failure with an ARCHIVELOG database, the pros and cons of recovering an ARCHIVELOG database, complete recovery operations, recovering ARCHIVELOG databases after media failure, and performing ARCHIVELOG database recovery using Oracle Recovery Manager (RMAN).

Implications of Instance Failure with an ARCHIVELOG Database

An Oracle database typically operates in ARCHIVELOG mode under the following circumstances:

➤ The backup window doesn't allow for shutting down the database to take an offline backup.

➤ The organization cannot afford to lose any data.

➤ The recovery process is simpler when using archived redo log files than manually applying lost transactions.

When a media failure occurs with an ARCHIVELOG mode database and complete recovery up to the time of failure is required, you must make sure the following items are available:

➤ A valid backup of the damaged or lost data files taken after the database was set to ARCHIVELOG mode

➤ All the archived redo log files from the time of the restored backup to the present time

Pros and Cons of Recovering an ARCHIVELOG Database

Operating your database in ARCHIVELOG mode has both pros and cons. The pros include the following:

➤ You can typically perform the recovery procedures while the database is open. The exception is when the data files for the **SYSTEM** tablespace or the data file containing rollback segments with active transactions are being recovered.

➤ When restoring files from a valid backup, you only need to restore a subset of the valid backup, the damaged or lost files.

➤ No data loss will be incurred for committed data. When you restore files from a valid backup and apply all the redo information generated using online and archived redo log files, the database will be current up to the present time.

➤ The total recovery time is dependent on the following factors:

  ➤ The amount of time spent locating the files

  ➤ The speed of the hardware in restoring the required files and in applying all the online and archived redo log files

The cons include the following:

➤ Additional disk space is required for the archived redo log files.

➤ The potential risk that the database will run out of space and subsequently hang is increased.

➤ Additional DBA maintenance overhead is incurred.

➤ All of the archived redo log files from the time of the last valid backup to the present time must be available. If one file is missing, complete recovery cannot be performed because all archived redo log files must be sequentially applied.

Complete Recovery Operations

You can use the following two basic methods to recover physical files:

➤ Recovering your database manually by executing either the **RECOVER** or the **ALTER DATABASE RECOVER** command

➤ Using the RMAN utility to automate recovery

The following steps are typically performed for a complete recovery up to the time of failure when a valid backup and all the applicable redo log files are available:

1. Determine which data files need recovery. The **V$RECOVER_FILE** view is helpful in this effort.

2. Make sure the status of the damaged or lost file is not **ONLINE**. You can query the **V$DATAFILE** and the **V$TABLESPACE** data dictionary views to obtain the status of the file.

3. Make sure that you restore only the damaged or lost file from backup. If you cannot restore a data file to its original location, relocate the restored data file, and inform the control file of the new location by using the **ALTER DATA-BASE RENAME DATAFILE** command. Restore any necessary archived redo log files. Also make sure the online redo log files are not restored.

> Restoring all the files from the backup will take your database back to a certain point in time, which is not desirable when you're performing a complete recovery up to the time of failure.

4. Make sure the database is in MOUNT or OPEN mode.

5. Use the **RECOVER** command to recover the restored files.

RECOVER Command

The **RECOVER** command performs media recovery on one or more tablespaces, one or more data files, or the entire database. The following **RECOVER** command syntax examples are typically issued during the recovery process to reconstruct the data files:

➤ RECOVER [AUTOMATIC] DATABASE—Recovers the entire database. This command is only applicable for a closed database recovery.

➤ RECOVER [AUTOMATIC] TABLESPACE *<tablespace_specification: number or name>*—Recovers a particular tablespace. The *<tablespace_specification>* is the number or the name of a tablespace in the current database. This command is only applicable for an open database recovery.

➤ RECOVER [AUTOMATIC] DATAFILE *<datafile_specification: number or name>*—Recovers a particular data file. You can specify any number of data files. This command is applicable for both open and closed database recovery.

The **AUTOMATIC** keyword in the **RECOVER** commands tells Oracle to generate automatically the name of the next archived redo log file needed to continue the recovery operation. Oracle uses the **LOG_ARCHIVE_DEST** and the **LOG_ARCHIVE_FORMAT** parameters to generate the next redo log file name. If the file is found, the contents of the redo log file are applied. If the file is not found, Oracle prompts you for a file name, displaying the generated file name as a suggestion. You can then accept the generated file name or replace it with a desirable fully qualified file name. If you didn't specify **AUTOMATIC**, Oracle prompts you for a file name, displaying the generated file name as a suggestion. You can then accept the generated file name or replace it with a desirable fully qualified file name.

Things to Remember When Using the RECOVER Command

You should consider the following when using the **RECOVER** command:

➤ The **ALTER DATABASE** tokens may be optionally included in front of the **RECOVER** command.

➤ You must be connected to Oracle as SYSOPER or SYSDBA.

➤ You cannot use the **RECOVER** command when connected through the multithreaded server.

➤ To perform media recovery on an entire database (all tablespaces), the database must be mounted and closed.

➤ To perform media recovery on a tablespace, the database must be mounted and open, and the tablespace must be offline.

➤ To perform media recovery on a data file not belonging to the **SYSTEM** tablespace, the database can remain open and mounted with the damaged data files offline.

➤ You must restore the damaged data files from a valid backup before using the **RECOVER** command. Also, make sure you can access all archived and online redo log files since the restored backup.

➤ You should restore copies of the archived redo log files needed for recovery to the destination specified in **LOG_ARCHIVE_DEST**, if necessary.

➤ During recovery, you can accept the suggested log name by pressing Return, cancel recovery by typing "Cancel", or type "AUTO" at the prompt for automatic file selection without further prompting. If you've enabled autorecovery (that is, **SET AUTO RECOVERY ON**), the recovery process proceeds without prompting you with file names. Status messages are displayed when each log file has been applied.

Recovering ARCHIVELOG Databases after Media Failure

You can perform complete recovery for an ARCHIVELOG database after media failure using four different techniques:

➤ Closed database recovery

➤ Open database recovery with database initially open

➤ Open database recovery with database initially closed

➤ Recovery for a data file with no backup

Closed Database Recovery

This recovery technique is typically used under the following circumstances:

➤ The database does not need to be available 24 hours a day and 7 days a week.

➤ The files that need recovery belong to the **SYSTEM** tablespace or contain active rollback segments.

➤ Recovery is needed for the whole database.

➤ Recovery is needed for a large number of the data files.

You should be aware that the closed database recovery technique means that the database will be unavailable to the business users during the recovery process.

Sample Recovery Scenario

Corrupted blocks have been discovered for data file df3 located on disk d3. Data file df3 belongs to the **SYSTEM** tablespace. The following are steps to recover data file df3:

1. Restore the file from the most recent valid backup, as illustrated by this sample code:

```
Unix:
SVRMGR> !cp /u1/backup/df3.ora /u2/oradata/
NT:
SVRMGR> !copy e:\orant\backup\df3.ora d:\orant\database\
```

2. Start the database in MOUNT mode, and then recover data file df3 to the point of failure by applying applicable archived log files and online redo log files, as illustrated by this sample code:

```
SVRMGR> startup mount pfile=initTEST.ora
...
SVRMGR> recover datafile '/u2/oradata/df3.ora';
ORA-00279: change 102772 ...12/30/99 20:01:22 needed for thread
1
ORA-00289: suggestion : /u1/archive/arch_7.rdo
ORA-00280: change 102772 for thread 1 is in sequence #7
Log applied.
...
Media recovery complete.
```

3. Upon recovery process completion, all the data files are synchronized. The database can be opened for normal use, as illustrated by the following sample code:

```
SVRMGR> alter database open;
```

4. Notify business users to reenter any data that was not committed before the media failure.

Open Database Recovery with Database Initially Open

This recovery technique is typically used under the following circumstances:

➤ Downtime cannot be tolerated because the database must be available 24 hours a day and 7 days a week.

➤ The files that need recovery don't contain active rollback segments or don't belong to the **SYSTEM** tablespace.

➤ Recovery is needed when a media failure has occurred that did not cause the database to be shut down.

➤ Recovery is needed when an accidental file loss has occurred that did not cause the database to be shut down.

➤ Recovery is needed when a file corruption has been detected that did not cause the database to be shut down.

Sample Recovery Scenario

A member of the DBA team accidentally deleted data file df3 using operating system (OS) commands. The database is open for normal use. The following are steps to recover data file df3:

1. Determine the tablespace to which the data file df3 belongs, as illustrated by the following code sample:

```
SQL> select file_id FID,
  2> file_name,
  3> tablespace_name TS_NAME,
  4> status
  5> from dba_data_files;
FID  FILE_NAME                              TS_NAME     STATUS
---- -------------------------------------  ----------  --------
   1 /u1/oradata/system01.ora               SYSTEM      AVAILABLE
   2 /u2/oradata/df3.ora                    APP03_DATA  AVAILABLE
...
```

2. Check to see if data file df3 is offline. You'll need to take the data file offline if it is currently online. The following sample code illustrates using a Structured Query Language (SQL) query to obtain the current status of all the data files. Offline data files may require recovery:

```
SQL> select df.file# file#, df.name, df.status, dh.status
  2> from v$datafile_header dh, v$datafile df
  3> where dh.file# = df.file#;
FILE# DF.NAME                              DF.STATUS DH.STATUS
----- -------------------------------------  -------- --------
    1 /u1/oradata/system01.ora              SYSTEM    ONLINE
    2 /u2/oradata/df3.ora                   RECOVER   OFFLINE
    3 /u1/oradata/rbs01.ora                 ONLINE    ONLINE
...
```

 When a tablespace is taken offline, all the data files belonging to the offline tablespace are also taken offline. This means that all the data residing in the offline tablespace is not accessible. To maximize availability for a tablespace comprised of multiple data files, you can take the data file requiring recovery offline so that other online data files in the tablespace remain available.

3. Because the data file is offline, you can restore the file from a valid backup, as illustrated by the following code sample:

```
Unix:
SVRMGR> !cp /u3/backup/df3.ora /u2/oradata/
NT:
SVRMGR> !copy e:\orant\backup\df3.ora d:\orant\database\
```

4. Use the **RECOVER** or the **ALTER DATABASE RECOVER** commands to recover the restored data file, as illustrated by the following sample code:

```
SVRMGR> recover datafile '/u2/oradata/df3.ora';
OR
SVRMGR> recover tablespace APP03_DATA;
```

5. Bring the data file df3 online when the recovery process is finished and all data files are synchronized, as illustrated by the following sample code:

```
SVRMGR> alter database
datafile '/u2/oradata/df3.ora' online;
OR
SVRMGR> alter tablespace APP03_DATA online;
```

When Oracle encounters a file problem, it will sometimes automatically take the data file offline. It is highly recommended that you always check the alert log for any errors and that you check the current status of data files before you begin the recovery process.

Open Database Recovery with Database Initially Closed

This recovery technique is typically used under the following circumstances:

➤ A media or hardware failure has caused the database system to go down.

➤ Downtime cannot be tolerated because the database must be available 24 hours a day and 7 days a week.

➤ The files that need recovery don't contain rollback segments or don't belong to the **SYSTEM** tablespace.

Sample Recovery Scenario

You've discovered that the disk controller to disk u3 failed, which caused the media failure. One data file, df3, resides on disk u3. The data file df3 does not belong to the **SYSTEM** tablespace and does not contain rollback segments. The data file df3 also should not prevent users from running their end-of-fiscal-year reports. The following are steps to recover data file df3:

1. Start and mount the database, as illustrated by the following code. The database will not open because data file df3 can't be opened:

```
SVRMGR> startup mount pfile=$HOME/initTEST.ora
Database mounted.
```

2. Issue the following query to obtain the tablespace number to which the data file belongs:

```
SQL> select df.file# file#, df.ts#, df.tablespace_name
TS_NAME,
  2> df.name, dh.error
  3> from v$datafile_header dh, v$datafile df
  4> where dh.file# = df.file#;
FILE# TS# TS_NAME    NAME                      ERROR
----- --- --------   ----------------------    ----------------
    1   0 SYSTEM     /u1/oradata/system01.ora
    2   1            /u3/oradata/df3.ora       FILE NOT FOUND
    3   2 RB_DATA    /u1/oradata/rbs01.ora
 ...
```

3. From the **V$DATAFILE** view, you've determined that the data file df3 is currently online. The data file df3 must be taken offline to open the database. The following code sample can be issued to take the data file df3 offline:

```
SVRMGR> alter database datafile
    2> '/u3/oradta/df3.ora' offline;
```

The **ALTER TABLESPACE** command will not work here because the database is not opened at this point.

4. Open the database for normal use, as illustrated by the following sample code:

```
SVRMGR> alter database open;
```

5. Restore the data file df3 to disk u4 because disk u3 is no longer available, as illustrated by the following sample code:

```
Unix:
SVRMGR> !cp /u2/backup/df3.ora /u4/oradata/
NT:
SVRMGR> !copy e:\orant\backup\df3.ora f:\orant\database\
```

6. Inform Oracle of the new data file location using the following sample code:

```
SVRMGR> alter database rename file '/u3/oradata/df3.ora'
    2> to '/u4/oradata/df3.ora';
```

7. Issue the following query to obtain the tablespace name that owns the data file df3:

```
SQL> select file_id f#, file_name,
  2> tablespace_name ts_name,
  3> status
  4> from dba_data_files;
F#   FILE_NAME                        TS_NAME    STATUS
---- -------------------------------- ---------- --------
   1 /u1/oradata/system01.ora     .   SYSTEM     AVAILABLE
   2 /u4/oradata/df3.ora              APP03_DATA AVAILABLE
   3 /u1/oradata/rb01.ora             RB_DATA    AVAILABLE
...
```

8. Recover the restored data file df3 using the **RECOVER** or **ALTER DATA-BASE RECOVER** commands, as illustrated by the following sample code:

```
SVRMGR> recover datafile '/u4/oradata/df3.ora';
OR
SVRMGR> recover tablespace APP03_DATA;
```

9. Bring the data file df3 online when the recovery process is finished and all data files are synchronized, as illustrated by the following sample code:

```
SVRMGR> alter database
datafile '/u4/oradata/df3.ora' online;
OR
SVRMGR> alter tablespace APP03_DATA online;
```

10. Notify business users to reenter any data that was not committed before the media failure.

Recovery of a Data File with No Backup

This recovery technique is typically used under the following circumstances:

➤ A media or user failure has caused a loss of a data file that has no available backup.

➤ All archived redo log files from the time the lost data file was created up to the current time are available.

➤ The files that need recovery don't contain rollback segments or don't belong to the **SYSTEM** tablespace.

During the recovery process, all archived redo log files need to be available on disk. If any archived redo log files are on a backup tape, they must be restored to disk first.

Sample Recovery Scenario

One of the application DBAs created the **TRAINING_DATA** tablespace on disk u5 yesterday, and that tablespace has not been incorporated into the backup strategy. The **TRAINING_DATA** tablespace contains a single data file df5, which is now lost. All of the archived redo log files generated since yesterday are available. The following are steps to recover data file df5:

1. Mount the database if it is closed. Take the data file df5 offline. Because the **TRAINING_DATA** tablespace contains one data file df5, we can optionally take the tablespace offline instead of the data file. Make sure the **IMMEDIATE** option is used in the **ALTER TABLESPACE** command to prevent a checkpoint that tries to write to a nonexistent data file. Open the database for normal use. The following sample code illustrates this action:

```
SVRMGR> alter tablespace TRAINING_DATA offline immediate;
Statement Processed.
```

2. Query the **V$RECOVER_FILE** view for the status of a backup and to confirm the recovery status, as shown here:

```
SVRMGR> selecLE NOT FOUND              0
```

3. Recreate the lost file, as illustrated by the following sample code:

```
SVRMGR> alter database create datafile '/u1/oradata/df5.ora'
    2> as '/u5/oradata/df5.ora';
Statement Processed.
SVRMGR> select * from v$recover_file;
FILE# ONLINE  ERROR           CHANGE#    TIME
---- ------  --------------  --------  --------
    5 OFFLINE                 118249    30-DEC-99
```

4. Recover the recreated data file using the following sample code:

```
SVRMGR> recover tablespace TRAINING_DATA;
```

5. All archived and redo log files are applied, and all the data files are synchronized.

6. Upon recovery process completion, bring the tablespace online (or bring the one data file online), as illustrated by the following code sample:

```
SVRMGR> alter tablespace TRAINING_DATA online;
```

7. Incorporate the data file in the backup strategy and notify users that the **TRAINING_DATA** tablespace is available for general use.

Additional Recovery Activities

DBAs may encounter several recovery activities in performing their day-to-day functions, including the following:

➤ Recovery of a file in Backup mode

➤ Clearing redo log files

➤ Recreating inactive redo log files

➤ Obtaining recovery status information

➤ Restoring archived redo log files to a different location

➤ Enabling automatic application of redo log files

➤ Locating files that need recovery

Recovery of a File in Backup Mode

While a DBA is performing an open database backup, a failure condition may occur that may cause the database to go down. You should be aware of the following issues when you encounter this situation:

➤ The backup files will not be valid if the OS backup has been terminated abnormally. A new backup will be required. The new backup is not good until it has been completed and the archived redo logs generated during the backup have been backed up.

➤ The database files in hot backup mode will be out of sync with the rest of the database because the file headers are frozen at the start of the open database backup.

➤ You can't issue the **ALTER TABLESPACE** command until the database is open. The database will not open until the database files are synchronized or offline. Taking the database files offline will not help the situation because the **ALTER TABLESPACE END BACKUP** command used to unfreeze the file headers requires database files to be online.

Note: During hot backups, Oracle will continue to write to the database data files that are in hot backup mode.

To perform recovery of a file in Backup mode, follow these steps:

1. Query the **V$BACKUP** view to determine which files are in hot backup mode, as illustrated by the following sample code:

```
SQL> select * from v$backup;
FILE# STATUS          CHANGE# TIME
---- -------------- ------ --------
    1 NOT ACTIVE          0
    2 ACTIVE         119865 30-DEC-99
    3 NOT ACTIVE          0
...
```

The above listing shows that file number 2 is in hot backup mode.

2. Issue the **ALTER DATABASE END BACKUP** command to unfreeze the file header, as illustrated by the following sample code:

```
SVRMGR> alter database datafile 2 end backup;
Statement processed.
SVRMGR> select * from v$backup;
SQL> select * from v$backup;
FILE# STATUS          CHANGE# TIME
---- -------------- ------ --------
    1 NOT ACTIVE          0
    2 NOT ACTIVE     119865 30-DEC-99
    3 NOT ACTIVE          0
...
```

3. Open the database for general use, as illustrated by the following sample code:

```
SVRMGR> alter database open;
```

Clearing Redo Log Files

If corruption has been detected for an online redo log file while the database is open, you can use the **ALTER DATABASE CLEAR UNARCHIVED LOGFILE** command to create or clear the online redo log file without shutting down the database. The **ALTER DATABASE CLEAR UNARCHIVED LOGFILE** command is useful when you can't drop the online redo log file because you only have two redo log groups, or because the corrupt redo log file is a member of the current redo log group. You are not allowed to clear a redo log file that is currently required for recovery.

You should take a backup after using the **ALTER DATABASE CLEAR UNARCHIVED LOGFILE** command because complete recovery can't be accomplished if the applicable archived redo log file was not generated.

You can also use the ALTER DATABASE CLEAR LOGFILE... UNRECOVERABLE DATAFILE command to clear a redo log file even though offline data files require the redo log file for recovery. The offline data files requiring this cleared redo log file will be unusable after this command has been issued. To recover the offline data files, you can restore them and perform an incomplete recovery to the point in time before the required redo log file was cleared, or you can drop the tablespace containing the unrecoverable data files.

Recreating Inactive Redo Log Files

When the online redo log files are damaged or lost, you may not be able to perform complete recovery up to the point of failure. However, you will not lose any data under the following conditions:

➤ The database configuration includes mirrored redo log files.

➤ The online redo log file has been archived.

➤ The status of the lost online redo log file is not current.

Sample Recovery Scenario

You've just created the quality assurance (QA) database. The LGWR background process abnormally terminated and aborted the database instance. You have not taken a backup of this new database, and you don't have the resources to recreate the database. To recover from this situation, follow these steps:

1. Restart the database instance, as illustrated by the following sample code:

```
SVRMGR> startup pfile=$HOME/initQA.ora
ORACLE instance started.
...
ORA-00313: open failed for members of log group 1 of thread 1
ORA-00312: online log 1 thread 1: '/u2/oradata/log1a.ora'
```

2. Query the **V$LOG** data dictionary view for the redo log file status, as illustrated by the following sample code:

```
SVRMGR> select GROUP#,THREAD#,BYTES,MEMBERS,
    2> ARCHIVED,STATUS,FIRST_CHANGE#
    3> From v$log;
```

GROUP#	THREAD#	BYTES	MEMBERS	ARC	STATUS	FIRST_CHANGE#
1	1	1048576	1	YES	UNUSED	0
2	1	104857	1	NO	CURRENT	188128

The above listing shows that there is a problem with log group 1 because the **FIRST_CHANGE#** is 0. Log group 1 is not active because log group 2 is the current group. The redo log file for log group 1 has been archived, so no recovery information has been lost. You were not successful in locating the redo log file from the file system. Although the redo log file is lost, recovery is not required because no data has been lost. In this situation, you do need to recreate the lost inactive redo log file, so the database can be opened for general use.

When you need to recreate the redo log file, perform the following steps:

1. Obtain the location of the redo log file from the data dictionary, as illustrated by the following sample code:

```
SVRMGR> select * from v$logfile;
GROUP#   STATUS  MEMBER
------   ------  ------------------
1                /u01/oradata/log1a.ora
2        STALE   /u02/oradata/log2a.ora
```

You can't drop log group 1 because at least two log groups must exist. You need to create a temporary group 3, drop log group 1, recreate log group 1, drop the temporary group 3, and remove the redo log file for group 3 from the OS. The following code sample illustrates this process:

```
SVRMGR> alter database add logfile group 3
     2> '/u1/oradata/log3a.ora' size 1M;
Statement processed.
SVRMGR> alter database drop logfile group 1;
Statement processed.
SVRMGR> alter database add logfile group 1
     2> '/u1/oradata/log1a.ora' size 1M;
Statement processed.
SVRMGR> alter database drop logfile group 3;
Statement processes.
SVRMGR> !rm /u1/oradata/log3a.ora
```

2. Open the database for general use, as illustrated by the following sample code:

```
SVRMGR> alter database open;
```

3. Implement multiplexing of the redo log files to minimize data loss in the future.

4. When the redo log groups are of the same size, you can optionally recreate the redo log file using two commands, as illustrated by the following code sample:

```
SVRMGR> !cp /u1/oradata/log2a.ora /u1/oradata/log1a.ora
SVRMGR> alter database clear logfile '/u1/oradata/log1a.ora';
```

Obtaining Recovery Status Information

Two data dictionary views provide database recovery status information to the server and user processes performing the media recovery:

➤ **V$RECOVERY_STATUS**—Provides overall database recovery information:

```
SQL> desc v$recovery_status;
Name                              Null?      Type
-------------------------------   --------   ----
RECOVERY_CHECKPOINT                          DATE
THREAD                                       NUMBER
SEQUENCE_NEEDED                              NUMBER
SCN_NEEDED                                   VARCHAR2(16)
TIME_NEEDED                                  DATE
PREVIOUS_LOG_NAME                            VARCHAR2(513)
PREVIOUS_LOG_STATUS                          VARCHAR2(13)
REASON                                       VARCHAR2(13)
```

➤ **V$RECOVERY_FILE_STATUS**—Provides information for each data file needing recovery:

```
SQL> desc v$recovery_file_status;
Name                              Null?      Type
-------------------------------   --------   ----
FILENUM                                      NUMBER
FILENAME                                     VARCHAR2(513)
STATUS                                       VARCHAR2(13)
```

Restoring Archived Redo Log Files to a Different Location

If you've restored the archived redo log files to a location other than the **LOG_ARCHIVE_DEST** directory, you will need to inform Oracle of the new location during the recovery process. You have three ways to let Oracle know about the new location for the restored archived redo log files:

➤ You can specify the location and name of the archived redo log file at the RECOVER prompt. The following sample code illustrates this:

```
SVRMGR> RECOVER DATAFILE 3;
ORA-00279: change 101109...12/27/99 18:00:05 needed for thread 1
ORA-00289: suggestion : /u1/archive/arch_23.rdo
ORA-00280: change 101109 for thread 1 is in sequence #23
Specify log: {<RET>=suggested | filename | AUTO | CANCEL}
/u2/archive/arch_23.rdo
Log applied.
...
```

➤ Issue the **ALTER SYSTEM ARCHIVE** command, as illustrated by the following code sample:

```
SVRMGR> ALTER SYSTEM ARCHIVE LOG START TO
     2> <new_location_specification>;
```

➤ Issue the **RECOVER FROM** *<location_specification>* command, as illustrated by the following code sample:

```
SVRMGR> RECOVER FROM '<new_location_specification>' DATABASE;
```

Automatic Application of Redo Log Files

You can perform one of the following actions to tell Oracle to apply the necessary archived and online redo log files automatically before and during the recovery process:

➤ Issue the Server Manager **SET AUTORECOVERY ON** statement before starting media recovery, as illustrated by the following code sample:

```
SVRMGR> SET AUTORECOVERY ON
```

➤ Provide **AUTO** when prompted for a redo log file, as illustrated by the following sample code:

```
Specify log: {<RET>=suggested | filename | AUTO | CANCEL}
/u2/archive/arch_23.rdo
Log applied.
...
```

➤ Provide the **AUTOMATIC** keyword option when issuing the **RECOVER** command, as illustrated by the following sample code:

```
SVRMGR> RECOVER AUTOMATIC TABLESPACE 3;
Media recovery complete.
```

Locating Files That Need Recovery

Three data dictionary views can be used to locate data files that need recovery:

➤ **V$RECOVER_FILE**—Displays the status of data files needing media recovery:

```
SQL> desc v$recover_file
 Name                               Null?    Type
 ------------------------------     -------- ----
  FILE#                                .      NUMBER
  ONLINE                                      VARCHAR2(7)
  ERROR                                       VARCHAR2(18)
  CHANGE#                                     NUMBER
  TIME                                        DATE


SQL> select * from v$recover_file;
 FILE#    ONLINE    ERROR     CHANGE#      TIME
 ----     ------    --------  ----------   --------
    3     OFFLINE             182173       29-DEC-99
```

➤ **V$LOG_HISTORY**—Lists information about all of the archived redo log files for the database:

```
SQL> desc v$log_history
 Name                               Null?    Type
 ------------------------------     -------- ----
  RECID                                       NUMBER
  STAMP                                       NUMBER
  THREAD#                                     NUMBER
  SEQUENCE#                                   NUMBER
  FIRST_CHANGE#                               NUMBER
  FIRST_TIME                                  DATE
  NEXT_CHANGE#                                NUMBER
```

➤ **V$RECOVERY_LOG**—Lists information about archived redo log files that
are needed to complete media recovery:

```
SQL> desc v$recovery_log;
 Name                              Null?     Type
 ------------------------------    --------  ----
 THREAD#                                     NUMBER
 SEQUENCE#                                   NUMBER
 TIME                                        DATE
 ARCHIVE_NAME                                VARCHAR2(513)


SQL> select * from v$recovery_log;
 THREAD#  SEQUENCE#  Time       ARCHIVE_NAME
 ------   --------   --------   ----------------------
      1         21  29-DEC-99  /u1/archive/arch_21.rdo
 ...
      1         31  31-DEC-99  /u1/archive/arch_31.rdo
      1         32  31-DEC-99  /u1/archive/arch_32.rdo
```

ARCHIVELOG Database Recovery Using RMAN

RMAN can be used to perform complete database recovery, recovery of a data file in
an open database, and recovery of a tablespace. For complete recovery of an entire
database, the database should be closed. For data file and tablespace recovery, the
unaffected portion of the database can remain open and available for normal use.

The basic RMAN recovery commands are **RESTORE** and **RECOVER**. You
can use RMAN to restore data files from backup sets or from image copies on
disk. You can also restore backup sets containing archived redo logs. The restored
files can optionally be directed to a new location. The RMAN **RECOVER** command is used to perform media recovery and to apply incremental backups. If you
use a recovery catalog, RMAN maintains information on all the essential metadata
concerning every backup that you have taken. If you do not use a recovery catalog, RMAN uses the control file for the necessary metadata. RMAN completely
automates the procedure for recovering and restoring your backups and copies.

Complete Database Recovery

The restore and recovery process for complete database recovery using RMAN is
as follows:

1. If the target database is open, perform a shutdown.

2. Start up and mount the target database.

3. Start RMAN, and connect to the target database and the recovery catalog, as illustrated by the following sample code:

```
$ rman target rman/rmanpwd@target_db \
rcvcat rman/rmanpwd@catalog_db
```

4. Create and execute the **RUN** command that will perform the restore and recovery operations, as illustrated by the following sample code:

```
RMAN> run {
   2> allocate channel c1 type DISK;
   3> restore database;
   4> recover database;
   5> sql "alter database open resetlogs";
   6> release channel c1; }
```

5. Take a backup.

Recovery of a Tablespace in an Open Database

Perform the following steps to recover a tablespace in an open database using RMAN:

1. Issue a query against the **V$INSTANCE** view to determine the status of the database, as illustrated by the following sample code:

```
SVRMGR> Select status from v$instance;
```

2. Issue a query against the **V$DATAFILE_HEADER** view to determine which data files need to be restored or recovered, as illustrated by the following sample code:

```
SVRMGR> select name, file#, tablespace_name,
   2>        status, error, recover
   3> from v$datafile_header
   4> where tablespace_name = 'APP01_DATA';
```

If the error column is not null, the data file is not accessible and may need to be restored or switched to an associated image copy.

3. Create and execute a **RUN** command script similar to the following sample code:

```
RMAN> run {
    2> allocate channel c1 type disk;
    3> sql "alter tablespace APP01_DATA offline immediate";
    4> restore tablespace APP01_DATA;
    5> recover tablespace APP01_DATA;
    6> sql "alter tablespace APP01_DATA online";
    7> release channel c1; }
```

4. Verify that the tablespace has been recovered.

5. Take a backup.

Recovery of a Data File in an Open Database

When a data file is not accessible due to a disk failure, it typically will need to be restored to a new location or switched to an associated image copy. For the purposes of this section, we will assume a data file needs to be restored to a new location. Perform the following steps to recover a data file in an open database using RMAN:

1. After users reported problems accessing information in data file number 3, which resides on disk number 3, you issued the following query to determine the location of the data file:

```
SQL> select file#, name, bytes from v$datafile;
FILE# NAME                                       BYTES
---- ------------------------------------       --------
    1 /u1/oradata/system01.ora               31457280
    2 /u2/oradata/app01.ora                  10485760
    3 /u3/oradata/app02.ora                  10485760
...
```

2. Because there is sufficient disk space on disk u2, we will restore the data file to disk u2 using the **SET NEWNAME** command. We'll also use the **SWITCH** command to tell Oracle that the restored data file is now current.

3. Use the **RECOVER** command to begin applying incremental backups, cumulative backups, redo log files, and archived redo log files to synchronize the database.

4. Bring the tablespace online when the recovery process is complete.

5. Inform users that the APP01 data is available for use and to reenter any data that was uncommitted before the system failure.

The following is a sample **RUN** command that can be used to recover a data file that has been restored to a new location:

```
RMAN> Run {
   2> Allocate channel c1 type disk;
   3> Sql "alter tablespace APP01_DATA offline immediate";
   4> Set newname for datafile '/u3/oradata/app03.ora'
   5> To '/u2/oradata/app03.ora';
   6> Restore (tablespace APP01_DATA);
   7> Switch datafile 3;
   8> Recover tablespace APP01_DATA;
   9> Sql "alter tablespace APP01_DATA online";
  10> Release channel c1; }
```

*Note: In the restoration process, RMAN uses the recovery catalog or the target database control file to determine which backups, archived redo log files, or image copies that it will use. The **RESTORE** command does not restore incremental backups with a level greater than 0. RMAN will apply these incremental backups to a level 0 backup during recovery.*

RMAN will only restore from backups that were taken or registered with RMAN.

Practice Questions

Question 1

> When you encounter a media failure for your database and you've determined all required archived redo log files are available since the most recent backup, to what point in time should you be able to recover the database?
>
> ○ a. To the point in time just before the media failure
>
> ○ b. To the point in time of the most recent backup
>
> ○ c. To the oldest redo log file sequence number
>
> ○ d. To the oldest archived redo log sequence number

The correct answer is a. When a media failure occurs for an ARCHIVELOG database and all required archived redo log files are available since the last backup, the database can be recovered up to the point in time before the media failure. Answers b, c, and d are incorrect because they imply incomplete recovery of the database. It is more likely that the recovery from a database media failure will require full media recovery rather than point-in-time recovery.

Question 2

> Your production database is operating in ARCHIVELOG mode and has been configured with two redo log groups. Which of the following commands needs to be run if you discovered that redo log group number 1 is corrupt and it is the current group?
>
> ○ a. **ALTER SYSTEM ARCHIVE LOG CURRENT GROUP 1**
>
> ○ b. **ALTER SYSTEM ACTIVE LOGFILE GROUP 1**
>
> ○ c. **ALTER DATABASE CLEAR UNARCHIVED LOGFILE GROUP 1**
>
> ○ d. **RECOVER DATAFILE**

The correct answer is c. The ALTER DATABASE CLEAR UNARCHIVED LOGFILE command is used to reinitialize (clear and recreate) an online redo log file that was not archived. This command can be used when there are only two redo log groups or when the corrupt redo log file belongs to the current redo log group. Answers a and b are incorrect because they are invalid command specifications. Answer d is incorrect because the RECOVER DATAFILE command is not applicable to redo log files.

Question 3

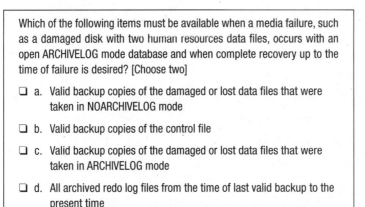

Which of the following items must be available when a media failure, such as a damaged disk with two human resources data files, occurs with an open ARCHIVELOG mode database and when complete recovery up to the time of failure is desired? [Choose two]

❑ a. Valid backup copies of the damaged or lost data files that were taken in NOARCHIVELOG mode

❑ b. Valid backup copies of the control file

❑ c. Valid backup copies of the damaged or lost data files that were taken in ARCHIVELOG mode

❑ d. All archived redo log files from the time of last valid backup to the present time

The correct answers are c and d. To perform complete recovery for an archiving database, you need to restore only the damaged or lost data files from the last valid backup and apply all the archived redo log files since the last valid backup. Answer a is incorrect because the data file backups taken in NOARCHIVELOG mode are not usable in an archiving database. Answer b is incorrect because it is not required for this sample scenario.

Question 4

Which data dictionary view provides information about all the archived redo log files for a database?

○ a. **V$RECOVERY_LOG**

○ b. **V$LOG_HISTORY**

○ c. **V$LOGFILE**

○ d. **V$REDO_LOGS**

The correct answer is b. The **V$LOG_HISTORY** data dictionary view provides information on all the archived redo log files in the database. Answer a is incorrect because the **V$RECOVERY_LOG** data dictionary view provides information about the archived logs that is needed to complete media recovery. **V$RECOVERY_LOG** is derived from the log history view, **V$LOG_ HISTORY**. Answer c is incorrect because the **V$LOGFILE** data dictionary view provides information on the online redo log files. Answer d is incorrect because it is an invalid data dictionary view.

Question 5

Your database is operating in ARCHIVELOG mode, and the available archived redo log files are numbered 102 through 121. In the event archived redo log number 112 is damaged, to what point in time can the database be restored?

○ a. Through archived redo log number 101

○ b. Through archived redo log number 102

○ c. Through archived redo log number 121

○ d. Through archived redo log number 111

○ e. Through archived redo log number 112

The correct answer is d. If an archived redo log file is damaged or lost, you can recover up through the previous archived log file, in this case redo log number 111. Answer a is incorrect because it is not one of the given available archived redo log files. Answer b is incorrect because subsequent archived redo log files are available. Answer c is incorrect because archived redo log files from number 112 through 121 are not usable. Answer e is incorrect because redo log number 112 is damaged and therefore unusable.

Question 6

Which of the following tablespaces cannot take advantage of online complete recovery?

○ a   **USER_DATA** tablespace

○ b. **APPLICATION_DATA** tablespace

○ c. **INDEX_DATA** tablespace

○ d. **TEMPORARY_DATA** tablespace

○ e. **SYSTEM** tablespace

The correct answer is e. When restoring data files belonging to the **SYSTEM** tablespace, the restore operation must be performed while the database is offline. Answers a, b, c, and d are incorrect because data files belonging to **NONSYSTEM** tablespaces can be restored while the database is open, but the **NONSYSTEM** tablespaces associated with the restored data files should be offline.

Question 7

Which RMAN command points the control file and the recovery catalog to the renamed data files when restoring data files after a media failure?

- ○ a. **ALTER TABLESPACE**
- ○ b. **RESTORE DATAFILE**
- ○ c. **RECOVER DATAFILE**
- ○ d. **SWITCH**
- ○ e. **SET NEWNAME**

The correct answer is d. The **SWITCH** command is used to point the control file and the recovery catalog to the renamed data files when restoring data files after a media failure. The **SWITCH** command is similar to the **ALTER DATABASE RENAME DATAFILE** command. Answers a, b, and c are incorrect because they cannot be used to point the control file and the recovery catalog to the renamed data files when restoring data files after a media failure. Answer e is incorrect because the **SET NEWNAME** command is used to restore data files to a new location, but it doesn't point the control file and the recovery catalog to the renamed data files.

Question 8

What does the following command sequence accomplish for a database in ARCHIVELOG mode?

```
RMAN> run {
    2> allocate channel c1 type disk;
    3> restore database; }
```

- ○ a. It recovers the entire database.
- ○ b. It restores the control file from the last full backup.
- ○ c. It restores all the files from the last full backup.
- ○ d. It restores only the data files from the last full backup.

The correct answer is d. The **RESTORE DATABASE** command only restores data files. Answer a is incorrect because the **RESTORE DATABASE** command does not recover the entire database. Answer b is incorrect because the **RESTORE DATABASE** command does not restore the control file. Answer c is incorrect because the **RESTORE DATABASE** command does not restore all files.

Question 9

You've issued the following command sequences:

```
SVRMGR> SET AUTORECOVERY ON
SVRMGR> RECOVER DATABASE;
```

Which part of the database is available for normal use while you perform recovery?

○ a. Read-only tablespaces

○ b. Any data file not needing recovery

○ c. Any table unaffected by the recovery procedure

○ d. Any tablespace unaffected by the recovery procedure

○ e. None

The correct answer is e. The sample command sequences will recover the whole database and require a closed database. Answers a, b, c, and d are incorrect because they are not accessible for normal use during the recovery of an entire database.

Question 10

Which data dictionary view provides information about data files needing recovery?

○ a. **V$RECOVERY_STATUS**

○ b. **V$RECOVER_FILE**

○ c. **V$LOG_HISTORY**

○ d. **V$DATAFILE**

The correct answer is b. The **V$RECOVER_FILE** view contains the names of data files that need to be recovered. Answer a is incorrect because the **V$RECOVERY_STATUS** view provides status information on the recovery process. Answer c is incorrect because the **V$LOG_HISTORY** view provides information on all the archived redo log files for the database. Answer d is incorrect because the **V$DATAFILE** view provides information on all the data files in the database, but does not indicate whether they need recovery.

Need to Know More?

 Velpuri, Rama. *Oracle8i Backup and Recovery Handbook*. Oracle Press, Berkeley, CA, 2000. ISBN 0-072-12717-1. This book provides information on how to maximize uptime and recover data without compromising mission critical systems. Actual corporate scenarios and case studies are included. Chapter 6 provides information on recovery strategies and methods. Chapter 10 provides information on case studies of recovery scenarios.

 http://technet.oracle.com provides the best information on Oracle's products and technologies. You can also access the following manuals online:

Dialeris, Connie. *Oracle8i Backup and Recovery Guide Release 2*. Oracle Corporation, Redwood City, CA, 1999. Part No. A76993-01. This manual provides guidance on data protection techniques and offers strategies for data storage, backup, and restore for Oracle 8i. Chapter 5 provides information on performing complete and incomplete media recovery.

Leverenz, Lefty. *Oracle8i Concepts Release 2*. Oracle Corporation, Redwood City, CA, 1999. Part No. A76965-01. This manual describes all features of the Oracle8i server running on all operating systems. Chapter 1 covers basic recovery concepts.

Lorentz, Diana. *Oracle8i Reference Release 2*. Oracle Corporation, Redwood City, CA, 1999. Part No. A76961-01. This manual describes the architecture, processes, structures, and other concepts of Oracle8i and provides detailed information on static and dynamic data dictionary views.

Lorentz, Diana. *Oracle8i SQL Reference Release 2*. Oracle Corporation, Redwood City, CA, 1999. Part No. A76989-01. This manual contains a complete description of the SQL used to manage information in an Oracle database.

 www.revealnet.com. This site from RevealNet provides Oracle administration reference software.

Incomplete Oracle Recovery with Archiving

Terms you'll need to understand:

✓ Incomplete recovery

✓ **RESETLOGS** option

✓ Cancel-based recovery

✓ Time-based recovery

✓ Change-based recovery

✓ **RECOVER DATABASE** command

✓ Tablespace point-in-time recovery (TSPITR)

Techniques you'll need to master:

✓ Understanding when to use incomplete recovery

✓ Understanding the types of incomplete recovery

✓ Performing incomplete recovery procedures

✓ Understanding recovery implications after losing current and active redo log files

✓ Using Recovery Manager (RMAN) in incomplete recovery

✓ Understanding TSPITR

When an Oracle database is operating in ARCHIVELOG mode and complete recovery cannot be performed or is not desirable after a media failure, incomplete recovery provides Oracle database administrators (DBAs) with additional recovery options. In incomplete recovery, the entire database is restored from a valid backup and recovered through the application of some of the redo information generated since the last valid backup. In other words, the database is rebuilt to a point in time before the time of failure. This chapter focuses on incomplete recovery concepts and procedures. Specifically, you will learn the types of incomplete recovery, when to use incomplete recovery, incomplete recovery procedures, recovery after current and active redo log loss, incomplete recovery using Oracle Recovery Manager (RMAN), and tablespace point-in-time recovery (TSPITR).

When to Use Incomplete Recovery

Incomplete recovery is usually performed under the following circumstances:

➤ *The control files are lost.* For example, your control file was lost due to a media failure, and your database is not multiplexing control files. You don't know the current structure of the database, but you do have a backup copy of an old control file. In this scenario, the database should be restored and recovered to a prior point in time with a different structure than the current database.

➤ *The online logs are lost due to hardware failure.* For example, your database is not configured for the multiplexing of online redo log files, and you lost your redo log files before archiving them along with a data file. In this scenario, the database should be recovered until the last archived log generated before the failure.

➤ *A user error requires recovery up until just before the error occurred.* For example, a user accidentally deleted accounting transactions before they were sent to the accounting system. In this scenario, the DBA would need to restore the whole database and then perform an incomplete recovery up until the point just before the user deleted the transactions. Other examples include if a user accidentally dropped a table, or if a user committed data with unwanted values due to a faulty Structured Query Language (SQL) **WHERE** clause construction.

➤ *An archived redo log file required for recovery is missing.* For example, an archive log file needed for complete recovery was lost, damaged, or corrupted (for example, due to media failure). In this scenario, your option would be to recover up to the missing log.

In all of the previous scenarios, the database must be opened with the **RESETLOGS** option. A **RESETLOGS** operation invalidates all redo information in the online redo log files, resets the current redo log sequence to 1, and synchronizes the data files with the control files and the online redo log files.

Because incomplete recovery takes a database back to a point in time before the time of failure, data loss may result from committed transactions after the time of recovery. Users may need to manually reenter data, so a DBA should use incomplete recovery judiciously.

Note: For distributed databases, an incomplete recovery performed at one location requires incomplete recovery to be performed at all the other database locations that are part of the distributed database network.

Performing an Incomplete Recovery

The following items must be in place before you can perform an incomplete recovery:

➤ A valid offline or online backup of all the database files

➤ All the archived redo log files from the valid backup until the designated time of recovery

There are four types of incomplete recovery:

➤ Cancel-based recovery

➤ Time-based recovery

➤ Change-based recovery

➤ Recovery using a backup control file

Cancel-Based Recovery

Cancel-based recovery enables the DBA to terminate the recovery process at a desired point in time in the past by entering CANCEL at the recovery prompt. This recovery method is used under the following circumstances:

➤ A current redo log file or group is damaged and therefore not available for recovery.

➤ An archived redo log file needed for complete recovery is damaged or lost.

Incomplete Recovery Using UNTIL CANCEL Technique

You are the new DBA for a case-tracking database. You discovered that the redo log files are not multiplexed and that one of the online redo log files is missing. The missing redo log file (log sequence number 23) has not been archived. The missing redo log file contains approximately 15 minutes of data from 10:00 A.M. A user also informed you that a table was dropped at 10:02 A.M. You've determined that an incomplete recovery should be performed using the **UNTIL CANCEL** technique, as illustrated below:

1. Make sure the database is shut down.

2. Take a full offline database backup.

3. Mount the database.

4. Restore all data files from the most recent valid backup before the backup taken in Step 2.

5. Recover the database until log sequence number 23, as illustrated in the following code.

```
SVRMGR> RECOVER DATABASE UNTIL CANCEL
...
ORA-00279: change 109101...12/28/99 9:59:01 needed for thread 1
ORA-00289: suggestion : /u2/oradata/archive/arch_23.ora
ORA-00280: change 109101 for thread 1 is in sequence #23
Specify log: {<RET>=suggested | filename | AUTO | CANCEL}
CANCEL
Media recovery cancelled.
```

6. Open the database using the **RESETLOGS** option.

7. Verify that the dropped table exists by querying the database.

8. Take a full offline database backup.

9. Notify users that the database is available and that any data entered after 10:00 A.M. will need to be reentered.

Time-Based Recovery

Time-based recovery enables the DBA to terminate the recovery process at a desired point in time in the past after the database has committed all changes up to the desired point in time. This recovery method is used under the following circumstances:

➤ An essential table was accidentally dropped.

➤ Unwanted database changes were made due to faulty SQL constructions.

➤ A nonmirrored online redo log file was damaged or lost.

➤ The approximate time of error has been determined.

Note: Oracle8i provides the LogMiner utility that enables the DBA to perform granular logical recovery by undoing Data Manipulation Language (DML) operations of one or more transactions. This minimizes the need for performing point-in-time recovery to recover from logical application errors, and it provides the exact time of the errors.

Incomplete Recovery Using UNTIL TIME Technique

You were informed that an essential table was dropped from the quality assurance (QA) database two hours ago, at 10:00 A.M. Because of the approximate time of failure and because the database structure has not changed since 9:59 A.M., an incomplete recovery should be performed using the UNTIL TIME technique, as illustrated below:

1. Shut down the database normally if the database is open.

2. Take a full offline database backup.

3. Mount the database.

4. Restore all data files from the most recent valid backup before the backup taken in Step 2, as illustrated by the following code:

```
UNIX:
SVRMGR> !cp /u2/oradata/backup/*.ora /u1/oradata/


NT:
SVRMGR> !copy d:\orant\database\backup\*.ora
d:\orant\database\
```

5. Restore applicable archived redo log files to the location specified by the **LOG_ARCHIVE_DEST** initialization parameter or to a new location by issuing the SQL **ALTER SYSTEM ARCHIVE LOG START TO** *<location_ specification>* or the Server Manager **SET LOGSOURCE** *<location_ specification>* commands.

6. Recover the database using the **RECOVER DATABASE UNTIL TIME** '*<time specification YYYY-MM-DD:HH24:MI:SS>*' command, as illustrated in the following code:

```
SVRMGR> RECOVER DATABASE UNTIL TIME '1999-12-28:10:00:00';
ORA-00279: change 101115 ...12/18/99 15:01:02 needed for
thread
ORA-00289: suggestion : /u2/oradata/backup/arch_9.ora
ORA-00280: change 101115 for thread 1 is in sequence #9
Log applied.
...
Media recovery complete.
```

7. Open the database with the **RESETLOGS** option to synchronize data files with control files and the redo log files, as illustrated by the following code:

```
SVRMGR> ALTER DATABASE OPEN RESETLOGS;
SVRMGR> ARCHIVE LOG LIST;
...
Oldest online log sequence 0
Next log sequence to archive 1
Current log sequence 1
```

8. Verify that the dropped table has been restored, as illustrated by the following code:

```
SVRMGR> select owner, table_name
    2> from dba_tables
    3> where table_name = 'DROPPED_TABLE_NAME';
OWNER           TABLE_NAME
-----           ----------
QA              ORGANIZATIONS
```

If the query in Step 8 returns no rows, the dropped table has not been restored, and you will need to perform incomplete recovery to a different point in time.

9. Take a full offline database backup.

10. Notify users that the database is available and to reenter data after the recovery point.

Change-Based Recovery

Change-based recovery enables the DBA to terminate the recovery process at a desired point in time in the past after the database has committed all changes up to the specified System Change Number (SCN). This recovery method is used when recovering databases in a distributed database environment.

Query the **V$LOG_HISTORY** view to obtain SCN ranges in the archived redo log files.

Recovery Using a Backup Control File

When performing an incomplete recovery using a backup control file, the DBA can terminate the recovery process when the desired type of recovery (**CANCEL**,

CHANGE, or **TIME**) has been completed or when the control files have been recovered. The **RECOVER DATABASE** command should indicate that an old copy of the control file is being used for recovery. This recovery method is used under the following circumstances:

➤ All control files are lost and can't be re-created. An old copy of the control file is available.

➤ The database needs to be returned to a prior point in time when the database structure was different.

Incomplete Recovery Using the Backup Control File Technique

You are the new DBA, and you accidentally issued the **DROP TABLESPACE APP01_DATA INCLUDING CONTENTS** command that dropped the **PERSONS** table. You've located a backup copy of the control file from yesterday. Using the alertSID.log file, you've determined that you made the error at 11:00 A.M. You've also determined that an incomplete recovery should be performed using the backup control file technique as follows:

1. Shut down the database.

2. Back up the control files.

3. Restore all data files and control files for the database at a point in time before the tablespace was dropped.

4. Attempt to open the database. An error indicating that the redo log files and the control files are not synchronized is returned, as illustrated with the following code:

```
ORA-00314: log 1 of thread 1, expected sequence# doesn't match
ORA-00312: online log 1 thread 1: '/u1/oradata/log1a.ora'
```

5. Make sure all offline data files are online because offline data files may be unrecoverable after recovery.

6. Recover the database using the **RECOVER DATABASE USING BACKUP CONTROLFILE** command, as illustrated by the following code sample:

```
SVRMGR> recover database until '1999-12-29:10:59:00'
    2> using backup controlfile;
```

7. Open the database with the **RESETLOGS** option.

8. Verify that the dropped table exists.

9. Take a full offline database backup.

10. Notify users that the database is available and that any data entered after 11:00 A.M. will need to be reentered.

RECOVER DATABASE Command

Incomplete recovery is typically performed using the following **RECOVER DATABASE** command syntax:

```
RECOVER [AUTOMATIC] DATABASE <option>
```

Table 12.1 describes command elements for the **RECOVER DATABASE** command.

Optionally, you may choose to use the SQL **ALTER DATABASE RECOVER** command syntax.

 Instead of using the SQL **RECOVER AUTOMATIC** command, you can use the **SET AUTORECOVERY ON** Server Manager command and enter "AUTO" at the recovery prompt to direct Oracle to apply redo log files automatically during the recovery process.

The following code samples illustrate the **RECOVER DATABASE** command.

➤ Cancel-based recovery is illustrated by the following code:

```
SVRMGR> RECOVER DATABASE UNTIL CANCEL;
```

➤ Time-based recovery is illustrated by the following code:

```
SVRMGR> RECOVER DATABASE UNTIL TIME '2000-01-02:10:11:01';
```

➤ Change-based recovery is illustrated by the following code:

```
SVRMGR> RECOVER DATABASE UNTIL SCN 118110;
```

➤ Recovery using a backup control file is illustrated by the following code:

```
SVRMGR> RECOVER DATABASE
    2> UNTIL TIME '2000-01-02:10:11:01'
    3> USING BACKUP CONTROLFILE;
```

Table 12.1 Elements and values of RECOVER DATABASE Command.	
Element	**Value**
AUTOMATIC	The **AUTOMATIC** keyword signals Oracle to apply archived and online redo log files automatically.
Option	UNTIL TIME 'YYYY-MM-DD:HH:MI:SS'; UNTIL CANCEL; UNTIL SCN *<integer>*; or USING BACKUP CONTROL FILE.

Incomplete Recovery Procedure

Follow these steps to perform an incomplete recovery for an archiving-enabled database:

1. Take a full offline backup of the current database.

2. Make sure the database is shut down because all data files, including the system data files, will be restored from a prior backup.

3. Restore all the data files to return the database to a past point in time. Don't restore the control file, parameter files, password file, or redo log files.

4. Mount the database.

5. Recover the database to a point in time before the failure.

6. Open the database with the **RESETLOGS** option.

7. Shut down the database cleanly, and take a full offline backup of the database.

8. Open the database for normal use.

Things to Consider When Performing Incomplete Recovery

You should remember to do the following when performing incomplete recovery:

➤ Make sure you perform all recovery steps in the proper sequence. Because the recovery process requires DBAs to perform multiple steps manually, it is prone to operator errors.

➤ You should take a full offline database backup (including control files and redo log files) before starting the recovery process. The benefits of this activity are as follows:

   ➤ It provides protection in the event of a recovery error or failure. For example, your recovery failed because you mistakenly recovered past the required point of recovery. Unless you have a backup of the control files and the redo log files, the current control files and the redo log files are not usable for future recovery operations.

➤ It provides time savings in the event of a recovery failure. For example, the data files can be restored from the new backup rather than from an older backup, which requires application of archived redo log files.

 If taking a full offline database backup is not possible, it is highly recommended that you archive the current redo log file using the **ALTER SYSTEM ARCHIVE LOG CURRENT** command and back up the control file using the **ALTER DATABASE BACKUP CONTROLFILE TO** *<location_specification>*.

➤ You should take a full offline database backup after you've confirmed a successful recovery. This backup can be used if recovery needs to be performed before the next routine backup.

➤ Make sure the recovery has resolved the failure before opening the database for normal use. If the recovery did not resolve the failure, recovery needs to be performed again. For example, a user informed you that he dropped a table at 10:10 A.M. You recovered the database to 10:09 A.M. before the table was dropped. You queried the database, and the dropped table does not exist. You later learned that the user's clock is ten minutes fast, and you should have recovered to 9:59 A.M.

➤ Take a control file backup whenever the database structure changes. A backup control file will be needed if the current database structure is different from the structure at the desired recovery point.

➤ Make sure you open the database with the **RESETLOGS** option after each incomplete recovery operation. The **RESETLOGS** option ensures database files are in sync and will automatically recreate missing redo log files when needed.

➤ Back up archived redo log files from the previous version of the database, and remove them from the system to prevent accidental mixing of archived redo log files from two different database versions.

➤ Be aware that database transactions can only be rolled forward to the desired point in time. Database transactions cannot be rolled back to the desired point in time. This is why all data files must be restored to return the database to a prior point in time. If all data files are not restored, the database cannot be opened because the database is in an unsynchronized state.

➤ During recovery, Oracle writes recovery progress information in the alert_SID.log file. You should check this file before and after recovery for SCN information, recovery errors, and so forth. The following code sample illustrates recovery progress information recorded in the alertSID.log file:

```
...
Media Recovery Log
ORA-279 ... RECOVER   database until time '1999...
Mon Dec 27 10:01:11 1999
ALTER DATABASE RECOVER   CONTINUE DEFAULT
Media Recovery Log /u1/oradata/archive/arch_19.ora
Incomplete recovery done UNTIL CHANGE 100213
Media Recovery Complete
Completed: ALTER DATABASE RECOVER   CONTINUE DEFAULT
Mon Dec 27 10:01:11 1999
Alter database open resetlogs
...
```

Recovery after Current and Active Redo Log Loss

When a current and active redo log file is damaged or lost, the database may be open, but in a hung state, or the database may be closed because of a media failure or the abnormal termination of a background process. The technique you use for recovery depends on whether the database is open or closed.

If the database is open, follow these steps:

1. Query the **V$LOG** view to determine the redo log file with a status of **CURRENT.**

2. Issue the **ALTER DATABASE CLEAR UNARCHIVED LOGFILE GROUP** *<number>* command to clear the current log file. This action will cause the log file to be overwritten or re-created, depending on whether it was corrupted or lost.

3. Take a full offline database backup to prevent having to perform incomplete recovery due to media failure before taking the backup because redo information has just been cleared.

If the database is closed, follow these steps:

1. Start up your instance, and mount the database.

2. Obtain the sequence number for the current redo log, as illustrated by following the code sample. You will recover your database up to this redo log.

```
SVRMGR> select sequence# seq_num from v$log
    2> where status = 'CURRENT';
seq_num
-------
    19
```

3. Restore all your data files (but not control files, redo log files, password files, or initSID.ora files) from the most recent backup.

4. Perform incomplete recovery using the cancel-based technique. You will cancel the recovery when Oracle prompts you with the suggested redo log number 19.

5. Open the database using the **ALTER DATABASE OPEN RESETLOGS** command.

6. If you lost a disk containing redo logs, and you do not have the minimum number of logs necessary for Oracle to use, you must create new redo log groups and drop the lost redo log group. You will need to issue a combination of **ALTER DATABASE ADD LOGFILE GROUP** and **ALTER DATABASE DROP LOGFILE GROUP** commands.

7. Take a full offline database backup.

8. Open the database for normal use.

RMAN Usage in an Incomplete Recovery

In RMAN, incomplete recovery is handled the same way as complete recovery. However, you will restore all data files from your most recent backup, not just the damaged ones.

 When RMAN performs a restore, the files being restored must either be registered with RMAN or must have been taken by RMAN.

The incomplete recovery procedure using RMAN is as follows:

1. Shut down the target database cleanly.

2. Start up, mount, but do not open, the target database. The recovery catalog should also be open.

3. Set the **NLS_LANG** and the **NLS_DATE_FORMAT** environment variable to the appropriate values for your environment, for example, **NLS_LANG=american** and **NLS_DATE_FORMAT='YYYY-MM-DD:HH24:MI:SS'**.

4. Start **RMAN** by connecting to both the target database and the recovery catalog as illustrated by the following code:

```
$ rman target username/passwd@target_db rcvcat
username/passwd@catalog_db
```

5. Create a run script that allocates appropriate channels, specifies the incomplete recovery type using the **SET UNTIL** command, performs the restore and recovery operations, and releases applicable channels.

6. Open the database using the **RESETLOGS** option as illustrated by the following code:

```
...
RMAN> sql "alter database open resetlogs";
...
```

7. Verify the incomplete recovery was successful and take a backup.

8. Notify users that the database is available and that they need to enter any uncommitted data entered before the system failure.

9. If a recovery catalog is being used, register a new incarnation of the database using the **RESET DATABASE** command as illustrated by the following code:

```
RMAN> reset database;
```

The following code sample illustrates a typical **RUN** command used for incomplete recovery:

```
D:\ORANT\BIN> rman80 target user/pass@proddb rcvcat
user/pass@catdb
RMAN> run {
   2> allocate channel c1 type disk;
   3> set until time = '2000-01-02:10:05:00';
   4> restore database;
   5> recover database;
   6> sql 'alter database open resetlogs';
   7> release channel c1; }
```

Working with Tablespace Point-In-Time Recovery

Tablespace point-in-time recovery (TSPITR) is a type of incomplete recovery that is appropriate when a user error has been discovered and the database cannot be returned to a prior point in time. For example, a defect in an application messed up data in an essential table. The messed-up table must be recovered, and the database cannot be taken back in time because other applications are performing other database tasks. You can perform TSPITR with or without the transportable tablespace feature. Refer to Chapter 13 for performing TSPITR with the transportable tablespace feature. You shouldn't have to use TSPITR if you've followed proper backup and recovery procedures. In the unlikely event you need to use TSPITR and because of the complexity associated with TSPITR, you should only perform this task with the assistance of Oracle Worldwide Customer Support Services.

You'll need the following when performing TSPITR:

➤ All data files associated with the tablespace that needs recovery

➤ All data files for the system tablespace

➤ All archived redo log files up to the desired recovery point

➤ A backup copy of your current control file

➤ Sufficient disk space and memory on your machine or another machine to create and run the clone database

Perform the following steps for TSPITR:

1. Determine if objects will be lost due to TSPITR. Use the **TS_PITR_OBJECTS_TO_BE_DROPPED** view for this purpose.

2. Analyze and resolve any dependencies for the production database. Use the **TS_PITR_CHECK** view for this purpose.

3. Prepare the production database for TSPITR by archiving the current redo log, taking the rollback segments in the recovery set offline, and taking the tablespaces in the recovery set offline. These activities will prevent any modifications to the recovery set during TSPITR.

4. Prepare the parameter files for the clone database. The following parameters should be appropriately specified: **CONTROL_FILES, LOCK_NAME_SPACE, DB_FILE_NAME_CONVERT,** and **LOG_FILE_NAME_CONVERT**.

5. Prepare the clone database for TSPITR. Copy the applicable recovery files to the clone database, and then start and mount the clone database using **ALTER DATABASE MOUNT CLONE DATABASE.**

6. Recover the clone database to the desired point in time with the **USING BACKUP CONTROLFILE** option of the **RECOVER DATABASE** command. Optionally, you can use incomplete recovery techniques such as time-based or cancel-based recovery.

7. Open the clone database using the **ALTER DATABASE OPEN RESET LOGS** command.

8. Export the clone database. You will export the metadata associated with the recovery set tablespaces, as illustrated by the following sample code:

```
$ Exp sys/passwd point_in_time_recovery=y
Recovery_tablespaces=ts1, ts2, ...,tsN
```

9. Copy the cloned files associated with the recovery set to the production database.

10. Import the metadata from the export dump file into the production database. This process will update the file headers and integrate them with the production database as illustrated by the following code:

```
$ imp sys/passwd point_in_time_recover=true
```

11. Back up the recovered tablespace in the production database.

12. Open the production database for normal use.

Refer to Chapter 13 for detailed information on using the EXPORT and IM-PORT utilities.

Practice Questions

Question 1

> When an archived redo log file is corrupt and not available for a complete recovery, what type of incomplete recovery should the DBA perform?
>
> ○ a. Recovery using a backup control file
>
> ○ b. Time-based recovery
>
> ○ c. Change-based recovery
>
> ○ d. Cancel-based recovery

The correct answer is d. Cancel-based recovery is appropriate when an archived redo log file that is needed for a complete recovery is damaged or lost. Answer a is incorrect because it is used when all control files are lost or when you are attempting to restore a database to a prior point in time when the database structure was different. Answer b is incorrect because the approximate time of error is not known. Answer c is incorrect because change-based recovery is used for recovering databases in a distributed database environment.

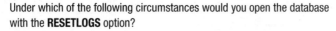

Question 2

Under which of the following circumstances would you open the database with the **RESETLOGS** option?

○ a. After performing complete recovery of a lost data file using the current control file

○ b. After restoring and recovering all the database files during complete recovery

○ c. After restoring and recovering all data files during incomplete recovery

○ d. After restoring and recovering damaged data files during incomplete recovery

○ e. After restoring and recovering all database files during incomplete recovery

The correct answer is c. The incomplete recovery procedure requires restoring all data files, mounting the database, recovering the data files before the time of failure, and opening the database with the **RESETLOGS** option. Answers a and b are incorrect because complete recovery operations don't require opening the database with the **RESETLOGS** option. Answers d and e are incorrect because the incomplete recovery procedure requires that all data files be restored (excluding control file, redo log files, or other configuration files).

Question 3

Which of the following situations requires the DBA to perform an incomplete recovery? [Choose three]

❑ a. All control files are lost, including corresponding mirrors.

❑ b. An archived redo log file needed for complete recovery is damaged.

❑ c. A user mistakenly drops an essential application table.

❑ d. The archived redo log directory runs out of space.

❑ e. A media failure occurs in an ARCHIVELOG mode database, and no data loss is tolerated.

The correct answers are a, b, and c. The typical failures that require an incomplete recovery include user errors that dropped an essential table or committed unwanted data updates; an archived redo log file required for recovery is damaged or missing; all the control files with corresponding mirrors are lost; and an online redo log file is damaged or lost. Answer d is incorrect because it only requires the DBA to free up space in the archived redo log directory. Answer e is incorrect because a complete recovery is needed.

Question 4

The QA administrator accidentally dropped an important table in an ARCHIVELOG mode database. You need to restore the database to a point in time before the user error was made. What type of recovery should you perform in this situation?

○ a. Complete database recovery

○ b. Tablespace recovery

○ c. Data file recovery

○ d. Incomplete recovery

The correct answer is d. Incomplete recovery is typically performed for databases in ARCHIVELOG mode that need to be recovered before the time of failure. Answers a, b, and c are incorrect because they pertain only to complete recovery situations.

Question 5

When using RMAN to perform an incomplete recovery, you want to recover the database to 10:00 A.M. on February 21, 2000. What command should you issue?

○ a. **SET UNTIL TIME = '2000-02-21:10:00:00'**

○ b. **RESTORE DATABASE UNTIL TIME '2000-02-21:10:00:00'**

○ c. **RESTORE DATABASE UNTIL CANCEL**

○ d. **SET RECOVERY UNTIL TIME = '2000-02-21:10:00:00'**

The correct answer is a. When incomplete recovery is managed by RMAN, you can set the time to which you want to recover using the **SET UNTIL TIME** command before issuing the **RESTORE DATABASE** command. Answers b, c, and d are incorrect because they are invalid command specifications.

Question 6

What recovery options enable you to recover to a prior point in time? [Choose three]

❑ a. Tablespace

❑ b. Cancel-based

❑ c. Data file

❑ d. Complete

❑ e. Time-based

❑ f. Change-based

The correct answers are b, e, and f. The incomplete recovery types include cancel-based recovery, time-based recovery, change-based recovery, and recovery using a backup control file. Answers a, c, and d are incorrect because they apply only to complete recovery.

Question 7

What data files must be restored when performing a cancel-based recovery?

○ a. Data files for the tablespace

○ b. Damaged data files

○ c. Undamaged data files

○ d. All data files for the database

The correct answer is d. In any type of incomplete recovery for an archiving database, you must restore all the data files from a valid backup. Answers a, b, and c are incorrect because they are only a subset of the data files required for an incomplete recovery.

Question 8

When performing incomplete recovery, what should you do immediately after shutting down the database?

○ a. Restore archived redo log files.

○ b. Restore data files.

○ c. Take a full offline database backup.

○ d. Open the database in MOUNT mode.

The correct answer is c. Oracle recommends that you take a full offline backup of the database after you shut down for protection in the event of recovery failure. Answers a, b, and d are incorrect because they are performed after taking a full offline database backup.

Question 9

> The database is in a hung state, and you suspect that a redo log file has been mistakenly dropped. Which view would you use to obtain information about the CURRENT redo log group?
>
> ○ a. **V$RECOVER_FILE**
>
> ○ b. **V$LOG**
>
> ○ c. **V$LOGFILE**
>
> ○ d. **V$LOG_HISTORY**

The correct answer is b. The **V$LOG** view provides information on the current redo log group, such as the redo log group sequence number. You can use the redo log group sequence number when issuing the **ALTER DATABASE CLEAR UNARCHIVED LOGFILE GROUP** command to reinitialize the damaged or lost file. Answer a is incorrect because the **V$RECOVER_FILE** view provides information on the status of files needing media recovery. Answers c and d are incorrect because these views don't indicate whether a redo log group is CURRENT.

Question 10

> What will the following RMAN command accomplish when performing an incomplete recovery?
>
> ```
> RMAN> RESET DATABASE;
> ```
>
> ○ a. It will synchronize the target database files.
>
> ○ b. It will change the database mode of the target database.
>
> ○ c. It will reinitialize the redo log files in the target database.
>
> ○ d. It will synchronize the recovery catalog database.
>
> ○ e. It will register the recovered database in the recovery catalog.

The correct answer is e. The RMAN **RESET DATABASE** command will update the recovery catalog with a new incarnation of the database that has been recovered. Answers a, b, c, and d are incorrect because the RMAN **RESET DATABASE** command doesn't perform these actions.

Need to Know More?

 Loney, Kevin and Marlene Theriault. *Oracle8i DBA Handbook*. Oracle Press, Berkeley, CA, 1999. ISBN 0-07212-188-2. This comprehensive guide for DBAs includes general backup and recovery concepts.

 Velpuri, Rama. *Oracle8i Backup and Recovery Handbook*. Oracle Press, Berkeley, CA, 2000. ISBN 0-072-12717-1. This book provides information on how to maximize uptime and recover data without compromising mission critical systems. Chapter 6 provides information on recovery methods. Chapter 10 provides sample recovery scenarios.

 http://technet.oracle.com. This site provides the best information on Oracle's products and technologies. You can also purchase the following manuals online:

Dialeris, Connie. *Oracle8i Backup and Recovery Guide Release 2*. Oracle Corporation, Redwood City, CA, 1999. Part No. A76993-01. This manual provides guidance on data protection techniques and offers strategies for data storage, backup, and restore for Oracle8i. Chapter 5 describes how to perform incomplete media recovery. Chapter 6 describes media recovery scenarios.

Lorentz, Diana. *Oracle8i Reference Release 2*. Oracle Corporation, Redwood City, CA, 1999. Part No. A76961-01. This manual describes the architecture, processes, structures, and other concepts of Oracle8i and provides detailed information on static and dynamic data dictionary views.

Lorentz, Diana. *Oracle8i SQL Reference Release 2*. Oracle Corporation, Redwood City, CA, 1999. Part No. A76989-01. This manual contains a complete description of the SQL used to manage information in an Oracle database.

 www.revealnet.com. This site from RevealNet provides Oracle administration reference software.

13

Oracle EXPORT and IMPORT Utilities

Terms you'll need to understand:

✓ Logical backup
✓ EXPORT utility
✓ Table mode EXPORT
✓ User mode EXPORT
✓ Tablespace mode EXPORT
✓ Full Database mode EXPORT
✓ IMPORT utility

✓ Table mode IMPORT
✓ User mode IMPORT
✓ Full Database mode IMPORT
✓ Complete EXPORT
✓ Cumulative EXPORT
✓ Incremental EXPORT
✓ Direct path EXPORT

Techniques you'll need to master:

✓ Using the EXPORT utility for logical backups

✓ Understanding the methods to invoke the EXPORT utility

✓ Understanding EXPORT modes

✓ Understanding EXPORT runtime parameters

✓ Using direct path EXPORT

✓ Understanding EXPORT issues when exporting database objects

✓ Understanding EXPORT compatibility restrictions

✓ Understanding the methods to invoke the IMPORT utility

✓ Understanding IMPORT modes

✓ Understanding IMPORT runtime parameters

✓ Using IMPORT to recover database objects

✓ Using transportable tablespaces for performing tablespace point-in-time recovery

The Oracle *EXPORT utility* enables Oracle database administrators (DBAs) to perform logical backups of the database. A logical backup involves making a copy of the logical database structures with or without the associated business data. A logical backup does not involve the physical database files with the exception of transporting tablespaces between different databases. The Oracle *IMPORT utility* enables DBAs to read a valid file generated by the EXPORT utility for moving data into an Oracle database and for the recovery of database objects and business data.

Note: Database objects imported from an EXPORT file will not be able to use the redo log history.

EXPORT and IMPORT Utility Overview

Oracle DBAs typically use the EXPORT and IMPORT utilities to perform the following tasks:

➤ Save database object definitions in an alternative Oracle binary format. This may help the DBA to maintain a baseline database structure for a particular schema.

➤ Move data from one Oracle version to another during database upgrades.

➤ Defragment Oracle database objects.

➤ Create a historical copy of an entire database or selective database objects.

➤ Recover from user failure errors, such as an accidental drop or a truncation of a database table.

➤ Create the structural definitions for database objects, such as tables based on information stored in the EXPORT dump file. This is achieved by configuring the IMPORT process to import data without rows.

➤ Create data extractions from a valid EXPORT dump file using the IMPORT modes of Table, User, or Full Database.

➤ IMPORT data from a complete, incremental, or cumulative EXPORT dump file.

➤ Transport tablespaces between databases.

Using the EXPORT Utility

Three methods invoke the EXPORT utility:

➤ An interactive dialog is available when the EXPORT executable name is specified at the operating system prompt with no parameters. The EXPORT utility prompts the user for input values while providing default values.

➤ The EXPORT Wizard of the Data Management tools within the Oracle Enterprise Manager (OEM) DBA Studio administrative toolset invokes the EXPORT utility.

➤ A command-line interface is available when the user wants to specify EX-PORT options explicitly on the command line. Any missing EXPORT options will assume default values. Optionally, the user may use a parameter file to specify EXPORT options explicitly. The following code shows an example of using the command-line interface of the EXPORT utility:

```
Unix:
$ exp scott/tiger tables=(dept,emp) rows=y file=scott.dmp

NT:
D:\ORANT\BIN> exp scott/tiger tables=(dept,emp) rows=y
file=scott.dmp
```

 Be aware that some EXPORT options are available only through the command-line interface. Using the command-line interface with a parameter file enables you to use all available EXPORT options.

EXPORT Modes

The *EXPORT modes* determine which portion of the database can be exported. The EXPORT utility can be run in four modes:

➤ Full Database mode

➤ Tablespace mode

➤ User mode

➤ Table mode

Full Database Mode

In the *Full Database mode*, all database objects except those owned by the **SYS** schema are exported and written to the EXPORT dump file. This file includes the business data and the *Data Definition Language (DDL)* statements needed to recreate the full database. This mode is available only to privileged database users, such as the DBA with the **EXP_FULL_DATABASE** role.

Tablespace Mode

In the *Tablespace mode*, you can use transportable tablespaces to move parts of the database to another database. When using Tablespace mode, no data is exported except the meta data (tablespace structural information). This method of transporting data is typically faster than the normal export/import method because it requires copying the physical data files and incorporating the tablespace structural information. When moving index tablespaces using this mode, you can avoid time-consuming index rebuilds, and you can achieve performance gains.

User Mode

In the *User mode*, all objects owned by a given schema are exported and written to the EXPORT dump file. Grants and indexes created by users other than the owner are not exported . Privileged database users, including the DBA, can EXPORT all objects owned by one or more schemas.

Table Mode

In the *Table mode*, specified tables owned by the user schema are exported and written to the EXPORT dump file. This mode also enables the user to specify partitions of a table to EXPORT. Privileged database users, including the DBA, can EXPORT specified tables owned by other database users.

 Know how to operate the EXPORT utility using the runtime parameters with the command-line interface.

EXPORT Runtime Parameters

The following sections describe typical runtime parameters that can be specified for the EXPORT utility and how to use them to write data from an Oracle database into an operating system file in a proprietary Oracle binary format.

USERID

The **USERID** parameter specifies the username and password of the user running the EXPORT utility. The USERID keyword does not have to be specified if it is the first parameter following the EXPORT executable name.

BUFFER

The **BUFFER** parameter specifies the size of the buffer used to fetch data rows. This parameter applies to the conventional path EXPORT and has no effect on a direct path EXPORT. The default is system dependent.

FILE

The **FILE** parameter specifies the name of the EXPORT dump file. The default value is **EXPDAT.DMP**.

COMPRESS

The **COMPRESS** parameter is a Y/N flag that specifies whether EXPORT should compress fragmented segments into single extents. This parameter affects the storage clauses that will be written in the EXPORT file for the applicable database objects. For the Large Object (LOB) data, extent compression is not performed, and the original values of initial extent size and the next extent size will be used. The default value is Y.

ROWS

The **ROWS** parameter is a Y/N flag that specifies whether data rows should be exported. If set to N, only the DDL for the applicable database objects will be written in the EXPORT file. The default is Y.

FULL

The **FULL** parameter is a Y/N flag that specifies whether a full database EXPORT will be performed. The default value is N.

OWNER

The **OWNER** parameter specifies a list of database users whose objects will be exported in User mode. It has no default value.

TABLES

The **TABLES** parameter specifies a list of tables to export in Table mode. It has no default value.

INDEXES

The **INDEXES** parameter is a Y/N flag that specifies whether indexes on tables will be exported. The default value is Y.

DIRECT

The **DIRECT** parameter is a Y/N flag that specifies whether a direct path EXPORT should be performed. A direct path EXPORT bypasses the buffer cache and the Structured Query Language (SQL) command-processing layer during the EXPORT and achieves significant performance gains for the EXPORT process. The default value is N.

INCTYPE

The **INCTYPE** parameter specifies whether the EXPORT is a complete, cumulative, or incremental EXPORT. This parameter does not have a default value. If the parameter is left unspecified, the EXPORT cannot be used as part of an incremental backup scheme.

PARFILE

The **PARFILE** parameter specifies the name of a parameter file to be read by the EXPORT utility. This file may contain entries for all of the EXPORT parameters described in this section. It has no default value.

HELP

The **HELP** parameter is a Y/N flag that specifies whether the EXPORT utility displays the EXPORT parameters on the screen with a brief explanation. The default value is N.

LOG

The **LOG** parameter specifies the file name to which you can record the screen output and error messages. By default, no log file is created.

CONSISTENT

This **CONSISTENT** parameter is a Y/N flag that specifies whether a read-consistent version of all the exported database objects are required. This parameter needs to be set to Y when tables that are related to each other are being modified during the EXPORT process. Additional rollback segment space should be considered when using this parameter.

STATISTICS

The **STATISTICS** parameter specifies whether **ANALYZE** commands for the exported objects should be written to the EXPORT dump file. It can be set to **ESTIMATE, COMPUTE,** or **NONE.** The default value is **ESTIMATE.**

TRANSPORT_TABLESPACE

The **TRANSPORT_TABLESPACE** parameter specifies whether to enable the export of the metadata for the transportable tablespace.

TABLESPACES

The **TABLESPACES** parameter specifies tablespaces to be transported. This is a new parameter in Oracle 8i.

POINT_IN_TIME_RECOVER

The **POINT_IN_TIME_RECOVER** parameter is a Y/N flag that is used to signal Oracle if you are exporting metadata for use in a tablespace point-in-time recovery. This is specific to release 8.

RECOVERY_TABLESPACES

The **RECOVERY_TABLESPACES** parameter specifies the tablespaces whose metadata should be exported during a tablespace point-in-time recovery. This is specific to release 8.

EXPORT Examples

The following are some examples of using the EXPORT utility:

➤ To execute a Table mode EXPORT:

```
$ exp dba9/password9 tables=(test1,test2) file=test.dmp
```

➤ To execute a User mode EXPORT:

```
$ exp dba9/password9 owner=tester file=tester.dmp
```

➤ To execute a User mode EXPORT for a remote database:

```
$ exp dba9/password9@remote_db owner=tester file=tester.dmp
```

➤ To EXPORT only the data definitions without the business data:

```
$ exp dba9/password9 owner=dvlp rows=n file=dvlp0.dmp
```

➤ To EXPORT a user's objects, excluding the grants to those objects and indexes:

```
$ exp dba9/password9 owner=prod grants=n
indexes=n file=prodx.dmp
```

➤ To EXPORT only a specific partition of the **PARTTAB** table:

```
$ exp dba9/password9 owner=user1 tables=parttab:
a file=parta.dmp
```

Things to Remember about EXPORTs

You should consider the following issues when exporting database objects:

➤ When sequences are cached, gaps in sequence numbers may occur because the exported sequence value is the next sequence number after the largest cached value. Sequence numbers that are cached, but unused, are lost when the sequence is subsequently imported.

➤ When exporting **LONG** data types, sufficient memory must be available to hold the contents of a row containing the **LONG** column. **LONG** columns can support lengths of up to 2 gigabytes (GB). Available system resources may restrict this function.

Note: Exporting LOB data does not require as much memory as exporting the **LONG** *data because the LOB data is loaded and unloaded in sections and all sections don't need to be held in memory at the same time.*

➤ When exporting foreign function libraries, only the library specification— name and location—is included in the Full Database mode and User mode EXPORT dump file.

➤ Directory alias definitions are written to the EXPORT dump file in Full Database mode.

➤ When exporting **BFILE**s, only the names and the directory aliases are written to the EXPORT dump file and subsequently restored by the IMPORT utility.

➤ When exporting array data, sufficient memory must be available to hold the maximum dimensions of the array even though the average dimensions in use may be much smaller.

➤ In all EXPORT modes, the EXPORT utility will write object type definitions for a table before writing the table definition. However, the object type definitions may not be complete. For example, if the object type for a column is owned by another user, the full definitions of object types from the other schema are not written to the EXPORT dump file.

➤ When exporting nested tables, the inner nested table is exported whenever the outer table is exported. The inner nested tables cannot be exported by themselves.

 Oracle recommends performing Full Database mode exports on a regular basis to preserve all object type definitions.

The EXPORT utility has some compatibility restrictions that you should be aware of:

➤ You can't run the Oracle6 EXPORT against an Oracle8i database.

➤ You can use Oracle7's EXPORT against an Oracle8i database with the exception that the EXPORT dump file is in the Oracle7 format and it won't contain any Oracle8i-specific database objects. When a lower version EXPORT utility is used against a higher version of the Oracle server, higher version-specific database objects will be excluded from the EXPORT dump file.

➤ The IMPORT utility prior to Oracle 7.3 cannot read a direct path EXPORT dump file.

➤ Oracle will return an error when you try to use a higher version of EXPORT with a lower version Oracle server.

Note: DBAs typically use the EXPORT version that matches the version of the Oracle server.

Using the IMPORT Utility

The IMPORT utility is typically used for the recovery of database objects and business data using a valid dump file created by the EXPORT utility. Three methods invoke the IMPORT utility:

➤ An interactive dialog is available when the IMPORT executable name is specified at the operating system prompt with no parameters. The IMPORT utility prompts the user for input values while providing default values.

➤ The IMPORT Wizard of the data management tools within the OEM DBA Studio administrative toolset invokes the IMPORT utility.

➤ A command-line interface is available when the user wishes to specify IMPORT options explicitly on the command line. Any missing IMPORT options will assume default values. Optionally, the user may use a parameter file to specify IMPORT options explicitly. The following code shows an example of using the command-line interface of the IMPORT utility under Windows NT:

```
D:\ORANT\BIN> imp scott/tiger tables=(dept,emp) rows=y
file=scott.dmp
```

Be aware that some IMPORT options are available only through the command-line interface. Using the command-line interface with a parameter file enables you to use all available IMPORT options.

IMPORT Modes

The IMPORT modes determine which portion of a valid EXPORT dump file can be imported. The IMPORT utility can be run in four modes:

> Table mode

> User mode

> Tablespace mode

> Full Database mode

Table Mode

In the *Table mode*, all specified tables in the operating user's schema are imported. A privileged database user, such as the DBA, can import specific tables owned by other database users.

User Mode

In the *User mode*, all database objects in the operating user's schema are imported. A privileged database user, such as the DBA, can import all database objects owned by one or more schema users.

Tablespace Mode

In the *Tablespace mode*, a privileged database user, such as the DBA, can transport a set of tablespaces from one database to another. All object definitions in the tablespaces (data dictionary meta data) will be imported. This mode does not load business data.

Full Database Mode

In the *Full Database mode*, all database objects except those owned by the **SYS** schema are imported. Only users with DBA privileges or users with **IMP_FULL_DATABASE** role can operate the IMPORT utility in this mode.

 Know how to operate the IMPORT utility using the runtime parameters with the command-line interface.

IMPORT Runtime Parameters

The following section describes typical runtime parameters that can be specified for the IMPORT utility and how to use them to read information from a valid EXPORT dump file into an Oracle database.

USERID

The **USERID** parameter specifies the username and password for the user running the IMPORT utility. The format for the command is **username/password**. Optionally, you may use Net8's **@connect_string** format. This parameter has no default value. You will be prompted for the userid and/or password if it is not entered.

FILE

The **FILE** parameter specifies the name of the EXPORT dump file to be imported. The default value is **expdat.dmp or EXPDAT.DMP** depending on the OS platform.

ROWS

The **ROWS** parameter is a Y/N flag that specifies whether rows should be imported. If set to N, only the DDL for the database objects will be run. The default value is Y.

IGNORE

The **IGNORE** parameter is a Y/N flag that specifies whether the IMPORT utility should ignore errors encountered when issuing the DDL **CREATE** commands. This is applicable to importing database objects that already exist in the target database. The default value is N.

FULL

The FULL parameter is a Y/N flag that specifies whether the full EXPORT dump file is imported. The default value is N.

TABLES

The **TABLES** parameter specifies a list of database tables to be imported. It has no default value.

INDEXES

The **INDEXES** parameter is a Y/N flag that specifies whether indexes on the database tables will be imported. The default value is Y.

INCTYPE

The **INCTYPE** parameter specifies the type of IMPORT being performed. Valid values are **SYSTEM** and **RESTORE**. This parameter has no default value.

PARFILE

The **PARFILE** parameter specifies the name of a parameter file to be read by the IMPORT utility. This file may contain entries for all the import parameters. It has no default value.

HELP

The **HELP** parameter is a Y/N flag that specifies whether the import utility will display the available IMPORT parameters on the screen with a brief explanation. The default value is N.

LOG

The **LOG** parameter specifies the name of the file to spool the feedback from the IMPORT session. Oracle appends an .log extension to the file unless the user specifies otherwise. This parameter has no default value.

DESTROY

The **DESTROY** parameter is a Y/N flag that specifies if Oracle will run the **CREATE TABLESPACE** commands found in the full EXPORT dump file and if it will overwrite any data files that exist. The default value is N.

FROMUSER

The **FROMUSER** parameter specifies a list of database accounts whose objects should be read from the EXPORT dump file. This parameter is applicable when the **FULL** parameter is set to N. It has no default value.

TOUSER

The **TOUSER** parameter specifies one or more database accounts into which database objects in the EXPORT dump file will be imported. This parameter value does not need to be set to the **FROMUSER** parameter value. It has no default value.

INDEXFILE

The **INDEXFILE** parameter specifies that Oracle write all **CREATE TABLE, CREATE CLUSTER,** and **CREATE INDEX** commands to a file rather than executing them. All but the **CREATE INDEX** commands will be commented out. This file is typically run after importing with **INDEXES=N.** It is very useful for separating tables and indexes into different tablespaces. This parameter requires that either the **FULL** parameter is set to Y or that a value is specified for the **FROMUSER** parameter. It has no default value.

ANALYZE

The **ANALYZE** parameter is a Y/N flag that specifies whether the IMPORT utility should execute the **ANALYZE** commands contained in the EXPORT dump file. The default value is Y.

SKIP_UNUSABLE_INDEXES

The SKIP_UNUSABLE_INDEXES parameter is a Y/N flag that specifies whether the IMPORT utility should skip partition indexes marked as unusable. This parameter enables you to defer index maintenance on selected index partitions until after row data has been inserted. Without this parameter, inserts that attempt to update unusable indexes will fail. The default value is N.

TRANSPORT_TABLESPACE

The TRANSPORT_TABLESPACE parameter specifies the import of transportable tablespace metadata from a valid export file.

TABLESPACES

The TABLESPACES parameter specifies the list of tablespaces to be transported into the database.

DATAFILES

The DATAFILES parameter specifies the list of data files to be moved into the database.

TTS_OWNERS

The TTS_OWNERS parameter specifies the owners of the data in the transportable tablespace set.

Understanding the IMPORT Process Flow for Table Database Objects

When you're importing database tables, the following IMPORT sequence of events takes place:

➤ The EXPORT dump file is read by the IMPORT utility.

➤ CREATE TABLE statements are executed, resulting in new tables being created. These newly created tables have the same data and attributes as the original source tables.

➤ Row data is imported into the database tables if the ROWS parameter is set to Y. If indexes were created along with the table, the indexes are updated along with the row data import.

➤ Index structures are created. To increase the performance of the IMPORT utility, the DBA can set the INDEXES parameter to N and then build the indexes after the IMPORT utility has successfully terminated. This approach also minimizes the number of rollback segments needed to support the IMPORT process.

➤ Database triggers are imported.

➤ Integrity constraints are enabled on the newly created tables.

➤ Bitmap index structures are created.

The order in which database tables are imported may be important under certain circumstances. For instance, if the child table contains a foreign key reference to the primary key of the parent table, and the child table is imported first, all rows that reference the parent table's primary key that have not been imported will be rejected if the constraints are in effect. A similar situation exists when a referential constraint on a table references itself. This problem does not apply to full database exports.

When importing into an existing table, DBAs typically disable the referential constraints and then reenable them after the import process has been successfully terminated.

Make sure you understand the order in which the IMPORT utility loads table objects into the database.

Understanding National Language Support Implications

When moving data between Oracle databases with different character sets, special consideration should be given to ensure that appropriate data conversion is performed. The EXPORT utility writes to the EXPORT dump file using the character set specified—such as 7-bit American Standard Code for Information Interchange (ASCII)—for the user session running the EXPORT utility. If the character set of the importing user session is different from the one in the EXPORT dump file, the IMPORT utility will translate the data to the character set of the importing user session. After the data is converted to the importing user session character set, it is then converted to the database character set. During the conversion, any characters in the EXPORT file that have no equivalent in the target character set are replaced with a default character that is character set dependent. The **NLS_LANG** environment variable can be set to the character set definition of the source database to protect against undesired data conversions and data loss.

Make sure you understand the National Language Support (NLS) considerations of loading data into the database.

 To ensure appropriate data conversion is performed, the target character set should be a superset of the source character set, or both character sets should be equivalent.

IMPORT Examples

The following are some examples of using the IMPORT utility:

➤ Importing a table exported by **USER1** into the **USER2** schema:

```
$ imp dba9/password9 fromuser=user1 touser=user2
file=user1.dmp tables=user1tab
```

➤ Importing using a parameter file named **IMPORT.par:**

```
$ imp dba9/password9 parfile=IMPORT.par
```

➤ Importing in Full Database mode excluding indexes:

```
$ imp dba9/password9 full=y indexes=n file=dball.dmp
```

➤ Importing partitions a and b from a table named **parttab** that is owned by **parttabowner:**

```
$ imp dba9/password9 fromuser=parttabtowner
tables=parttab:a,parttab:b
```

Using EXPORT for Logical Backups

When the EXPORT utility is run in the Full Database mode, you can make a logical backup of the entire database or just the database objects that have changed since the last EXPORT. This mode will EXPORT all table and data definitions. The **FULL EXPORT** parameter must be set to Y to run in the Full Database mode. When you're running EXPORT in the Full Database mode, three types of exports can be performed:

➤ Complete

➤ Cumulative

➤ Incremental

The **INCTYPE EXPORT** parameter can be used to specify the desired type of EXPORT. These three types of EXPORTs facilitate backup strategies involving EXPORTs.

Complete EXPORTs

Complete EXPORTs form the basis for a backup strategy involving EXPORTs. A complete EXPORT is equivalent to a full database EXPORT with the additional updates performed against the tables that track incremental and cumulative EXPORTs. The **SYS** schema owns three tables that enable EXPORT to track incremental and cumulative EXPORTs—INCEXP, INCFIL, and INCVID. A complete EXPORT dump file contains all database objects from the source database and can be used to perform point-in-time recovery up to the time that the complete EXPORT was taken. The following example code shows how to invoke the EXPORT utility under Windows NT to create a complete EXPORT file:

```
D:\ORANT\BIN> exp DBA9/PASSWORD9 FULL=Y INCTYPE=COMPLETE
FILE='TESTCOMP.DMP'
```

Cumulative EXPORTs

A cumulative EXPORT contains database tables that have changed since the last cumulative or complete EXPORT. A cumulative EXPORT essentially combines several incremental EXPORTs into a single cumulative EXPORT file. You can discard the incremental EXPORT files taken before a cumulative EXPORT because they are rolled up into the cumulative EXPORT file. The following example code shows how to invoke the EXPORT utility to create a cumulative EXPORT file:

```
D:\ORANT\BIN> exp DBA9/PASSWORD9 FULL=Y INCTYPE=CUMULATIVE
FILE='TESTCUM.DMP'
```

Incremental EXPORTs

An incremental EXPORT contains database tables that have changed since the last incremental, cumulative, or complete EXPORT. An incremental EXPORT file contains table definitions with all of the table's data rows. The following example code shows how to invoke the EXPORT utility to create an incremental EXPORT file:

```
D:\ORANT\BIN> exp DBA9/PASSWORD9 FULL=Y INCTYPE=INCREMENTAL
FILE='TESTINC.DMP'
```

Note: Incremental EXPORTs are more suitable for environments where database changes affect relatively smaller tables.

The incremental and cumulative EXPORTs provide several benefits to DBAs:

➤ They facilitate in the restoration of accidentally dropped tables.

➤ Smaller EXPORT files are generated because only tables that contained changed rows are exported.

➤ EXPORT time is reduced because only database objects that have changed since the last incremental or cumulative EXPORT are written to the current EXPORT file.

Using EXPORT's Direct Path Method

The EXPORT utility uses one of two paths in extracting data from an Oracle database: the *conventional* path or the *direct* path. The conventional path EXPORT uses most of the same mechanisms for extracting data as a SQL SELECT statement would use. Data is read into the buffer cache from disk, evaluated, and passed to a user, such as an EXPORT client, and written to an operating system file. Direct path EXPORTs, on the other hand, run faster because the data is extracted from the Oracle data files and passed directly to the EXPORT client for processing, bypassing the buffer cache and the SQL command-processing layer. Direct path EXPORTs eliminate the need to perform unnecessary data conversions because the data is in the format that EXPORT needs. The IMPORT utility can work with data extracted using either the conventional or direct path EXPORT.

Be aware that the formats of the data and the column specifications in the EXPORT dump files generated by direct path and conventional path EXPORTs are different.

Before using direct path EXPORT, the catexp.sql script, typically located in the rdbms/admin directory, must be run. The catexp.sql script is typically run as part of the catalog.sql script. Two methods invoke direct path EXPORT:

➤ Command-line option

➤ Parameter file

Command-Line Option

You can invoke the direct path EXPORT by using the **DIRECT** command-line parameter at the operating system prompt, as shown by the following code sample under Unix:

```
$ exp dba9/password9 full=y direct=y
```

Parameter File

You can invoke the direct path EXPORT by using a parameter file that contains all the user-specified parameters. The EXPORT utility reads the contents of the parameter file at runtime. The following code example shows the contents of a parameter file named EXPORT.par and demonstrates how the parameter file is used from the operating system prompt:

```
Contents of the EXPORT.par file:
    USERID=DBA9/PASSWORD9
    TABLES=(TESTTAB1,TESTTAB2)
    FILE=EXP_PAR.DMP
    DIRECT=Y
```

To run the EXPORT utility with the EXPORT.par parameter file, issue the following command at the operating system prompt under Unix:

```
$ exp parfile=EXPORT.par
```

 You can find out whether an EXPORT dump file was created using the direct or conventional path by looking in the log file produced by the EXPORT session, on the screen while EXPORT is running or at the EXPORT dump file when it is imported later.

Things to Remember about Direct Path EXPORT

When using the direct path EXPORT, you should be aware of the following limitations:

➤ The direct path option of EXPORT is not available when you're using the EXPORT utility interactively.

➤ The direct path EXPORT requires matching character sets on the client machine and the server machine because no character-set conversion will be performed.

➤ When using the direct path EXPORT involving database tables that contain columns defined with Oracle8-specific data types, such as **LOB, BFILE, REF, NESTED TABLE, VARRAY,** and other object types, only the table definitions are exported.

➤ The **BUFFER** parameter defines the buffer size EXPORT uses when unloading data on the conventional path. This parameter is not used by the direct path EXPORT.

Using IMPORT to Recover Database Objects

The IMPORT utility can be used to recover data and database objects from a valid EXPORT dump file. It is commonly used to support the following recovery activities:

➤ Creating table definitions from the EXPORT dump file. You need to specify IMPORT without the data rows.

➤ Extracting data from a valid EXPORT dump file when running in the Table, User, or Full Database mode.

➤ Importing data from a cumulative, incremental, or complete EXPORT file.

➤ Recovering an accidentally dropped table.

Restoring Database Objects Using Incremental, Cumulative, and Complete EXPORT Files

The order in which incremental, cumulative, and complete EXPORTs are made is important. A complete EXPORT must be made before database objects can be restored. After this has been accomplished, the database object restoration process is as follows:

1. Run IMPORT with parameter **INCTYPE** set to **SYSTEM** using the most recent incremental EXPORT file. Use a cumulative EXPORT file if no incremental EXPORTs have been made. This imports the system objects.

2. Run IMPORT with the parameter **INCTYPE** set to **RESTORE** using the most recent complete EXPORT file.

3. Run IMPORT with the parameter **INCTYPE** set to **RESTORE** using all cumulative EXPORT files after the last complete EXPORT.

4. Run IMPORT with the parameter **INCTYPE** set to **RESTORE** using all incremental EXPORT files after the last cumulative EXPORT.

Performing Tablespace Point-In-Time Recovery

You can perform perform tablespace point-in-time recovery using two methods: the traditional operating system (OS) method or Oracle8i's transportable tablespace feature. The traditional OS method requires the creation of a clone database, and both the primary and the clone database may reside on the same computer. The transportable tablespace method provides more flexibility because it supports recovering dropped tablespaces, it does not need a clone database, and it does not require the primary and the target databases to be on the same computer.

To perform tablespace point-in-time recovery using the transportable tablespace feature, follow these steps:

1. Construct the target database by restoring from an available backup. The target database can be on a different computer than the primary database.

2. If the target database was created using the clone database procedure, place all files in the recovery set and the auxiliary set online. Otherwise, if the target database was created as a normal database on a different computer than the primary database, take all data files not in the recovery and auxiliary set offline.

3. Recover the target database to the desired point in time.

4. Open the target database with the **RESETLOGS** option.

5. Set the tablespaces in the recovery set to read-only.

6. Run the EXPORT utility to generate the transportable set.

7. Drop the tablespace(s) in the recovery set from the primary database.

8. Copy the data files associated with the transportable tablespaces and the EXPORT file to the primary database.

9. Run the IMPORT utility to move the transportable set into the primary database.

10. Make the recovered tablespace read/write if necessary.

11. Make a backup of the recovered tablespace(s) in the primary database.

Practice Questions

Question 1

Which EXPORT parameter is used to specify the location to log EXPORT errors?

○ a. **PARFILE**

○ b. **INDEXFILE**

○ c. **HELP**

○ d. **BUFFER**

○ e. **LOG**

The correct answer is e. The **LOG** parameter enables the user to specify the name of the file to which informational and error messages encountered by EXPORT are written. Answer a is incorrect, because the **PARFILE** parameter enables the user to specify the name of the parameter file to be read by the EXPORT utility. Answer b is incorrect, because the **INDEXFILE** parameter specifies that Oracle write all **CREATE TABLE, CREATE CLUSTER,** and **CREATE INDEX** commands to a file rather than executing them. Answer c is incorrect, because the HELP parameter specifies whether the on-line help is displayed on the screen. Answer d is incorrect, because the **BUFFER** parameter specifies the size of the buffer used to fetch data rows.

Question 2

When you are performing an EXPORT of your database, what type of backup is it?

○ a. Physical database backup.

○ b. Logical database backup.

○ c. It is not a backup.

The correct answer is b. The EXPORT utility enables DBAs to perform logical backups of all database objects so that they can be subsequently re-created using the IMPORT utility. Answer a is not correct because the EXPORT utility does not back up the physical file structures of the database. Answer c is incorrect because the EXPORT utility enables users to perform logical database backups.

Question 3

> How can EXPORTs be incorporated in a backup and recovery strategy?
>
> ○ a. In conjunction with the redo log files to perform complete recovery
>
> ○ b. Instead of operating the database in ARCHIVELOG mode
>
> ○ c. When a new database needs to be created
>
> ○ d. In place of offline backups

The correct answer is c. A logical backup serves to supplement a physical backup because it can be used to restore a single table, all objects under a user schema, or an entire database. Answer a is incorrect because redo log files cannot be used with database objects recovered from an EXPORT dump file. Answer b is incorrect because EXPORTs should be performed as a safety net and should not replace operating the database in ARCHIVELOG mode. Answer d is incorrect because EXPORTs should not be used in place of offline backups.

Question 4

> Which EXPORT parameter enables you to specify the names of database tables to EXPORT?
>
> ○ a. **PARFILE**
>
> ○ b. **TABLES**
>
> ○ c. **OWNER**
>
> ○ d. **ROWS**
>
> ○ e. **FILE**

The correct answer is b. The **TABLES** parameter enables you to specify the names of database tables to be exported. Answer a is incorrect, because the **PARFILE** parameter specifies the name of a parameter file to be read by the EXPORT utility. Answer c is incorrect, because the **OWNER** parameter specifies a list of database users whose objects will be exported in user mode. Answer d is incorrect, because the **ROWS** parameter specifies whether data rows should be exported. Answer e is incorrect, because the **FILE** parameter specifies the name of the EXPORT dump file.

Question 5

> What are two limitations when using the direct path option of EXPORT?
> [Choose two]
>
> ❑ a. The EXPORT utility will compete with other database users for
> shared memory.
>
> ❑ b. The **BUFFER** parameter will have no effect.
>
> ❑ c. The client-side and the server-side character sets must be the
> same.
>
> ❑ d. Tables containing **LONG** columns will not be exported.
>
> ❑ e. The EXPORT utility must be run using the interactive interface.

The correct answers are b and c. When using the direct path option of EXPORT, the **BUFFER** parameter is ignored, and the character sets for the client machine and the server machine must be equivalent. Answer a is incorrect because direct path EXPORTs bypass the buffer cache and the SQL command-processing layer so that they don't compete with other database users for shared memory. Answer d is incorrect because tables containing **LONG** columns are supported by the direct path option of EXPORT. Answer e is incorrect because direct path EXPORTs require the use of the command-line interface.

Question 6

> What EXPORT mode should be used to EXPORT selected tables in a user's
> schema?
>
> ○ a. Full database
>
> ○ b. Tablespace
>
> ○ c. Table
>
> ○ d. User

The correct answer is c. In the Table mode of EXPORT, specified tables are exported. Answer a is incorrect because, with EXPORTs made in Full Database mode, all database objects except the database objects owned by **SYS** are exported. Answer b is incorrect because this Tablespace export mode cannot be used to export selected tables in a user's schema. Answer d is incorrect because, in the User mode of EXPORT, all the objects in a user's schema are exported.

Question 7

When importing database tables, what order does the IMPORT utility use to perform the following tasks?

1. Data imported
2. Indexes created
3. Triggers imported
4. Integrity constraints enabled
5. Bitmap indexes created
6. Tables created

○ a. 6,2,5,1,4,3

○ b. 6,1,2,3,4,5

○ c. 6,2,1,3,4,5

○ d. 6,1,2,4,3,5

The correct answer is c. When importing tables, the IMPORT utility will perform the following tasks: (1) create the tables, (2) create the indexes, (3) import the data, (4) import the database triggers, (5) enable integrity constraints, and (6) create the bitmap indexes. Answer a is incorrect because bitmap indexes are performed last. Answers b and d are incorrect because data is imported after the indexes are built.

Question 8

What EXPORT parameter should be set when you're exporting data and the users are performing updates to the database?

- ○ a. **CONSTRAINTS=Y**
- ○ b. **CONSISTENT=Y**
- ○ c. **DIRECT=Y**
- ○ d. **IGNORE=Y**

The correct answer is b. When the database is open and in use during an EXPORT, setting the **CONSISTENT** parameter to Y will enable a read-consistent view of the data. Answer a is incorrect because it specifies whether constraints will be exported. Answer c is incorrect because it specifies whether the direct path EXPORT will be performed. Answer d is incorrect because it is not a valid EXPORT parameter.

Question 9

What IMPORT parameter should be used when importing the metadata for transportable tablespace(s) from a valid export file?

- ○ a. **TRANSPORT_TABLESPACE**
- ○ b. **TTS_OWNERS**
- ○ c. **TABLESPACES**
- ○ d. **INCTYPE**

The correct answer is a. The IMPORT parameter **TRANSPORT_TABLESPACE** specifies that the metadata associated with transportable tablespace(s) are to be IMPORTed. Answer b is incorrect because it specifies the list of users who own the data in the transportable tablespace set. Answer c is incorrect because it is an invalid IMPORT parameter. Answer d is incorrect because it specifies the type of incremental import.

Question 10

> Which of the following statements is true for performing tablespace point-in-time recovery with the transportable tablespace feature?
>
> ○ a. Primary and clone databases must reside on the same computer.
>
> ○ b. Dropped tablespace(s) cannot be recovered.
>
> ○ c. Dropped tablespace(s) can be recovered.
>
> ○ d. A clone database is mandatory.

The correct answer is c. With the transportable tablespace feature, you can recover dropped tablespaces. Answer a is incorrect because the transportable tablespace feature doesn't require primary and target databases to reside on the same computer. Answer b is incorrect because dropped tablespaces can be recovered by the transportable tablespace feature. Answer d is incorrect because the transportable tablespace feature doesn't need a clone database.

Need to Know More?

 Loney, Kevin and Marlene Theriault. *Oracle8i DBA Handbook*. Oracle Press, Berkeley, CA, 1999. ISBN 0-07212-188-2. This comprehensive guide for DBAs includes general backup and recovery concepts.

 Velpuri, Rama. *Oracle8i Backup and Recovery Handbook*. Oracle Press, Berkeley, CA, 2000. ISBN 0-072-12717-1. This book provides information on how to maximize uptime and recover data without compromising mission critical systems. Actual corporate scenarios and case studies are included.

 http://technet.oracle.com. This site provides the best information on Oracle's products and technologies. You can also purchase the following manuals online:

Baylis, Ruth. *Oracle8i Administrator's Guide Release 2*. Oracle Corporation, Redwood City, CA, 1999. Part No. A76956-01. This manual describes basic database administration, Oracle server configuration, database storage management, schema object management, and database security for Oracle8i.

Dialeris, Connie. *Oracle8i Backup and Recovery Guide Release 2*. Oracle Corporation, Redwood City, CA, 1999. Part No. A76993-01. This manual provides guidance on data protection techniques and offers strategies for data storage, backup, and restore for Oracle 8i.

Leverenz, Lefty. *Oracle8i Concepts Release 2*. Oracle Corporation, Redwood City, CA, 1999. Part No. A76965-01. This manual describes all features of the Oracle8i server running on all operating systems.

Lorentz, Diana. *Oracle8i Reference Release 2*. Oracle Corporation, Redwood City, CA, 1999. Part No. A76961-01. This manual describes the architecture, processes, structures, and other concepts of Oracle8i. It provides detailed information on static and dynamic data dictionary views.

Rich, Kathy. *Oracle8i Utilities Release 2*. Oracle Corporation, Redwood City, CA, 1999. Part No. A76955-01. This manual describes how to use the Oracle8i utilities for data transfer, data maintenance, and database administration.

 www.revealnet.com. This site from RevealNet provides Oracle administration reference software.

Oracle Standby Database

Terms you'll need to understand:

✓ Standby database

✓ Manual Recovery mode

✓ Managed Recovery mode

✓ Read-Only mode

✓ **ALTER DATABASE OPEN READ ONLY** command

✓ **ALTER DATABASE MOUNT STANDBY DATABASE** command

✓ **ALTER DATABASE ACTIVATE STANDBY DATABASE** command

✓ **RECOVER STANDBY DATABASE** command

Techniques you'll need to master:

✓ Understanding the features of a standby database

✓ Configuring initialization parameters

✓ Creating, maintaining, and activating a standby database

✓ Understanding the operating modes of a standby database

✓ Propagating structural changes of the primary database

✓ Understanding Nologging operations of the primary database

A standby database is typically used when downtime must be minimized and high availability must be maintained. A standby database can provide access to data if the primary database fails and if recovery time does not meet business operational requirements.

Nologging Standby Database Features

The features of a standby database are as follows:

➤ A standby database is a physical copy of a primary database. The data files, archived redo log files, and customized control files are transferred from the primary database and are applied to the standby database to achieve synchronization. The databases normally reside on physically different machines to protect against hardware failure.

➤ The standby database is normally kept mounted and in Recovery mode because the archived redo log files are regularly transferred from the primary database. In Oracle8i, database administrators (DBAs) typically take the automated approach of redo log file transfers provided by NET8.

➤ The standby database can operate in Managed Recovery mode. In this mode, Oracle keeps the standby database synchronized with the primary database by automatically transferring the archived redo log files from the primary database to the standby database and then applying them.

➤ You can issue the **ALTER DATABASE OPEN READ ONLY** command to open a standby database in Read-Only mode. In this mode, queries can be issued, but Data Manipulation Language (DML) activity is not permitted. To return the standby database to Recovery mode, you need to shut down the database, issue the **STARTUP NOMOUNT** command, and issue the **ALTER DATABASE MOUNT STANDBY DATABASE** command.

➤ All archived redo log files can be transferred to the standby database and can be applied to the standby database by performing recovery. If the current redo log file cannot be transferred before the standby database is activated, the standby database cannot be brought to the time of failure, and data loss may occur. It is critical to apply all the redo log files to the standby database before activation because the redo log files are of no use after the standby database is activated.

➤ The standby database becomes the primary database after activation. All user connections are directed to this primary database while the failure on the other machine is under investigation. When the failure on the other machine has been fixed, the failed database can be set up as the new standby database by creating a new standby control file.

Things to Consider When Using a Standby Database

When using a standby database, you should be aware of the following standby database characteristics:

➤ The standby database feature was introduced in Oracle 7.3. Pre-Oracle 7.3 versions cannot use the standby database feature.

➤ The standby database feature was designed to protect against hardware failure. Therefore, the standby and the primary databases should reside on separate machines.

➤ The standby and the primary databases must have the same version, release, and patch of the Oracle server and the operating system because physical OS-specific database file transfers take place between the two machines. The standby database machine may use a different disk configuration.

 Oracle recommends that identical names be maintained on both the primary and the standby databases for the database name, data files, redo log files, and control files.

Important Initialization Parameters

The majority of the database initialization parameters are identical for the primary and standby database. However, initialization parameters, such as **CONTROL_FILES, LOG_FILE_NAME_CONVERT**, and **DB_FILE_NAME_CONVERT** may be different. The following are key database initialization parameters when using the standby database feature:

➤ COMPATIBLE—This parameter specifies the compatibility level of the features that can be used in a database. This parameter must be identical in the primary and the standby databases.

➤ CONTROL_FILES—This parameter is used to define the control files of the primary and the standby databases. This parameter should be different if the standby and the primary databases are on the same machine or on the same cluster.

➤ **DB_FILES**—This parameter determines the maximum number of database files that can be opened for a database. The maximum valid value is the maximum number of files, subject to operating system constraint, that will ever be specified for the database, including files to be added by **ADD DATAFILE** statements. This parameter should be the same in the primary and the standby databases.

➤ **DB_FILE_NAME_CONVERT**—This parameter enables you to use different naming conventions for the standby and the primary database data files.

➤ **LOG_FILE_NAME_CONVERT**—This parameter enables you to use different naming conventions for the standby and the primary database log files.

➤ **STANDBY_ARCHIVE_DEST**—This parameter is used by the remote file server (RFS) process on the standby database to determine the directory in which to place the archived redo log files. Oracle uses this parameter in conjunction with the **LOG_ARCHIVE_FORMAT** parameter to generate the log file name for the standby database.

 Database initialization parameters should be changed with caution because any inconsistencies between the primary and the standby databases could lead to performance degradation or database malfunction.

Creating, Maintaining, and Activating a Standby Database

Three tasks are involved in getting the standby database operational: creating the standby database, maintaining the standby database, and activating the standby database.

Creating the Standby Database

The process for creating a standby database consists of the following steps:

1. Take a backup of the primary database data files.

2. Create the standby database control file.

3. Archive the current online redo logs for the primary database.

4. Transfer the standby database control file, data files, and archived redo log files to the standby database location.

5. Mount the standby database.

The following is a step-by-step example of how to create a standby database:

1. Copy the init.ora file from the primary database to the standby database. Make applicable adjustments in the **CONTROL_FILES, DB_FILE_NAME_ CONVERT,** and **LOG_FILE_NAME_CONVERT** database parameters of the standby database. Other database parameters, such as **LOG_ARCHIVE_ DEST, LOG_ARCHIVE_FORMAT, USER_DUMP_DEST,** and **BACKGROUND_DUMP_DEST** may also require modification.

2. Issue the following command at the primary database to create the control file for the standby database:

```
SQL> alter database create standby controlfile
SQL> as <filename specification>;
```

3. Copy the standby database control file created in Step 2 to the standby database at the locations specified by the **CONTROL_FILES** parameter of the standby database.

4. Back up the data files of the primary database. You can take online or offline backups. Copy the backed up data files to the applicable location in the standby database.

5. If an online backup is taken in Step 4, archive the current online redo log files of the primary database by issuing the following command:

```
SQL> alter system archive log current;
```

6. Copy the archived log files generated by Step 5 to the standby database. This will ensure complete recovery can be performed on the standby database.

7. Start the standby database in NOMOUNT mode as illustrated by the following code:

```
SQL> startup pfile=$ORACLE_HOME/initSTANDBY.ora NOMOUNT
```

8. Mount the standby database using the following command:

```
SQL> alter database mount standby database;
```

9. Issue the following **RECOVER** command and apply the archived redo log files to the standby database so that it is synchronized with the primary database:

```
SQL> recover standby database;
```

The standby database may be kept in Standby Recovery mode, which enables the Oracle processes to recover the database by applying archived redo log files to the data files and which disables normal user connections.

Maintaining the Standby Database

The standby database needs to be synchronized with the primary database on a regular basis. The synchronization process consists of the following maintenance tasks:

➤ Transfer archived redo log files from the primary database to the standby database on a regular basis using NET8 service.

➤ Apply the archived redo log files to the standby database by using the **RECOVER** command or take the automated approach that comes with the Managed Recovery mode.

➤ Clear out unarchived redo log files in the primary database to avoid incomplete recovery and invalidating the standby database.

➤ When Nologging operations occur in the primary database, a backup of the applicable tablespace needs to be taken and copied to the standby database.

Using NET8 Service for Archived Redo Log Transfers

When you use the NET8 service for transferring archived redo log files, you must make sure that the NET8 service is configured at the primary site to connect to the standby site. The **LOG_ARCHIVE_DEST_n** database initialization parameters can be used to automatically transfer the archived redo log files. The **LOG_ARCHIVE_DEST_n** parameters enable the archive processes to archive to the standby database location.

Activating the Standby Database

When the primary database fails, the standby database can be activated so that it becomes the primary database. To activate the standby database, perform the following steps:

1. Attempt to archive the current redo log files of the primary database, and transfer them to the standby database as illustrated by the following code:

```
SQL> alter system archive log all;
```

2. Make sure that the standby database is mounted in Exclusive mode.

3. Issue the **RECOVER** command at the standby database to apply the primary database's archived redo log files as illustrated by the following code:

```
SQL> recover standby database;
```

4. Cancel the recovery, and activate the standby database. Issue the **ALTER DATABASE ACTIVATE STANDBY DATABASE** command to reset the standby bit in the control file and to take the standby database back to NOMOUNT mode as illustrated by the following code:

```
SQL> alter database activate standby database;
```

5. Shut down the new primary database and take a backup.

6. Open the new primary database, and enable normal user connections as illustrated by the following code:

```
SQL> alter database mount;
SQL> alter database open;
```

 Unarchived online redo log files copied from the primary database to the standby database will not be usable by the standby database, and an error will be returned.

Operating Modes of a Standby Database

There are three operating modes for a standby database: Manual Recovery mode, Managed Recovery mode, and Read-Only mode.

Manual Recovery Mode

In *Manual Recovery mode,* recovering the standby database is a manual process that involves transferring the archived redo log files from the primary database using File Transfer Protocol (FTP) or the Unix **rcp** command. The DBA then applies the archived redo log files manually when they become available.

Managed Recovery Mode

A standby database in *Managed Recovery mode* will wait for the archived redo log files from the primary database and then will automatically apply them when the files become available. This eliminates the need for the DBA to supply filenames manually during the recovery process. DBAs are responsible for the manual or automated transfer of the archived redo log files. To put the standby database in Managed Recovery mode, perform the following steps:

1. Start the standby database in NOMOUNT mode as illustrated by the following code:

```
SQL> startup nomount pfile=initSTANDBY.ora
```

2. Mount the standby database as illustrated by the following code:

```
SQL> alter database mount standby database;
```

3. Place the standby database in Managed Recovery mode as illustrated by the following code:

```
SQL> recover managed standby database timeout 60;
```

The **TIMEOUT** option of the **RECOVER** command enables you to specify a timeout interval in minutes. The timeout interval is the amount of time that the recovery process waits until Oracle writes the requested archived redo log files to the designated location before applying the archived redo log files.

Read-Only Mode

Read-Only mode enables users to query an open database without making any modifications. This can reduce resource consumption on the primary database by allowing the standby database to serve as a reporting database. When the standby database is placed in Read-Only mode to support queries, it is unavailable for managed recovery, and its role as a disaster recovery database will be limited.

To place the standby database in Read-Only mode when the database is in Manual Recovery mode, perform the following steps:

1. Cancel the recovery as illustrated by the following code:

```
SQL> recover cancel
```

2. Open the database in Read-Only mode as illustrated by the following code:

```
SQL> alter database open read only;
```

To place the standby database in Read-Only mode when the database is in Managed Recovery mode, perform the following steps:

1. Cancel the recovery as illustrated by the following code:

```
SQL> recover managed standby database cancel;
```

2. Open the database in Read-Only mode as illustrated by the following code:

```
SQL> alter database open read only;
```

To change the standby database from Read-Only mode to Manual Recovery mode, perform the following steps:

1. Make sure all active user sessions are terminated.

2. Issue the **RECOVER STANDBY DATABASE** command to enable Manual Recovery mode as illustrated by the following code:

```
SQL> recover standby database;
```

To change the standby database from Read-Only mode to Managed Recovery mode, perform the following steps:

1. Make sure all active user sessions are terminated.

2. Issue the **RECOVER MANAGED STANDBY DATABASE** command to enable Manual Recovery mode as illustrated by the following code:

```
SQL> recover managed standby database;
```

Propagating Structural Changes of the Primary Database

When the physical structure of the primary database is altered, the standby database's control file will need to be updated to maintain synchronization. The following database operations in the primary database will cause the physical structure to change:

➤ Adding new data files

➤ Altering redo log files

➤ Altering the control file

Adding New Data Files

When a data file has been added to the primary database, the same data file needs to be added to the standby database. To add a data file to the standby database, perform the following steps:

1. Copy the data file from the primary database to the standby database.

2. Add the data file to the standby database as illustrated by the following code:

```
SQL> alter database create datafile
SQL> '/oradata/MYSID/standby/app10.dbf' as
SQL> '/oradata/MYSID/standby/app10.dbf';
```

3. Recreate the control file for the standby database.

Altering the Redo Log Files

Modifying the online redo log file groups, such as adding or dropping groups, will require no changes to be made on the standby database. However, clearing log files on the primary database using the ALTER DATABASE CLEAR UNARCHIVED LOGFILE command or using the RESETLOGS option upon opening the database or backing up the control file invalidates the standby database.

Altering the Control File

When the control file on the primary database has been changed, the standby database control file will need to be refreshed. For example, a CREATE CONTROLFILE command is used to increase the maximum number of data files that can be associated with the primary database. To refresh the control file at the standby database, perform the following procedure:

1. Create the standby database control file at the primary database location by issuing the following command:

```
SQL> alter database create standby controlfile
  2> as 'my_standby_control.ctl';
```

2. Archive the current online redo log files of the primary database as illustrated by the following code:

```
SQL> alter system archive log current;
```

3. Stop the recovery process at the standby database by entering CANCEL at the Specify Log prompt.

4. Transfer the standby control file, archived redo log files, and a copy of any data files to the standby database location.

5. Mount the standby database as illustrated by the following code:

```
SQL> alter database mount standby database;
```

6. Restart the recovery process on the standby database as illustrated by the following code:

```
SQL> recover standby database;
```

Handling Nologging Operations of the Primary Database

Nologging or unrecoverable operations on the primary database are not recorded in the redo log files. Therefore, the recovery process on the standby database has no information to apply. To record these changes in the standby database, you need to perform the following procedure:

1. Take an online or offline copy of all the data files associated with the tablespace affected by the Nologging or unrecoverable operation at the primary database.

2. Take the affected data files offline at the standby database, and drop the associated tablespace.

3. Transfer the affected data files and the current archived redo log files from the primary database to the standby database.

4. Perform recovery at the standby database.

Practice Questions

Question 1

What is the implication when a data load has been performed in the primary database using the Nologging option?

○ a. The data cannot be recovered from the redo log files, so the standby database will be invalidated.

○ b. Nologging operations have no effect on the standby database.

○ c. The data cannot be recovered from the redo log files. However, all DML operations will be automatically transferred if the standby database is operating in Managed Recovery mode.

○ d. The control file of the standby database needs to be recreated using the **STANDBY_NOLOGGING** option set to true.

The correct answer is a. Data loads in the primary database using the Nologging option cannot be recovered from the redo log files. The standby database must receive the affected data files and the current archived redo log files and initiate recovery operations. Answer b is incorrect because Nologging operations on the primary database do affect the standby database. Answer c is incorrect because DML actions for the Nologging operations are not recorded in the redo log files, so they will not be recorded in the standby database regardless of the Recovery mode. Answer d is incorrect because it is an invalid option specification.

Question 2

A new data file has been added in the primary database. Which initialization parameter will convert the name of the added data file for the standby database?

- ○ a. **DB_STANDBY_FILE_NAME_CONVERT**
- ○ b. **DB_FILE_NAME_CONVERT**
- ○ c. **DB_FILES**
- ○ d. **DB_DATA_FILES**

The correct answer is b. The **DB_FILE_NAME_CONVERT** initialization parameter converts the name of the added data file so that the recovery process can open and write to it. Answer a is incorrect because it is an invalid initialization parameter specification. Answer c is incorrect because **DB_FILES** specifies the total number of files associated with a particular instance of a database. Answer d is incorrect because it is an invalid initialization parameter specification.

Question 3

After you create a standby database, in which mode does this new database operate? [Choose two]

- ❏ a. Transfer
- ❏ b. Closed
- ❏ c. NOMOUNT
- ❏ d. Recovery
- ❏ e. Read-Only

The correct answers are d and e. The standby database is normally continually kept mounted and in Recovery mode. Answer a is incorrect because it is an invalid mode. Answer b is incorrect because the standby database is normally in Recovery mode. Answer c is incorrect because the standby database is always mounted.

Question 4

> What command must be issued when your primary database is down and you need to use the standby database?
>
> ○ a. **SQL> startup standby database recover;**
>
> ○ b. **SQL> startup standby database activate;**
>
> ○ c. **SQL> alter database activate standby database;**
>
> ○ d. **SQL> activate standby database;**

The correct answer is c. The **ALTER DATABASE ACTIVATE STANDBY DATABASE** command is used to activate the standby database. This command resets the standby bit in the control files and places the database in NOMOUNT mode. Answers a, b, and d are incorrect because they are invalid command specifications.

Question 5

> You decided to create a standby database for your 24x7 primary database. What command do you need to issue to create the control file of the standby database?
>
> ○ a. **COPY CONTROLFILE <*filename*> AS STANDBY <*filename*>;**
>
> ○ b. **CREATE STANDBY CONTROLFILE AS <*filename*>;**
>
> ○ c. **MOVE CONTROLFILE TO STANDBY DATABASE;**
>
> ○ d. **ALTER DATABASE CREATE STANDBY CONTROLFILE AS <*filename*>;**

The correct answer is d. The **ALTER DATABASE CREATE STANDBY CONTROLFILE AS** command creates the standby control file. This file is then copied to the applicable location specified by the **CONTROL_FILES** parameter of the standby database. Answers a, b, and c are incorrect because they are invalid command specifications.

Question 6

> You just cleared the online redo log files of the primary database. What is the implication of this action on the standby database?
>
> ○ a. The standby database is automatically updated.
>
> ○ b. The standby database is activated.
>
> ○ c. The standby database is invalidated.
>
> ○ d. The standby database is not affected.

The correct answer is c. Clearing the online redo log files of the primary database invalidates the standby database. Answers a and b are incorrect because these actions don't take place. Answer d is incorrect because the standby database is impacted by this action.

Question 7

> What is the main justification for creating a standby database?
>
> ○ a. To provide another database for users to access
>
> ○ b. To protect against instance failure
>
> ○ c. To protect against hardware failure
>
> ○ d. To provide an alternate testing environment

The correct answer is c. The standby database feature was designed to protect against hardware failure. The standby database typically resides on another machine. Answer a is incorrect because a standby database is not accessible until activation. Answer b is incorrect because instance failure recovery is performed by Oracle automatically and doesn't require a standby database. Answer d is incorrect because standby databases are typically used for disaster recovery purposes and not for testing purposes.

Question 8

Which command will enable you to automatically apply available archived redo log files from the primary database to the standby database?

○ a. **ALTER DATABASE ACTIVATE STANDBY MODE=RESYNC;**

○ b. **STARTUP NOMOUNT MODE=RESYNC_STANDBY;**

○ c. **ALTER DATABASE STANDBY AUTO RESYNC;**

○ d. **RECOVER MANAGED STANDBY DATABASE;**

The correct answer is d. The standby database will automatically apply the available archived redo log files from the primary database if it is put into Managed Recovery mode. Answers a, b, and c are incorrect because they are invalid command specifications.

Question 9

You added a log file group in the primary database. What effect does this action have on the standby database?

○ a. The standby database is automatically updated.

○ b. The standby database is not affected.

○ c. The standby database is activated.

○ d. The standby database is invalidated.

The correct answer is b. Adding or dropping redo log files of the primary database does not impact the standby database because only the archived redo log files are used to synchronize the standby database with the primary database. Answers a, c, and d are incorrect because these actions don't occur.

Need to Know More?

 Loney, Kevin and Marlene Theriault. *Oracle8i DBA Handbook*. Oracle Press, Berkeley, CA, 1999. ISBN 0-07212-188-2. This comprehensive guide for DBAs includes general backup and recovery concepts. Chapter 2 provides an overview of standby databases.

 Velpuri, Rama. *Oracle8i Backup and Recovery Handbook*. Oracle Press, Berkeley, CA, 2000. ISBN 0-072-12717-1. This book provides information on how to maximize uptime and recover data without compromising mission-critical systems. Actual corporate scenarios and case studies are included. Chapter 6 covers standby databases.

 http://technet.oracle.com. This site provides the best information on Oracle's products and technologies. You can also purchase the following manuals online:

Anderson, Rick et al. *Standby Database Concepts and Administration Release 2*. Oracle Corporation, Redwood City, CA, 1999. Part No. A76995-01. This manual provides information that you will need to create, manage, and maintain a standby database.

Lorentz, Diana. *Oracle8i Reference Release 2*. Oracle Corporation, Redwood City, CA, 1999. Part No. A76961-01. This manual describes the architecture, processes, structures, and other concepts of Oracle8i and provides detailed information on static and dynamic data dictionary views.

 www.revealnet.com. This site from RevealNet provides Oracle administration reference software.

Additional Oracle Recovery Issues

. . . .

Terms you'll need to understand:

✓ Fast-Start recovery

✓ Parallel recovery

✓ **RECOVERY_PARALLELISM**

✓ **CREATE CONTROLFILE** command

✓ **RESYNC CATALOG FROM BACKUP CONTROLFILE** command

Techniques you'll need to master:

✓ Understanding methods for minimizing downtime

✓ Reconstructing lost or damaged control files

✓ Understanding read-only tablespace recovery

✓ Recovering from recovery catalog loss

In this chapter, you will learn additional methods to minimize downtime, recovery implications of read-only tablespaces, how to recover from recovery catalog loss, and how to resolve lost or damaged control files.

Methods for Minimizing Downtime

Reducing the amount of time spent in database recovery will minimize downtime and maximize data availability. The Oracle database provides several ways to enhance recovery performance, including:

➤ Using Fast-Start recovery

➤ Starting Oracle with missing data files

➤ Recovering temporary or index tablespaces

➤ Using parallel recovery

Fast-Start Recovery

Fast-Start recovery is an Oracle database feature introduced in Oracle 7.3 that allows for fast instance recovery. Instance recovery has two main phases: the roll-forward phase and the rollback phase. In the roll-forward phase, Oracle applies transaction data recorded in the online redo log files that has not been recorded in the data files, including the contents of rollback segments. In the rollback phase, instead of waiting for all transactions to be rolled back before making the database available, Oracle enables the database to be opened as soon as cache recovery is complete. This is called Fast-Start recovery. This also means that the database is available at the end of the roll-forward phase of instance recovery and that the majority of the rollback activities are deferred to the individual user processes when blocks are subsequently requested. Fast-Start recovery improves database recovery with minimal performance overhead for subsequent transactions requesting data blocks containing uncommitted data.

Starting Oracle with Missing Data Files

When you lose a data file after your database shuts down, you will not be able to start the database because of the missing file. In this situation, Oracle minimizes downtime by enabling you to bring the unaffected parts of the database up for normal use while you perform recovery operations on the tablespace containing the lost or damaged data file. Follow these steps to start an ARCHIVELOG database that has a missing data file:

1. Start the instance, and then mount, but do not open, the database, as illustrated by the following code sample:

```
SVRMGR> STARTUP MOUNT
```

2. Take the missing data file offline using the **ALTER DATABASE DATAFILE** *<filename>* **OFFLINE** command. For an ARCHIVELOG mode database, you use the **ALTER DATABASE DATAFILE** *<filename>* **OFFLINE IMMEDIATE** command, as shown here:

```
SVRMGR> ALTER DATABASE DATAFILE '/u1/oradata/app01.ora'
OFFLINE immediate;
```

3. Open the database so that users can access the unaffected parts of the database as illustrated by the following code:

```
SVRMGR> ALTER DATABASE OPEN;
```

4. Restore the lost data file from a valid backup.

5. Perform either tablespace or data file recovery. Because the **APP01_DATA** tablespace contains a single data file, which has been lost, I'll use the **RECOVER TABLESPACE** command as illustrated by the following code:

```
SVRMGR> RECOVER TABLESPACE APP01_DATA;
```

6. Bring the tablespace back online with the **ALTER TABLESPACE** *<tablespace_name>* **ONLINE** command as illustrated by the following code:

```
SVRMGR> ALTER TABLESPACE APP01_DATA ONLINE;
```

The recovery operation for a missing data file will recover through the current online redo log files so that the log sequence number in the headers of the recovered files will synchronize with the rest of the database. This also ensures that no committed transactions are lost.

Recovering Temporary or Index Tablespaces

When a loss of the temporary or index tablespaces has occurred, database administrators (DBAs) typically recreate the tablespace instead of restoring the data files associated with the damaged tablespace and then recovering the temporary or index tablespace. The recovery steps for a temporary and an index tablespace are as follows:

1. Start the instance, if necessary.

2. Shut down the instance if startup failed.

3. Mount the database.

4. Issue a query against the **V$RECOVER_FILE** and the **V$DATAFILE** views to get the file names associated with the file numbers.

5. Take the file offline, and drop it.

6. Open the database.

7. Drop the temporary tablespace.

8. Create the temporary tablespace by using the same file name as in Step 4.

9. To drop the index tablespace, the primary key constraints need to be disabled before issuing the **DROP TABLSPACE CASCADE CONSTRAINTS** command.

10. Drop the index tablespace.

11. Create the index tablespace.

12. Reenable the applicable primary key and foreign key constraints.

13. Take a full backup, if necessary.

Parallel Recovery

Oracle's parallel recovery feature enables you to use several processes to apply changes from the redo log files. You can run a recovery in parallel to take advantage of available machine processing power and database resources so that the database recovery is completed faster and downtime is minimized. Parallel recovery is most beneficial when the data files being recovered reside on different disks. A typical parallel recovery involves a master process (recovery session) that reads and dispatches redo entries from the redo log files to the child processes (recovery processes). The child processes are responsible for applying the changes from the redo entries to the data files.

You can accomplish parallel recovery by performing either of the following activities:

➤ Setting initialization parameters for parallel recovery

➤ Issuing the **RECOVER** command with the appropriate options

Setting Initialization Parameters for Parallel Recovery

The **RECOVERY_PARALLELISM** initialization parameter specifies the default number of recovery processes per session. The number of recovery processes must not be greater than the value of the **PARALLEL_MAX_SERVERS** initialization parameter. This parameter is typically derived by multiplying one or two processes by the number of disks containing data files. This parameter value determines the degree of parallelism when the **PARALLEL** option is not specified with the **RECOVER** command.

You will need to be familiar with the parallel recovery feature and the associated initialization parameters.

Issuing the **RECOVER** Command with the Appropriate Options

You can use the **RECOVER** command in Server Manager to specify the number of recovery processes for performing media recovery. The **RECOVER** command syntax pertaining to parallel recovery from Server Manager is as follows:

```
SVRMGR> RECOVER OBJECT_LIST [ NOPARALLEL|PARALLEL (DEGREE n)];
```

Refer to Table 15.1 for the **RECOVER** command elements and corresponding actions.

The **NOPARALLEL** keyword and the specification of **PARALLEL (DE-GREE 1 INSTANCE 1)** have the same effect.

Multiple Oracle Enterprise Manager (OEM) sessions can be manually spawned so that multiple **RECOVER DATAFILE** commands can operate on a different set of data files at the same time. To enable automatic parallel recovery, you can use Oracle Recovery Manager's (RMAN's) **RESTORE** and **RECOVER**

Table 15.1	**RECOVER command elements and the corresponding actions.**
ELEMENT	**ACTION**
OBJECT_LIST	Specifies that parallel operations will be performed at the database, tablespace, or data file levels.
PARALLEL	Specifies parallel recovery is desired.
DEGREE	Used in conjunction with the **PARALLEL** element to specify the number of recovery processes used to apply redo entries to the data files. **DEGREE DEFAULT** tells Oracle to use two times the number of data files being recovered as the desired number of recovery processes.
NOPARALLEL	Specifies serial recovery.

commands. In this case, Oracle uses a single process to read the log files and dispatches redo entries to multiple recovery processes, which apply the redo entries to the data files. With RMAN, you only need one session to perform recovery because RMAN automatically starts the recovery processes.

Reconstructing Lost or Damaged Control Files

Several situations require you to reconstruct or replace a lost or damaged control file for your database, including:

➤ Loss of all control files for your database due to media failure

➤ The need to change the name of the database

➤ The need to change option settings that are fixed at the time that the control file was created (**MAXLOGFILES, MAXDATAFILES, MAXLOGMEMBERS,** and others)

You can recover from lost or damaged Oracle control files in the following ways:

➤ Use the multiplexed copy of your control file. This means that you didn't lose all of your control files. To recover, just shut down the database using the **NORMAL** or **IMMEDIATE** option, copy your control file, and start the database again.

➤ Use the **CREATE CONTROLFILE** command to create a new file. You will need to know all the files for your database. The **ALTER DATABASE BACKUP CONTROLFILE TO TRACE** command can be run periodically to provide a current listing of files for your database.

➤ When all control files are lost, you can recover by using the backup binary copy of your control file.

Oracle recommends that you mirror your control files to minimize total control file loss.

When the "ORA-01207: file is more recent than control file—old control file" error message is encountered during a recovery operation, it indicates that you need to recover your database using a backup control file. To recover from this situation, follow these steps:

1. Copy the backup control file that was created using the **ALTER DATA-BASE BACKUP CONTROLFILE** command to the location of the lost control file.

2. Perform database recovery using the backup control file, as shown here:

```
SVRMGR> RECOVER DATABASE USING BACKUP CONTROLFILE;
```

3. Open the database with the **RESETLOGS** option, as illustrated by the following code:

```
SVRMGR> ALTER DATABASE OPEN RESETLOGS;
```

Read-Only Tablespace Recovery Issues

A *read-only tablespace* is a tablespace that has its status set to prevent any subsequent updates until the status is reset. The tablespace status is changed by issuing the Structured Query Language (SQL) **ALTER TABLESPACE** *<tablespace_name>* **READ ONLY** command. Typically, a tablespace is put into Read-Only mode to minimize the frequency of backups for the data. A read-only tablespace typically contains static data that infrequently changes, such as lookup tables. The following are types of recovery scenarios associated with read-only tablespaces:

➤ You are performing a tablespace recovery for a read-only tablespace, TS1. The most recent backup contains the data file for the TS1 tablespace when it was read-only. To recover TS1, you need to restore TS1 from the most recent backup and bypass applying redo entries.

➤ You are performing a tablespace recovery for a writable tablespace, TS2. The most recent backup contains the data file for the TS2 tablespace when it was read-only. To recover TS2, you need to restore TS2 from the most recent backup and apply redo entries from the point in time when the TS2 tablespace was set to writable.

➤ You are performing a tablespace recovery for a read-only tablespace, TS3. The most recent backup contains the data file for the TS3 tablespace when it was writable. Because you didn't back up TS3 after setting it to read-only, you need to restore TS3 from the most recent backup and recover up to the point in time when the tablespace was set to read-only.

Things to Consider When Working with Read-Only Tablespaces

You should consider the following issues when working with read-only tablespaces:

➤ In the event that you cannot restore your read-only tablespace data files to the proper location, perhaps because a failed disk cannot be replaced immediately, you can use the **ALTER DATABASE RENAME FILE** command to specify a new location.

➤ When recovering a read-only tablespace with a backup control file, follow the same procedures that you would for normal offline tablespaces, with one exception. You need to bring the tablespace online after the database is open.

➤ When you recreate a control file with the **CREATE CONTROLFILE** command and your database contains read-only tablespaces, you need to follow special procedures. The trace script file produced by the **ALTER DATABASE BACKUP CONTROLFILE TO TRACE** command contains the special handling procedures. The following code snippet is an excerpt from a sample trace script file generated from a database that contains a read-only tablespace:

```
...
# Recovery is required if any of the datafiles are restored
# backups, or if the last shutdown was not normal or immediate.

RECOVER DATABASE
# The database can now be opened normally.
ALTER DATABASE OPEN;
# The backup control file does not list read-only and normal
# offline tablespaces so that
# Oracle can avoid performing recovery on them. Oracle checks
# the data dictionary and finds information on these absent
# files and marks them 'MISSINGxxxx'. It then renames
# the missing files to acknowledge them without having to
#
recover them.
ALTER DATABASE RENAME FILE 'MISSING0003'
    TO 'D:\ORANT\DATABASE\READONLY.ORA';
# Online the files in read-only tablespaces.
ALTER TABLESPACE "READONLY_DATA" ONLINE;
```

Recovering from Recovery Catalog Loss

The recovery catalog is an important feature in Oracle8i database backup and recovery. The recovery catalog database is no different than any other Oracle database. You should include the recovery catalog database in your regular backup schedule. In the event that you cannot recover the recovery catalog using normal recovery mechanisms, you can choose one of the following options to rebuild the recovery catalog partially:

➤ Use the **CATALOG** command in RMAN to catalog all the available data file backups, archived redo logs, and the backup control files.

➤ Use the **RESYNC CATALOG FROM BACKUP CONTROLFILE** command to repopulate the recovery catalog with information extracted from a backup control file. The **RESYNC CATALOG FROM BACKUP CONTROLFILE** command also enables you to re-create information about backup sets and/or backup pieces.

RMAN does not verify that the files it finds listed in the backup control file actually exist. After resynchronization, you may have recovery catalog records for items that don't exist. To remove these nonexistent items, use the **CHANGE...UNCATALOG** commands.

Practice Questions

Question 1

> The data file for a read-only tablespace, TS1, is damaged. The most recent backup was taken when tablespace TS1 was read-only. What action do you need to perform to recover tablespace TS1?
>
> O a. No recovery action is needed.
>
> O b. Put tablespace TS1 in Read-Write mode, and restore from the most recent backup.
>
> O c. Restore from the most recent backup.
>
> O d. Restore from the most recent backup, and apply redo entries from the redo log files.

The correct answer is c. You only need to restore from the most recent backup because no changes were made. Answer a is incorrect because you need to restore from the most recent backup. Answer b is incorrect because you don't need to set tablespace TS1 to Read-Write mode. Answer d is incorrect; you don't need to apply redo entries from the redo log files because no changes were made.

Question 2

> Which of the following actions can be used to open an ARCHIVELOG mode database with a missing data file?
>
> O a. Mount the database, take all tablespaces offline, and open the database.
>
> O b. Restore the data file, and open the database.
>
> O c. Mount the database, take the tablespace with the missing data file offline, and open the database.
>
> O d. Restore all data files using OS mechanisms, open the database, and perform database recovery.

The correct answer is c. You need to perform the following actions to recover from a lost data file while the unaffected part of the database is available for normal use: mount the database, take the tablespace with the missing data file offline, open the database, restore the data file from the most recent backup, recover thc data file, and bring the tablespace online. Answers a, b, and d are incorrect because they don't perform the prescribed recovery actions for starting Oracle with a missing data file.

Question 3

If you tried to open the database and Oracle displayed the following sample error message, what action would you need to take to resolve the error?

```
SVRMGR> ALTER DATABASE OPEN;
ORA-00283:  Recovery session canceled due to errors
ORA-01122:  database file 2 failed verification
            check
ORA-01110:  data file 2: '/u1/oradata/app02/
            app02.ora'
ORA-01207:  file is more recent than control file -
            old control file
```

○ a. You need to restore a backup data file.

○ b. You need to recover a data file.

○ c. You need to restore a backup control file.

○ d. You need to recover the control file.

The correct answer is c. This error is generated because you restored a data file and tried to open the database with the current control file. The database will not open because the files are out of sync. To resolve this error, you need to restore the backup control file associated with the backup data file. Answers a, b, and d are incorrect because these actions don't resolve the given error.

Question 4

> When all control files and corresponding mirrors are lost, how would you re-create a control file?
>
> ○ a. You can only restore from a backup control file because a control file cannot be recreated.
>
> ○ b. Use the **ALTER DATABASE BACKUP CONTROLFILE** command.
>
> ○ c. Use the **CREATE CONTROLFILE** command.
>
> ○ d. Use the **RECOVER DATABASE USING BACKUP CONTROLFILE** command, and open the database with the **RESETLOGS** option.

The correct answer is c. You need to use the **CREATE CONTROLFILE** command to create a new control file when all control files are lost. Answer a is incorrect because a control file can be recreated. Answer b is incorrect because the **ALTER DATABASE BACKUP CONTROLFILE** command creates a backup control file. Answer d is incorrect because the **RECOVER DATABASE USING BACKUP CONTROLFILE** command performs recovery using a backup control file.

Question 5

> Your ARCHIVELOG database has grown by 50 percent within the last month. What can you do to minimize recovery time in the event of a media failure?
>
> ○ a. Perform recovery only on weekends.
>
> ○ b. Recover the damaged files only from the most recent backup.
>
> ○ c. Perform recovery after hours.
>
> ○ d. Recover the database using parallel recovery operations.
>
> ○ e. Recover all the data files from the most recent backup, and perform point-in-time recovery.

The correct answer is d. Parallel recovery helps to reduce recovery time in the event of a media failure. Answers a and c are incorrect because recovery time is not reduced when serial recovery operations are deferred to after hours and weekends. Answer b is incorrect because this action is a serial operation and a complete recovery requires applying redo information generated since the most recent backup. Answer e is incorrect because performing point-in-time recovery is a serial operation and requires the application of some of the redo information generated since the most recent backup.

Question 6

What information is needed to create a new control file for an existing database?

- ○ a. The database name and the names and locations of data files and redo log files
- ○ b. Only the database name
- ○ c. Only the names of the data files
- ○ d. Only the location of the parameter file

The correct answer is a. When using the **CREATE CONTROLFILE** command to create a new control file, you need to know the names and locations of all the database files. Answers b and c are incorrect because they are subsets of the information needed. Answer d is incorrect because the control file does not record the location of the parameter file.

Question 7

When performing parallel recovery, how many processes per disk drive are typically allocated?

- ○ a. 5
- ○ b. 3
- ○ c. 1 or 2
- ○ d. 4
- ○ e. 6

The correct answer is c. To minimize input/output (I/O) contention during parallel recovery operations, DBAs typically allocate one or two processes per disk drive. Answers a, b, d, and e are incorrect because they will incur higher I/O overhead with marginal performance benefit.

Question 8

> How can you change the **MAXLOGMEMBERS** parameter?
>
> ○ a. Use the **ALTER DATABASE** command.
>
> ○ b. Use the **ALTER SYSTEM** command.
>
> ○ c. Use the **ALTER SESSION** command.
>
> ○ d. Recreate the control file using the **CREATE CONTROLFILE** command.
>
> ○ e. Change the initSID.ora parameter file, and restart the instance.

The correct answer is d. You must re-create the control file to change the **MAXLOGMEMBERS** parameter. Answers a, b, c, and e are incorrect because they don't support changing the **MAXLOGMEMBERS** parameter.

Question 9

> The data file for a read-only tablespace, TS1, is damaged. The most recent backup was taken when tablespace TS1 was read-write. What action do you need to perform to recover tablespace TS1?
>
> ○ a. Restore from the most recent backup, and recover up until the time when the tablespace was set to read-only.
>
> ○ b. Recover to the point in time when the tablespace became read-write.
>
> ○ c. Recovery action cannot be performed for this tablespace.
>
> ○ d. Restore from the most recent backup, and set the tablespace to read-only.

The correct answer is a. When a tablespace changes from read-write to read-only, you need to restore from the most recent backup and recover up until the time when the tablespace was set to read-only. Answer b is incorrect because you need to recover up to the point when the tablespace was set to read-only. Answer c is incorrect because you can restore and recover this tablespace. Answer d is incorrect because you should not set the tablespace to read-only.

Need to Know More?

 Velpuri, Rama. *Oracle8i Backup and Recovery Handbook*. Oracle Press, Berkeley, CA, 2000. ISBN 0-072-12717-1. Chapter 6 describes recovery principles such as creating a control file and recovering tablespace and data files. Chapter 10 provides case studies, such as recovery with a backup control file and read-only tablespace recovery.

 http://technet.oracle.com. This site provides the best information on Oracle's products and technologies. You can purchase the following manuals online:

Brenman, Dreskin, Herbert, et al. *Oracle8i Error Messages Release 2*. Oracle Corporation, Redwood City, CA, 1999. Part No. A76999-01. This manual describes the error messages that may appear while using Oracle products.

Dialeris, Connie. *Oracle8i Backup and Recovery Guide Release 2*. Oracle Corporation, Redwood City, CA, 1999. Part No. A76993-01. This manual provides guidance on data protection techniques and offers strategies for data storage, backup, and restore for Oracle 8i. Chapter 6 discusses media recovery scenarios, such as recovering after control file loss and data file loss.

Leverenz, Lefty. *Oracle8i Concepts Release 2*. Oracle Corporation, Redwood City, CA, 1999. Part No. A76965-01. This manual describes all features of the Oracle8i server running on all operating systems.

Lorentz, Diana. *Oracle8i Reference Release 2*. Oracle Corporation, Redwood City, CA, 1999. Part No. A76961-01. This manual describes the architecture, processes, structures, and other concepts of Oracle8i and provides detailed information on static and dynamic data dictionary views.

 www.revealnet.com. This site from RevealNet provides Oracle administration reference software.

Sample Test

Question 1

Which of the following are roles of the database administrator (DBA) in the development and execution of a backup and recovery strategy? [Choose three]

- ❑ a. To implement the strategy
- ❑ b. To provide recommendations on how to minimize data loss
- ❑ c. To provide recommendations on how to minimize downtime
- ❑ d. To provide the necessary corporate resources and support for implementation

Question 2

Which of the following initSID.ora parameters specifies the number of OS blocks written to the redo logs between the most recent redo entry and the checkpoint position before a checkpoint is initiated?

- ○ a. **LOG_CHECKPOINT_TIMEOUT**
- ○ b. **LOG_CHECKPOINT_INTERVAL**
- ○ c. **LOG_BUFFER**
- ○ d. **LOG_CKPT_BLOCKS**

Question 3

What Server Manager command statement will display the current database log mode?

○ a. **SELECT * FROM V$DATAFILE**

○ b. **SELECT * FROM V$LOGFILE**

○ c. **ARCHIVE LOG LIST**

○ d. **SHOW ARCHIVE LOG**

○ e. **ARCHIVE LOG ALL**

Question 4

What file(s) contain the most recent business transactions issued against the database for recovery purposes?

○ a. Control file

○ b. Data files

○ c. Online redo log files

○ d. Offline archived redo log files

Question 5

Which of the following are valid **RUN** commands? [Choose three]

❑ a. **RMAN> RUN { host "ls -l"; }**

❑ b. **RMAN> ALTER SYSTEM SWITCH LOGFILE;**

❑ c. **RMAN> RUN { sql "alter system switch logfile"; }**

❑ d. **RMAN> RUN { execute script DailyBackup; }**

❑ e. **RMAN> RUN { sql alter system switch logfile; }**

Question 6

> Which of the following functions can be accomplished using RMAN's **REPORT** command?
>
> ○ a.   Display the current physical schema of the target database.
>
> ○ b.   List the number of the copies of each backup set.
>
> ○ c.   List obsolete data files.
>
> ○ d.   List obsolete backups.

Question 7

> What type of EXPORT is appropriate when you only need database objects that have changed since the last EXPORT of any type?
>
> ○ a.   Complete
>
> ○ b.   Incremental
>
> ○ c.   Full
>
> ○ d.   Cumulative

Question 8

> When a user reboots a PC without disconnecting from the database, what kind of failure occurs?
>
> ○ a.   Statement failure
>
> ○ b.   User process failure
>
> ○ c.   Media failure
>
> ○ d.   Instance failure

Question 9

Which of the following statements are true about loading data into a table using the **NOLOGGING** option? [Choose two]

❏ a. The inserts are written in the redo log files.

❏ b. The inserted data is fully recoverable without taking a backup subsequent to the load operation.

❏ c. Processing costs are reduced because the inserts are not recorded in the redo log files.

❏ d. The amount of recorded redo will decrease.

❏ e. The amount of recorded redo will increase.

Question 10

You are the DBA for a reporting database that is updated monthly. Which backup strategy should you use?

○ a. Back up before updates are made

○ b. Back up daily

○ c. Back up weekly

○ d. Back up after updates are made

Question 11

Your production database has 15 data files spread across 3 disk drives. How many backup sets are created by the following command sequence?

```
RMAN> RUN {
2> ALLOCATE CHANNEL c1 TYPE 'SBT_TAPE';
3> BACKUP
4> (DATABASE FILESPERSET = 3);
5> RELEASE CHANNEL c1; }
```

○ a. None

○ b. One

○ c. Two

○ d. Three

○ e. Four

○ f. Five

Question 12

Which of the following statements is NOT true about the large pool?

○ a. The **LARGE_POOL_SIZE** parameter configures the size of the large pool.

○ b. The large pool increases the speed and efficiency of backup and restore operations when using RMAN.

○ c. The large pool is an area of the SGA that RMAN uses for buffering information in memory when IO slaves are needed.

○ d. The large pool is a mandatory memory area.

Question 13

Which of the following would be suitable circumstances in which to operate a database in NOARCHIVELOG mode?

○ a. Control files are multiplexed.

○ b. Redo log files are multiplexed.

○ c. The database can be shut down regularly to perform OS backups.

○ d. You can perform online backups while the database is in use.

Question 14

What is the minimum number of redo log groups you need to configure for your Oracle database?

○ a. One

○ b. Two

○ c. Three

○ d. Four

Question 15

Which of the following statements is NOT true about the recovery catalog?

○ a. The recovery catalog should be created in a database that is separate from the target database.

○ b. The recovery catalog must be used when stored scripts are required.

○ c. The recovery catalog should be used when incremental block level backups are required.

○ d. The recovery catalog should be used when historical information about backup, restore, and recovery operations needs to be retained.

○ e. The recovery catalog should reside in the same database as the target database.

Question 16

Which EXPORT mode can be used to export all objects owned by user Steve?

○ a. Full database

○ b. Tablespace

○ c. Table

○ d. User

Question 17

Which of the following initialization parameter settings will enable check summing for the online redo log files?

○ a. **DB_BLOCK_CHECKSUM=Y**

○ b. **DB_BLOCK_CHECKSUM=TRUE**

○ c. **LOG_BLOCK_CHECKSUM=Y**

○ d. **LOG_BLOCK_CHECKSUM=TRUE**

Question 18

When one of the Oracle background processes fails and the database shuts down, where are the errors recorded?

○ a. **CORE_DUMP_DEST**

○ b. **LOG_ARCHIVE_DEST**

○ c. **USER_DUMP_DEST**

○ d. **BACKGROUND_DUMP_DEST**

Question 19

Which of the following commands is used to perform an online backup of the control file?

○ a. **ALTER DATABASE BACKUP CONTROLFILE TO TRACE**

○ b. **ALTER SYSTEM BACKUP CONTROLFILE TO TRACE**

○ c. **ALTER SYSTEM BACKUP CONTROLFILE TO** *<filename>*

○ d. **ALTER DATABASE BACKUP CONTROLFILE TO** *<filename>*

○ e. **ALTER SESSION BACKUP CONTROLFILE TO** *<filename>*

Question 20

How will your backup strategy affect recoverability?

○ a. It will help you determine additional storage device needs.

○ b. It determines whether complete or incomplete recovery can be performed.

○ c. It will help you get management support.

○ d. It will not affect recoverability.

Question 21

After you placed the tablespace **LOOKUP_DATA** in Read-Only mode, you took a backup of **LOOKUP_DATA**. How often do you need to perform subsequent backups?

○ a. Each time that a data file is added to the database.

○ b. Each time that the control file is changed.

○ c. Each time that a database backup is performed.

○ d. Subsequent backups are not required.

Question 22

Which Oracle background process performs automatic instance recovery?

- ○ a. LGWR
- ○ b. DBWR
- ○ c. PMON
- ○ d. SMON
- ○ e. ARCH

Question 23

What is the maximum number of archive processes that you can configure?

- ○ a. 1
- ○ b. 5
- ○ c. 2
- ○ d. 9
- ○ e. 10

Question 24

Which of the following are NOT features of RMAN? [Choose two]

- ❏ a. It supports incremental block level backups.
- ❏ b. It is the only way to back up an Oracle database.
- ❏ c. It is compatible with all versions of Oracle.
- ❏ d. It detects corrupted blocks.
- ❏ e. It compresses unused blocks.

Question 25

Which command would you issue to register a new version of the database in the recovery catalog after performing incomplete recovery with the **RESETLOGS** option?

○ a. **RMAN> restore database;**

○ b. **RMAN> recover catalog;**

○ c. **RMAN> restore catalog;**

○ d. **RMAN> reset catalog;**

○ e. **RMAN> reset database;**

Question 26

What is the first task performed by IMPORT when importing data into your database?

○ a. Enabling database constraints

○ b. Rebuilding indexes

○ c. Importing data

○ d. Creating tables

Question 27

Which file are log switches recorded to?

○ a. alert.log

○ b. smon.trc

○ c. lgwr.trc

○ d. initSID.ora

○ e. config.ora

Question 28

The control file is lost because of media failure, and you must restore it to a new location. Which steps must you perform before opening the database? [Choose two]

❑ a. Edit the initialization parameter file with the new location.

❑ b. Use the **RENAME CONTROLFILE** command to change the control file location.

❑ c. Restore the control file to the new location.

❑ d. Use the **ALTER DATABASE RENAME CONTROL FILE** command to change the control file location.

Question 29

What types of files will RMAN back up? [Choose three]

❑ a. Archived redo log files

❑ b. Parameter files

❑ c. Password files

❑ d. Control files

❑ e. Data files

❑ f. OS files

Question 30

Why do you need to regularly test the validity of your backup and recovery strategy?

○ a. Testing helps management determine the costs associated with downtime.

○ b. Testing reduces the likelihood of media failures.

○ c. Testing helps to identify business, operational, and technical needs that may have changed.

○ d. Testing is the only way to ensure optimal database configuration.

Question 31

One of the data files of tablespace **APP2_DATA** has been damaged because of media failure. What recovery should you perform?

○ a. Tablespace recovery

○ b. Table recovery

○ c. Database recovery

○ d. Import recovery

○ e. Data file recovery

Question 32

Which of the following database events will trigger a checkpoint?

○ a. When a user commits a transaction

○ b. When the **SHUTDOWN ABORT** command is issued by the DBA

○ c. When the DBA adds a new data file

○ d. When a log switch occurs

Question 33

What command can you issue to manually archive the oldest online redo log file group that has not yet been archived?

○ a. **ALTER SYSTEM ARCHIVE LOG SEQUENCE**

○ b. **ALTER SYSTEM ARCHIVE LOG LOGFILE**

○ c. **ALTER SYSTEM ARCHIVE LOG CHANGE**

○ d. **ALTER SYSTEM ARCHIVE LOG NEXT**

Question 34

Which of the following are benefits provided by the Backup Manager?
[Choose two]

- ❑ a. It is compatible with the Enterprise Backup Utility (EBU).

- ❑ b. It is the only option to back up an Oracle database.

- ❑ c. It makes it easy to create and schedule backup jobs.

- ❑ d. It has a user-friendly GUI.

- ❑ e. It is provided as part of any client installation.

Question 35

What does the following RMAN command accomplish?

```
RMAN> CHANGE DATAFILECOPY
        '/u1/oradata/appl1data.bak' DELETE;
```

- ○ a. It marks the data file copy as unavailable.
- ○ b. It removes the data file copy from the control file and the recovery catalog.
- ○ c. It removes the data file copy from the control file, recovery catalog, and physical media.
- ○ d. It marks the data file copy as available.

Question 36

When you import data into an existing table, what parameter needs to be set
to direct IMPORT to continue processing if create errors are encountered?

- ○ a. **CONSISTENT=Y**
- ○ b. **INDEXES=Y**
- ○ c. **IGNORE=Y**
- ○ d. **LOG=Y**

Question 37

What utility enables the DBA to check for data corruption in both online and offline data files?

- ○ a. DBVERIFY
- ○ b. ANALYZE
- ○ c. EXPORT
- ○ d. TKPROF

Question 38

Which of the following **SHUTDOWN** commands should you use before taking a closed (offline) database backup? [Choose three]

- ❑ a. **SHUTDOWN NORMAL**
- ❑ b. **SHUTDOWN IMMEDIATE**
- ❑ c. **SHUTDOWN TRANSACTIONAL**
- ❑ d. **SHUTDOWN ABORT**

Question 39

What will the following command sequence accomplish?

```
RMAN> RUN {
    2> ALLOCATE CHANNEL c1 TYPE DISK;
    3> COPY LEVEL 0
    4> DATAFILE 1 TO '/u1/oradata/backup/app1.ora',
    5> DATAFILE 2 TO '/u1/oradata/backup/app2.ora';
    6> RELEASE CHANNEL c1; }
```

- ○ a. It will create an image copy backup that can be used in an incremental backup strategy.
- ○ b. It will create an image copy backup of the OS blocks since the last full backup.
- ○ c. It will create an OS file copy of two data files.
- ○ d. It will create an OS file copy of two backup sets.

Question 40

How will minimizing recovery time benefit the business?

- ○ a. It helps to prevent failures from occurring.
- ○ b. It reduces the amount of data loss.
- ○ c. It reduces the cost of downtime.
- ○ d. It reduces the need to update the backup and recovery strategy regularly.

Question 41

Your production database is running in ARCHIVELOG mode. Due to a media failure, you need to recover the database, and you have a lot of archived redo log files. What command should you issue to direct Oracle to apply the archived redo log files automatically when the recovery process is initiated?

- ○ a. **RECOVER DATAFILE**
- ○ b. **SET AUTORECOVERY ON**
- ○ c. **ALTER DATABASE CLEAR LOGFILE**
- ○ d. **ALTER SYSTEM ACTIVE LOGFILE**

Question 42

What takes place when a checkpoint occurs? [Choose two]

- ❑ a. SMON coalesces contiguous free extents into larger free chunks.
- ❑ b. DBWR writes all modified data blocks in the database buffer cache to disk.
- ❑ c. PMON frees resources held by failed user processes.
- ❑ d. LGWR writes all modified data blocks in the database buffer cache to disk.
- ❑ e. LGWR writes the redo log entries from the redo log buffer to the online redo log files.

Question 43

You need to perform an incomplete recovery because you've discovered that an archived redo log file is missing. After you've performed the incomplete recovery, which of the following statements is true?

○ a. Committed transactions will be lost prior to the point of recovery.

○ b. All uncommitted transactions prior to the point of the failure will be committed.

○ c. All transactions after the point of recovery will be lost.

○ d. Committed transactions after the point of failure will be recovered when the applicable redo log files are applied.

Question 44

What does the following command accomplish?

```
$rman target scott/pwd@PROD1 rcvcat rman/pwd
```

○ a. It connects user SCOTT to the local **PROD1** database and uses a local recovery catalog.

○ b. It connects user SCOTT to the remote **PROD1** database and uses a remote recovery catalog.

○ c. It connects user SCOTT to the remote **PROD1** database and uses a local recovery catalog.

○ d. It connects user SCOTT to the local **PROD1** database and uses a remote recovery catalog.

○ e. It connects user RMAN to the remote **PROD1** database and uses a local recovery catalog.

Question 45

A large number of data rows were accidentally deleted before month-end closing. An audit system has not been implemented that could identify the user that performed the delete operation. Which of the following Oracle utilities can help you identify the user that performed this delete operation?

- ○ a. DBMS_REPAIR
- ○ b. LogMiner
- ○ c. DBVERIFY
- ○ d. DBMS_UTILITY
- ○ e. DBMS_LOGMINER

Question 46

What EXPORT parameter should you set when exporting data while users are performing updates to the database?

- ○ a. **IGNORE=Y**
- ○ b. **CONSTRAINTS=Y**
- ○ c. **DIRECT=Y**
- ○ d. **CONSISTENT=Y**

Question 47

When a user enters bad data that violates integrity constraints into a database table, which type of failure is this?

- ○ a. Statement failure
- ○ b. User process failure
- ○ c. Instance failure
- ○ d. Media failure

Question 48

What events will occur after you issue the following command?

```
SVRMGR> ALTER TABLESPACE SALES_DATA BEGIN BACKUP;
```

- ○ a. Data file header blocks for the **SALES_DATA** tablespace will be updated.
- ○ b. An offline backup begins.
- ○ c. An online backup ends.
- ○ d. Transactions occurring within the **SALES_DATA** tablespace will not be recorded in the redo logs.
- ○ e. Data file header blocks for the **SALES_DATA** tablespace are frozen to prevent updates.

Question 49

What will the following command sequence accomplish?

```
RMAN> RUN {
   2> ALLOCATE CHANNEL c1 TYPE DISK;
   3> ALLOCATE CHANNEL c2 TYPE DISK;
   4> COPY
   5> DATAFILE 1 TO '/u1/oradata/backup/app1.ora',
   6> DATAFILE 2 TO '/u1/oradata/backup/app2.ora';
   7> }
```

- ○ a. An incremental backup will be performed.
- ○ b. Two files will be copied in parallel.
- ○ c. A level 2 backup will be performed.
- ○ d. One channel will be idle.

Question 50

> Which **V$** view is used to query for the names of all data files in the database?
>
> ○ a. **V$CONTROLFILE**
>
> ○ b. **V$DATABASE**
>
> ○ c. **V$DATAFILE**
>
> ○ d. **V$DATABASE_FILE**
>
> ○ e. **V$DATA_FILE**

Question 51

> Which of the following circumstances do not require the DBA to perform an incomplete recovery? [Choose two]
>
> ❑ a. A loss of all control files, including corresponding mirrors, occurs.
>
> ❑ b. An archived redo log file needed for complete recovery is damaged.
>
> ❑ c. A user mistakenly drops an essential application table.
>
> ❑ d. The archived redo log directory runs out of space.
>
> ❑ e. A media failure occurs in an ARCHIVELOG database, and a valid backup and all archived redo log files are available to perform recovery operations to meet the zero data loss service-level agreement.

Question 52

> By default, which archive mode is in effect for an Oracle database?
>
> ○ a. ARCHIVELOG mode with automatic archiving
>
> ○ b. NOARCHIVELOG mode
>
> ○ c. ARCHIVELOG mode with manual archiving
>
> ○ d. None of the above

Question 53

The disk in which the **RBS_TS** tablespace resides failed in a NOARCHIVELOG database. To what point in time can you recover the database?

○ a. Last redo log

○ b. Last export

○ c. Last full backup

○ d. Point of failure

Question 54

Which RMAN commands will cause an automatic resync of the recovery catalog with its target database? [Choose four]

❏ a. **BACKUP**

❏ b. **COPY**

❏ c. **RESTORE**

❏ d. **SWITCH**

❏ e. **RESET DATABASE**

Question 55

What does the following command accomplish?

```
Rman> list backupset of datafile
      '/u1/oradata/app01.ora';
```

○ a. It adds app01.ora to the current backup set.

○ b. It displays the status of the copy of app01.ora.

○ c. It displays all backup sets that contain app01.ora.

○ d. It displays all data files in the same backup set as app01.ora.

Question 56

What command is required for RMAN to read from or write to the OS?

○ a. **CHANGE**

○ b. **CATALOG**

○ c. **COPY**

○ d. **BACKUP**

○ e. **ALLOCATE CHANNEL**

Question 57

Which of the following commands can you use to create the script file for creating a new control file?

○ a. **ALTER SYSTEM**

○ b. **ALTER INSTANCE**

○ c. **ALTER DATABASE**

○ d. **ALTER SESSION**

○ e. **ALTER CONTROL FILE**

Question 58

What database components can you recover using the **RECOVER** command with the **PARALLEL** keyword? [Choose three]

❑ a. Database

❑ b. Data files

❑ c. Tablespaces

❑ d. Tables

❑ e. Control file

❑ f. Redo log file

❑ g. Rollback segments

Question 59

In an Oracle8i instance failure recovery, when are uncommitted transactions rolled back?

○ a. Before the roll forward is completed

○ b. During the roll forward process

○ c. As soon as the database starts

○ d. When the data blocks associated with the uncommitted transactions are subsequently requested

Question 60

Which option of the **RECOVER MANAGED STANDBY DATABASE** command can you specify to indicate a time interval to wait for a specified archived redo log file to be written to the standby database control file's directory?

○ a. **WAIT_TIME**

○ b. **WAIT**

○ c. **WRITE_WAIT**

○ d. **TIMEOUT**

Answer Key

1. a, b, c	21. d	41. b
2. b	22. d	42. b, e
3. c	23. e	43. c
4. c	24. b, c	44. c
5. a, c, d	25. e	45. b
6. d	26. d	46. d
7. b	27. a	47. a
8. b	28. a, c	48. e
9. c, d	29. a, d, e	49. b
10. d	30. c	50. c
11. f	31. e	51. d, e
12. d	32. d	52. b
13. c	33. d	53. c
14. b	34. c, d	54. a, b, c, d
15. e	35. c	55. c
16. d	36. c	56. e
17. d	37. a	57. c
18. d	38. a, b, c	58. a, b, c
19. d	39. a	59. d
20. b	40. c	60. d

Question 1

The correct answers are a, b, and c. In creating and executing a backup and recovery strategy, database administrators (DBAs) are responsible for providing recommendations to management on how to minimize downtime, minimize data loss, and carry out the strategy. Answer d is incorrect because providing necessary corporate resources and support for implementation is management's role.

Question 2

The correct answer is b. The **LOG_CHECKPOINT_INTERVAL** initialization parameter specifies the number of OS blocks written to the redo logs between the most recent redo entry and the checkpoint position before a checkpoint is initiated. Recovery from instance failure starts from the latest checkpoint in the current online redo log file. Answer a is incorrect because the **LOG_CHECKPOINT_TIMEOUT** initialization parameter specifies the number of seconds passed between the most recent redo entry and the checkpoint position before a new checkpoint is initiated. Answer c is incorrect because the **LOG_BUFFER** initialization parameter specifies the size of the redo log buffers in bytes. Answer d is incorrect because it is an invalid initialization parameter.

Question 3

The correct answer is c. The **ARCHIVE LOG LIST** command shows the database log mode, the archive destination, the oldest online log sequence, the next log sequence to archive, the current log sequence, and whether automatic archiving is in effect. Answers a, b, and e are incorrect because they don't provide information about the current database log mode. Answer d is incorrect because it is an invalid command specification.

Question 4

The correct answer is c. The online redo log files record the most recent business transactions issued against the database during normal use. Answer a is incorrect because the control file stores the names and the status of all the data files. Answer b is incorrect because data files contain the actual business data. Answer d is incorrect because the offline archived redo log files contain earlier database changes.

Question 5

The correct answers are a, c, and d. The **RUN** command enables you to execute OS commands, SQL statements, stored scripts, backup commands, and so on. Answers b and e are incorrect because they are invalid commands.

Question 6

The correct answer is d. The **REPORT** command can be used to list backups that are obsolete. Answers a, b, and c are incorrect because the **REPORT** command doesn't perform these functions.

Question 7

The correct answer is b. An incremental export will export only the database objects that have changed since the last export of any type. Answer a is incorrect because a complete export contains all database objects except those owned by the SYS schema. Answer c is incorrect because it is an invalid export type. Answer d is incorrect because a cumulative export contains database tables that have changed since the last cumulative or complete export.

Question 8

The correct answer is b. User process failure occurs when a user process that is connected to the Oracle instance terminates abnormally. The sample scenario is an example of an abnormal termination of a user process. Answers a, c, and d are incorrect because the sample scenario doesn't cause these errors.

Question 9

The correct answers are c and d. When loading data using the direct load operation with the **NOLOGGING** option, the inserts are not recorded in the redo log files. The data should be backed up after the load to ensure the data is fully recoverable. The direct load operation reduces processing costs because the inserts are not recorded in the redo log files. Answer a is incorrect because the inserts are not written in the redo log files for direct load operations. Answer b is incorrect because you need to take a backup after the direct load operation to ensure the data is fully recoverable. Answer e is incorrect because the amount of recorded redo decreases, not increases, for direct load operations.

Question 10

The correct answer is d. The backup schedule should match the frequency of data updates. Answer a is incorrect because for this sample scenario you should take a backup after the data has been changed. Answers b and c are incorrect because more frequent backups of static data are not necessary.

Question 11

The correct answer is f. The **FILESPERSET** option of the **BACKUP** command specifies the number of files included in each backup set. For the sample command, five backup sets with three files in each backup set will be created. Answers a, b, c, d, and e are incorrect because they don't match the five backup sets the sample command will create.

Question 12

The correct answer is d. The large pool is an optional, not mandatory, Oracle8i memory area. Answers a, b, and c are incorrect because they are true statements about the large pool.

Question 13

The correct answer is c. If you can regularly shut down a database for backups, you could consider operating the database in NOARCHIVELOG mode if any lost data can be tolerated. Answers a and b are incorrect because these files should be multiplexed independent of the Database Log mode. Answer d is incorrect because ARCHIVELOG mode enables you to perform online backups while the database is open and in use.

Question 14

The correct answer is b. The LGWR process writes redo log files in a circular fashion, so two redo log groups are required to support this operation. By default, Oracle creates two redo log groups. Answers a, b, and d are incorrect because they don't match the default number of two.

Question 15

The correct answer is e. The recovery catalog should reside in a database that is separate from the target database. Answers a, b, c, and d are incorrect because they are true statements about the recovery catalog.

Question 16

The correct answer is d. The EXPORT User mode will export all the objects in a user's schema. Users can back up their own schema. A privileged user, such as the DBA, can export all objects owned by one or more schemas. Answer a is incorrect because it will export all database objects except those owned by the SYS schema. Answer b is incorrect because it is an invalid export mode. Answer c is incorrect because it will only export specified tables owned by the user schema.

Question 17

The correct answer is d. When the **LOG_BLOCK_CHECKSUM** parameter is set to **TRUE**, check summing for the online redo log files will be enabled. Answers a and c are incorrect because they are invalid parameter specifications. Answer b is incorrect because the **DB_BLOCK_CHECKSUM** parameter applies to check summing of data files.

Question 18

The correct answer is d. When Oracle background processes encounter errors, they will write the error trace files to the location specified by the initialization parameter **BACKGROUND_DUMP_DEST**. Answers a, b, and c are incorrect because the background processes don't write error trace files to these locations.

Question 19

The correct answer is d. The **ALTER DATABASE BACKUP CONTROLFILE TO** *<filename>* command is used to take an online backup of the control file. Answer a is incorrect because it only creates a text script trace file that may subsequently be modified and executed to create the binary control file. Answers b, c, and e are incorrect because they are invalid command specifications.

Question 20

The correct answer is b. Your backup strategy determines the type of recovery that can be performed. Answers a and c are incorrect because they don't affect recoverability. Answer d is incorrect because your backup strategy does affect recoverability.

Question 21

The correct answer is d. The data in a read-only tablespace is static. You only need to back up the **LOOKUP_DATA** tablespace immediately after it becomes read-only. Answers a, b, and c are incorrect because read-only tablespaces don't need to be backed up under these circumstances.

Question 22

The correct answer is d. The SMON process performs instance recovery and free space coalescing. Answers a, b, c, and e are incorrect because these processes perform other functions.

Question 23

The correct answer is e. The maximum number of archive processes that can be configured is 10. Answers a, b, c, and d are incorrect because they are less than the maximum archive processes that can be configured.

Question 24

The correct answers are b and c. Recovery manager (RMAN) is not the only way to back up an Oracle database because you could choose to use OS mechanisms. RMAN does not support backing up pre-Oracle8 databases. Answers a, d, and e are incorrect because these are RMAN features.

Question 25

The correct answer is e. You should issue the **RESET DATABASE** command after you've performed an incomplete recovery and opened the database with the **RESETLOGS** option so that the new version of the database is registered in the recovery catalog. Answers a, b, c, and d are incorrect because they are invalid commands.

Question 26

The correct answer is d. IMPORT performs the following steps when data is imported: It (1) creates the tables, (2) builds the indexes, (3) imports the data, (4) imports the database triggers, and (5) enables the integrity constraints. Answers a, b, and c are incorrect because they are not the first tasks performed by IM-PORT when importing data into your database.

Question 27

The correct answer is a. Log switches are recorded in the alert.log file. Answers b, c, d, and e are incorrect because log switches are not recorded in these files.

Question 28

The correct answers are a and c. When your control file is lost due to a media failure, you must restore the control file to the new location and edit the initialization parameter with the new location before opening the database. Answers b and d are incorrect because they are invalid commands.

Question 29

The correct answers are a, d, and e. RMAN will back up data files, control files, and archived redo log files. It will create an image copy or a backup set of either data files or archived redo log files. Answers b, c, and f are incorrect because RMAN will not back up these file types.

Question 30

The correct answer is c. Testing helps to assess the effectiveness of the backup and recovery strategy and to identify any new or changed requirements. Answer a is incorrect because the costs associated with downtime depend on business, operational, and technical factors and not testing. Answer b is incorrect because testing does not affect the likelihood of media failures. Answer d is incorrect because testing is not the only way to ensure optimal database configuration.

Question 31

The correct answer is e. Because only one data file in a tablespace is damaged, you only need to recover the one damaged file. Answers a, b, c, and d are incorrect because these types of recovery are not appropriate for the sample scenario.

Question 32

The correct answer is d. Checkpoints occur during log switches. Answers a, b, and c are incorrect because they don't trigger a checkpoint.

Question 33

The correct answer is d. The **NEXT** option of the **ALTER SYSTEM ARCHIVE LOG** command archives the oldest redo log file group that has not yet been archived. Answer a is incorrect because the **SEQUENCE** option pertains to Oracle Parallel Server and specifies the thread associated with the redo log group to be archived. Answer b is incorrect because the **LOGFILE** option specifies the file name of the redo log group member to be archived. Answer c is incorrect because the **CHANGE** option specifies archiving based on the System Change Number (SCN).

Question 34

The correct answers are c and d. The Backup Manager is a GUI tool within the Oracle Enterprise Manager (OEM) administrative toolset that can be used to create and schedule backup jobs easily. Answer a is incorrect because the Backup Manager is not compatible with the Enterprise Backup Utility (EBU). Answer b is incorrect because using the Backup Manager is not the only way to back up an Oracle database. Answer e is incorrect because the Backup Manager is not provided as part of any client installation.

Question 35

The correct answer is c. The **CHANGE DATAFILECOPY DELETE** command removes specified files from the control file, recovery catalog, and from the physical media. Answers a and d are incorrect because the **CHANGE... AVAILABLE** and **CHANGE...UNAVAILABLE** commands mark files as available or unavailable. Answer b is incorrect because the removal of the data file copy from the physical media has been omitted.

Question 36

The correct answer is c. The **IGNORE** parameter will ignore any create errors encountered during the IMPORT process. Answers a and b are incorrect because these parameters serve other purposes. Answer d is incorrect because it is an invalid parameter specification.

Question 37

The correct answer is a. The DBVERIFY utility is used to verify the structural integrity of data blocks in the online and offline data files. Answer b is incorrect because ANALYZE computes statistics for tables and indexes. Answer c is incorrect because EXPORT is used to perform logical backups of the database. Answer d is incorrect because TKPROF is used for SQL tuning and optimization.

Question 38

The correct answers are a, b, and c. A closed (offline) database backup is an OS backup of the database files that is made after the database has been shut down cleanly using either **SHUTDOWN NORMAL, SHUTDOWN IMMEDIATE**, or **SHUTDOWN TRANSACTIONAL**. Answer d is incorrect because closed database backups performed after a **SHUTDOWN ABORT** are not reliable.

Question 39

The correct answer is a. The sample command sequence allocates the **c1** channel of type **DISK** and copies two data files at level 0. The level 0 copies can be used in an incremental backup strategy. Answer b is incorrect because the sample command sequence doesn't perform this function. Answers c and d are incorrect because the sample command sequence doesn't create OS file copies.

Question 40

The correct answer is c. A reduction in recovery time will shorten total downtime and will reduce the costs associated with downtime. Answer a is incorrect because appropriate database configuration prevents failures from occurring. Answer b is incorrect because the amount of data loss depends on the availability of valid backups. Answer d is incorrect because minimizing recovery time does not affect the frequency of updates to the backup and recovery strategy.

Question 41

The correct answer is b. Automatic recovery can be enabled using the **SET AUTORECOVERY ON** command. The redo log files must be in the location specified by the **LOG_ARCHIVE_DEST** initialization parameter. You will be prompted for the redo log file names if automatic recovery is not enabled. Answer a is incorrect because automatic recovery has not been specified using the

AUTOMATIC keyword of the **RECOVER DATAFILE** command. Answer c is incorrect because it performs another function. Answer d is incorrect because it is an invalid command specification.

Question 42

The correct answers are b and e. During a checkpoint event, the DBWR process writes all modified data blocks in the database buffer cache of the System Global Area (SGA) to the database files, and the LGWR process writes all redo log entries in the log buffer to disk. Answers a and c are incorrect because they are triggered independent of a checkpoint. Answer d is incorrect because the LGWR process writes the redo log entries from the redo log buffer to the online redo log files.

Question 43

The correct answer is c. When you perform an incomplete recovery for an ARCHIVELOG database, all the changes made to the data after the point of failure are lost. To recover the lost data, users must manually reenter the data. Answer a is incorrect because no committed transactions are lost prior to the point of recovery. Answer b is incorrect because uncommitted transactions prior to the point of failure will not be committed. Answer d is incorrect because the archived redo log files after the point of failure are not usable and therefore the committed transactions after the point of failure will be lost.

Question 44

The correct answer is c. The sample command connects user SCOTT to the remote **PROD1** database and uses a local recovery catalog. Answers a and d are incorrect because the sample command connects user SCOTT to the remote, not local, **PROD1** database. Answer b is incorrect because the sample command uses a local, not remote, recovery catalog. Answer e is incorrect because the sample command connects user SCOTT, not user RMAN, to the remote **PROD1** database.

Question 45

The correct answer is b. Using the LogMiner utility, you can query the **USERNAME** column of the **V$LOGMNR_CONTENTS** view to identify the user that performed the delete operation. Answer a is incorrect because

DBMS_REPAIR is used to identify logical block corruption in tables, partitions, or indexes. Answer c is incorrect because the DBVERIFY utility is used to verify the validity of a backup and to identify data corruptions in data files. Answer d is incorrect because DBMS_UTILITY does not provide any audit information. Answer e is incorrect because it is a nonexistent utility.

Question 46

The correct answer is d. Setting the **CONSISTENT** parameter to **Y** when exporting data from an online database will ensure that the exported data is read-consistent. Answers a, b, and c are incorrect because these parameters serve other functions.

Question 47

The correct answer is a. Statement failure occurs when a SQL statement fails, such as when a user enters bad data that violates integrity constraints into the database table. Oracle automatically handles these errors. Answers b, c, and d are incorrect because the sample scenario doesn't cause these failures.

Question 48

The correct answer is e. When a tablespace is placed in Backup mode using the **ALTER TABLESPACE BEGIN BACKUP** command, no changes can be made to the data file header blocks associated with the tablespace. Answers a, b, and c are incorrect because these events don't occur while a tablespace is in Backup mode. Answer d is incorrect because it is a bogus database event.

Question 49

The correct answer is b. The sample command sequence creates two disk channels. The **COPY** command will use the two channels to copy the two data files simultaneously. Answer a is incorrect because the sample command sequence performs an RMAN full backup. Answer c is incorrect because the sample command sequence does not perform an incremental (level 2) backup. Answer d is incorrect because both allocated channels will be used at the same time to copy the two data files.

Question 50

The correct answer is c. The **V$DATAFILE** view provides the names and locations of the data files that comprise the database. Answers a and c are incorrect because these views don't provide the names of data files for the database. Answers d and e are incorrect because they are invalid views.

Question 51

The correct answers are d and e. When the archive redo log directory runs out of space, the DBA only needs to free up space for additional redo log files. When a media failure occurs in an **ARCHIVELOG** database and no data loss is tolerated, complete recovery needs to be performed. Answers a, b, and c are incorrect because they require the DBA to perform an incomplete recovery.

Question 52

The correct answer is b. By default, an Oracle database operates in NOARCHIVELOG mode. Answers a, c, and d are incorrect because they are not the default database mode.

Question 53

The correct answer is c. For a nonarchiving database, you can only restore the database to the last full backup when a failure occurs. Data loss may result because redo log files are overwritten. Answers a and d are incorrect because they pertain to archiving databases. Answer b is incorrect because exports provide logical backups that supplement physical backups.

Question 54

The correct answers are a, b, c, and d. The **BACKUP, COPY, RESTORE,** and **SWITCH** commands will cause RMAN to perform an automatic resynchronization of the recovery catalog with its target database. Answer e is incorrect because the **RESET DATABASE** command creates database incarnation information in the recovery catalog, but does not perform the automatic resynchronization operation.

Question 55

The correct answer is c. The **LIST BACKUPSET** command will display all the backups that contain the specified data file or tablespace, or all the archived log files. Answers a, b, and d are incorrect because the given command doesn't perform these functions.

Question 56

The correct answer is e. The **ALLOCATE CHANNEL** command must be issued for RMAN to read from or write to the OS. Answers a and b are incorrect because these commands are not required for RMAN to read from or write to the OS. Answers c and d are incorrect because these commands are dependent on the **ALLOCATE CHANNEL** command to read from or write to the OS.

Question 57

The correct answer is c. The **ALTER DATABASE BACKUP CONTROL FILE TO TRACE** command outputs a trace script file that can be used to start the database, recreate the control file, and recover and open the database. Answers a and d are incorrect because these commands don't generate the trace script file to create a new control file. Answers b and e are incorrect because they are invalid commands.

Question 58

The correct answers are a, b, and c. Parallel recovery operations can be performed at the database, tablespace, and data file levels. Answer d is incorrect because tables can be restored only from an EXPORT file. Answers e, f, and g are incorrect because these are not valid levels for parallel recovery operations.

Question 59

The correct answer is d. Uncommitted transactions are rolled back when the data blocks associated with the uncommitted transactions are subsequently requested. Answers a, b, and c are incorrect because rollback activities don't take place at these times.

Question 60

The correct answer is d. The **TIMEOUT** option of the **RECOVER MANAGED STANDBY DATABASE** command enables you to specify a time interval to wait for a specified archived redo log file to be written to the standby database control file's directory. Answers a, b, and c are incorrect because they are nonexistent options.

Glossary

ALLOCATE CHANNEL command
A Recovery Manager (RMAN) command that establishes a connection between RMAN and a target database instance. Each connection initiates an Oracle server session on the target database instance that performs the work of backing up, restoring, and recovering backup sets and copies. When multiple connections are established, each connection operates on a separate backup set or file copy.

ALTER DATABASE CLEAR UNARCHIVED LOGFILE command
A Structured Query Language (SQL) command that reinitializes an online redo log without archiving the redo log. This command makes backups unusable if the redo log is needed for recovery.

ALTER DATABASE RECOVER command
A SQL command that is used to perform media recovery for the database, specified tablespaces, or specified data files.

ALTER DATABASE RENAME FILE command
A command that renames data files or redo log files. It renames only files in the control file. It does not rename them on the operating system (OS) file system. The file name must be specified using the OS file-naming conventions.

ARCH background process
This is an optional background process that copies the online redo log files to a designated archival destination.

archived redo log
A copy of one of the filled members of an online redo log group made when the database is in ARCHIVELOG mode. As each online redo log is filled and before it is overwritten, Oracle copies the log to one or more archival destinations.

ARCHIVELOG mode
The mode of the database in which Oracle copies filled online redo logs to disk. This mode can be set at

database creation or by using the **ALTER DATABASE** command.

automatic archiving

The process of automatically performing online redo log group archiving using the ARCH background process. You can enable automatic archiving either using the **ALTER SYSTEM** command or by setting the initialization parameter **LOG_ARCHIVE_START** to **TRUE**.

availability

The accessibility of the database for normal business use.

background processes

Noninteractive processes that run in an operating system environment and that perform some service or task. The Oracle server uses these processes to consolidate distinct functions of the server that would otherwise be handled by multiple Oracle programs running for each connected client application. The background processes send and receive information to and from the System Global Area (SGA). They asynchronously perform functions, such as database writes; monitor other Oracle processes; perform and coordinate tasks on behalf of concurrent users of the database; and provide better database performance and reliability. Oracle has five essential background processes: SMON, DBWR, LGWR, PMON, and CKPT.

backup

The process of making copies of files on another storage device so that they can be restored if the computer loses that information.

BACKUP command

An RMAN command that creates one or more backup sets that contain one or more physical backup pieces.

Backup Manager

One of the DBA tools within the Oracle Enterprise Manager (OEM) administrative toolset. It provides a graphical user interface (GUI) that enables DBAs to manage their database backup and recovery environment.

backup piece

An OS file that contains the backed-up data files, control files, or archived redo logs. A backup piece is a physical file in an RMAN-specific format that belongs to only one backup set. A backup set usually contains only one backup piece.

backup set

An RMAN-specific logical grouping of one or more backup pieces that make up a full or incremental backup of the objects specified in the **BACKUP** command. There are two types of backup sets: *data file backup sets* and *archivelog backup sets*. Data file backup sets are backups of any data files or a control file. This type of backup set is compressed, which means that it contains only data file blocks that have been used; unused blocks are not included. Archivelog backup sets are backups of the archived redo logs.

cancel-based recovery

An incomplete recovery type that enables the DBA to terminate the recovery process at a desired point in time in the past by entering CANCEL at the recovery prompt.

CATALOG command

An RMAN command that enables you to add information about an OS data file copy, archived redo log copy, or control file copy to the recovery catalog and control file. Specifically, it enables you to perform the following: (1) catalog a data file copy as a level 0 backup that facilitates performing a subsequent incremental backup, (2) record Oracle8i database backups created before RMAN was installed, and (3) record Oracle7 backups of read-only or offline normal files made before migrating to Oracle8i.

CHANGE command

An RMAN command used to set the status of a backup or copy as unavailable or available; delete a backup or copy from the OS and update its status to deleted; and check whether backups, image copies, and archived redo logs are available and, if they are not, mark them as expired.

change-based recovery

An incomplete recovery type that enables the DBA to terminate the recovery process at a desired point in time in the past after the database has committed all changes up to the specified system change number (SCN).

channel

A connection between RMAN and the target database. Each allocated channel starts a new Oracle server session; the session then performs backup, restore, and recovery operations. The type of channel determines whether the Oracle server process will attempt to read or write and whether it will work through a third-party media manager. If the channel is of type disk, the server process attempts to read backups from or write backups to disk. If the channel is of type sbt_tape, the server process attempts to read backups from or write backups to a third-party media manager.

checkpoint

A pointer indicating that all changes prior to the SCN specified by a redo record have been written to the data files by DBWR. Each redo record in the redo log describes a change or a set of atomic changes to database blocks. A checkpoint for a redo entry confirms that the changes described in previous redo entries have been written to disk, not just to memory buffers.

closed (offline) database backup

A backup of one or more database files taken while the database is closed. Typically, closed backups are also known as whole database backups. If you closed the database cleanly, all the files in the backup are consistent. If you shut down the database using a **SHUTDOWN ABORT** or the instance terminated abnormally, the backups are inconsistent.

complete EXPORT

A type of export that can be performed with EXPORT in the full database mode. It is equivalent to a full database export with the additional updates performed against the tables that track incremental and cumulative exports.

complete recovery

The process in which a database is restored and recovered through the application of all redo information generated (in the online and archived redo log files) since the last available backup.

CONTROL_FILE_RECORD_KEEP_TIME

The initSID.ora parameter that specifies the number of days that the RMAN information is stored in the control file before being overwritten.

COPY command

An RMAN command that creates an image copy of a file. The following types of files can be copied: data files (current or copies), archived redo logs, and control files (current or copies).

CREATE CONTROLFILE command

A SQL command used to recreate a control file under the following circumstances: (1) when all copies of your existing control files have been lost through media failure, (2) when you want to change the name of the database, and (3) when you want to change the maximum number of redo log file groups, redo log file members, archived redo log files, data files, or instances that can concurrently have the database mounted and open.

cumulative EXPORT

A type of export that contains database tables that have changed since the last cumulative or complete export. It combines several incremental exports into a single cumulative export file.

data file copy

A copy of a data file on disk created by the RMAN COPY command or an OS utility.

database administrator (DBA)

A person responsible for the operation and maintenance of an Oracle server or a database application. The database administrator monitors the database's use to customize it to meet the needs of the business users of an organization.

database buffers

The memory buffers in the SGA of an instance that hold the most recently used data blocks that are read from the database files.

DBMS_REPAIR

An Oracle-provided package procedure that can be used to help identify and repair block corruptions.

DBVERIFY

An Oracle-provided utility that can be used to determine if there are block corruptions in data files.

direct path EXPORT

One of the two paths used by EXPORT to extract data from an Oracle database. In direct path EXPORT, the data is extracted from the Oracle data files and passed directly to the

EXPORT client for processing, bypassing the buffer cache and the SQL command-processing layer.

disaster

Any event that prevents an organization from providing critical business functions for a period of time. A disaster could be one of the following representative incidents: natural disasters (flood, fire, earthquake, and so on), blackouts, hardware failure, viruses, theft, and key personnel departure.

disaster recovery plan

The document that defines the resources, actions, tasks, and data required to manage the business recovery process in the event of a business interruption. The plan is designed to assist in restoring the business process following a catastrophic event by minimizing risk and optimizing recovery time.

downtime

Period of time during which a database is unavailable for normal business processing.

dynamic performance views

A set of performance views maintained by the Oracle server. These views are continuously updated while a database is open and in use. By default, these views are available only to the user SYS and to users granted **SELECT ANY TABLE** system privilege or the **SELECT_CATALOG_ROLE** role.

EXPORT utility

An Oracle-provided utility that enables DBAs to perform logical backups of the database. A *logical backup* involves making a copy of the logical database structures with or without the associated business data.

Fast-Start recovery

An Oracle database feature first introduced in Oracle 7.3 that allows for a fast instance recovery, meaning that the database can be opened as soon as cache recovery is complete. The database is available at the end of the roll-forward phase of instance recovery, and the bulk of the rollback activities are deferred to the individual user processes when blocks are subsequently requested.

fast-start on-demand rollback

A rollback strategy that improves the performance of transaction rollbacks done by SMON. The server process will perform the following actions when it encounters data to be rolled back: (a) roll back the block that the user transaction is trying to access and (b) pass the remaining block recovery to SMON, which may use parallel operations.

full backup

An RMAN backup that is not incremental.

full database mode EXPORT

An EXPORT of the whole database.

full database mode IMPORT

An IMPORT of the whole database.

image copy

A copy of a single data file, archived redo log file, or control file that is usable for subsequent recovery operations. It is created by the RMAN **COPY** command or an OS utility, such as the Unix dd.

IMPORT utility

An Oracle-provided utility that is typically used for the recovery of database objects and business data using a valid dump file created by the EXPORT utility.

incarnation

A separate version of a physical database as used by RMAN. The incarnation of the database changes when you open it with the **RESETLOGS** option. The RMAN **RESET DATABASE** command issued after opening in RESETLOGS mode will create a new incarnation of the database.

incomplete recovery

The process in which a database is restored and recovered through the application of some of the redo information generated since the last available backup.

incremental backup

An RMAN backup in which only modified blocks are backed up. Incremental backups are classified by level. An incremental level 0 backup is equivalent to a full backup in that they both back up all blocks that have ever been used. The difference is that a full backup will not affect blocks backed up by subsequent incremental backups, whereas an incremental backup will affect blocks backed up by subsequent incremental backups.

incremental EXPORT

A type of export that contains database tables that have changed since the last incremental, cumulative, or complete EXPORT.

initialization parameter file

A file that contains information to initialize the database and instance.

instance failure

A failure that occurs when a problem arises that prevents a database instance from continuing to work. Instance failure can result from a hardware or a software problem.

instance recovery

The recovery of an instance in the event of software or hardware failure so that the database is again available to users. If the instance terminates abnormally, instance recovery automatically occurs at the next instance startup.

large pool

An optional Oracle8i memory area. It is used to allocate sequential input/output (I/O) buffers from shared memory. RMAN uses the large pool for performing backup and restore operations. This pool does not have a least recently used (LRU) list.

LIST command

An RMAN command that enables you to produce a detailed listing of specified backups or image copies recorded in the recovery catalog or target control file.

LOG_ARCHIVE_DEST_N

The initialization parameter that specifies up to five archiving destinations. These archiving locations can be on the local machine or on a remote site where the standby database is located.

LOG_ARCHIVE_DEST_STATE_N

The initialization parameter that enables DBAs to change the state of an archive destination. The default state for an archive destination is ENABLE. To temporarily halt archiving to a mandatory destination, you can set the state of that destination to DEFER. You can define multiple destinations and set them to DEFER in the initialization parameter file. These destinations can be enabled on demand when other destinations encounter errors or require maintenance.

LOG_ARCHIVE_MIN_SUCCEED_DEST

The initialization parameter that specifies the minimum number of destinations the ARCn process should successfully write before overwriting the online redo log files.

log switch

The point at which LGWR stops writing to the active redo log file and switches to the next available redo log file. This happens when either the active redo log file is completely filled or a manual switch has been requested by the operator.

LOGGING mode

The default mode that enables full redo or undo data logging for instance and media recovery. In this mode, full recovery is supported from the most recent backup.

logical backup

Backups in which the EXPORT utility uses SQL to read database data and then write it into an Oracle-proprietary binary file. Logical backups are typically used to move data into different Oracle databases on possibly different platforms.

LogMiner

An Oracle-provided utility which consists of a set of PL/SQL packages and dynamic performance views that can be used to analyze the redo log files. It can provide a resolution for logical corruption by building redo and undo SQL statements from the contents of the redo logs.

Managed Recovery mode

The automatic process of recovering the standby database. This mode allows automatic transfer of the redo log files to remote locations in the LOG_ARCHIVE_DEST_N parameter and configures tnsnames.ora and listener.ora files and their associated utilities.

manual archiving

The manual process of archiving redo log files using the ALTER SYSTEM ARCHIVE LOG command.

media failure

The failure that occurs when the storage device for Oracle files is damaged. This usually prevents Oracle from reading or writing data.

multiplexed archived redo log file

The automated process of maintaining more than one identical copy of a redo log. The initSID.ora parameters **LOG_ARCHIVE_DUPLEX_DEST** and **LOG_ARCHIVE_MIN_SUCCEED_DEST** determine whether multiple archived copies of a redo log file are desired.

multiplexed control file

The automated process of maintaining more than one identical copy of a database's control file. You can create multiple entries in the **CONTROL_FILES** initialization parameter to multiplex the control file.

NOARCHIVELOG mode

The mode of the database in which Oracle does not require filled online redo logs to be archived to disk. You can specify the mode at database creation or change it by using the **ALTER DATABASE** command.

Nologging mode

The database mode in which full redo or undo data logging are not performed. Some minimal logging is performed for data dictionary changes and new extent invalidations.

offline backup

An OS backup of the database files that is made after the database has been shut down cleanly.

online (open) backup

A physical file backup of the database made while the database is open and running in ARCHIVELOG mode.

online redo log

A set of two or more files that record all changes made to Oracle data files and control files. Oracle generates a redo record in the redo buffer whenever a change is made to the database. The LGWR background process is responsible for flushing the contents of the redo buffer into the online redo log. You can create multiple members in each redo log group to enable multiplexing of the online redo logs.

open (online) database backup

A physical file backup of the database made while the database is open and running in ARCHIVELOG mode.

operating system backup

A backup of the database files using OS commands or utilities.

Oracle database

A collection of related, physically stored data that is treated as a unit and managed by the Oracle relational database management system (RDBMS). An Oracle database is subdivided into a physical and logical structure that enables the management of physical data storage to be independent from the access to logical storage structures.

Oracle Enterprise Manager (OEM)

A management framework used to manage the complete Oracle environment. OEM consists of a console, a suite of DBA tools and services, and a network of management servers and Oracle Intelligent Agents.

Oracle instance

A set of memory structures and background processes that access a set of database files.

parallel recovery

An Oracle database feature that enables you to use several processes to apply changes from the redo log files. Parallel recovery is most beneficial when the data files being recovered reside on different disks.

physical database backup

A set of physical database files that have been copied from one place to another. The files include data files, archived redo logs, or control files. You can use RMAN or OS commands to make physical database backups.

Program Global Area (PGA)

A memory area reserved for a user process. This memory area is private to the user process and is not shareable. In a Multithreaded Server (MTS) configuration, part of the PGA may reside in the SGA.

read-only tablespace

A tablespace with a status that has been changed to freeze it from subsequent updates. You put a tablespace in Read-Only mode by executing the SQL statement **ALTER TABLESPACE** *<tablespace>* **READ ONLY**. Typically, you put a tablespace in Read-Only mode to reduce the frequency with which it is backed up.

recover

The process of applying redo data or incremental backups to database files to reconstruct lost changes and to make a file current to a specific point in time.

RECOVER command

An RMAN command that applies redo logs or incremental backups to a restored backup set or copy to recover it to a specified point in time.

RECOVER DATABASE command

The Server Manager command used to recover a database that is mounted, but not open. This is the Oracle-recommended method of recovering a database vs. using the SQL **ALTER DATABASE RECOVER** command.

recovery catalog

A set of Oracle tables and views used by RMAN to store information about Oracle databases. RMAN uses this data to manage the backup, restore, and recovery of Oracle databases. If a recovery catalog is not available, RMAN uses information from the target database control file.

recovery catalog database

An Oracle database that contains a recovery catalog schema.

Recovery Manager (RMAN)

An Oracle utility that automates the backup, restore, and recovery operations for Oracle databases. You can use it with or without a recovery catalog. If you don't use a recovery catalog, RMAN uses the database's control file to store information necessary for backup and recovery operations.

RECOVERY_PARALLELISM

An initSID.ora parameter that specifies the default number of recovery processes per session.

redo log buffers

The memory buffer in the SGA in which Oracle writes redo records. The background process LGWR is responsible for flushing the buffers into the current online redo log.

redo log group

The group to which each online redo log belongs. A group has one or more identical members.

REGISTER DATABASE command

An RMAN command that is used to register the target database in the recovery catalog.

REPORT command

An RMAN command that enables you to perform detailed analyses of the recovery catalog content.

RESET DATABASE command

An RMAN command that enables you to create a new database incarnation record in the recovery catalog.

RESETLOGS option

An option that can be used to open the database. This option resets the current redo log sequence to 1. A RESETLOGS operation invalidates all redo in the online redo logs.

restore

The process of bringing back an original copy of a file from a valid backup.

RESTORE command

An RMAN command that restores files from backup sets or from copies on disk to the current location, overwriting the files with the same name.

RESYNC CATALOG command

An RMAN command that enables you to perform a full resynchronization, which creates a snapshot control file. It then compares the recovery catalog to either the current control file of the target database or the snapshot control file and updates it with information that is missing or changed.

RESYNC CATALOG FROM BACKUP CONTROLFILE command

An RMAN command used to extract information from a backup control file and to rebuild the recovery catalog from that information.

RUN command

An RMAN command that enables you to compile and execute one or more statements within the enclosed braces following the **RUN** keyword.

server process

A process created by Oracle to receive requests from a user process and to carry out the requests.

SET AUTORECOVERY ON command

A Server Manager command that automates the application of the default file names of archived redo logs needed during recovery.

SET NEWNAME command
An RMAN command used to specify a new location when restoring files. If you restore data files to a new location, Oracle considers them data file copies and records the same in the control file and recovery catalog.

shared pool
A memory area in the SGA that holds the library cache and the data dictionary cache.

snapshot control file
A copy of a database's control file taken by RMAN. RMAN uses the snapshot control file to read a consistent version of a control file when resynchronizing the recovery catalog or backing up the control file.

standby database
A database that is a replica of your production database. The standby database is typically kept in a different geographical location from the production database and is in a state of constant recovery. The standby database can be configured to read-only mode to enable users to query the standby database without making any changes. This can reduce resource consumption on the primary database by enabling the standby database to serve as a reporting database.

stored scripts
A sequence of RMAN commands stored in the recovery catalog.

SWITCH command
An RMAN command used to specify that a data file copy is now the current data file and that the control

file reflects this information. A switch is equivalent to using the **ALTER DATABASE RENAME DATAFILE** command. Oracle renames the files in the control file, but does not actually rename them on your operating system. Switching also deletes the data file copy records in the recovery catalog and the control file.

SYSDBA role
A special database administrator role that contains all system privileges with the **ADMIN OPTION** and the **SYSOPER** system privilege.

System Change Number (SCN)
A stamp that defines a committed version of a database at a point in time. Oracle assigns every committed transaction a unique SCN.

System Global Area (SGA)
A shared memory region that holds data and control information for one Oracle database instance. Oracle automatically allocates memory for an SGA whenever the instance is started. The SGA is deallocated when the instance is shut down. Each Oracle instance has one, and only one, SGA.

table mode EXPORT
An EXPORT mode that exports specified tables owned by the operating user's schema. In this mode, privileged database users, including the DBA, can export specified tables owned by other database users.

table mode IMPORT
An IMPORT mode that imports specified tables in the operating user's

schema. In this mode, privileged database users, including the DBA, can import specific tables owned by other database users.

tablespace point-in-time recovery

A type of incomplete recovery that is appropriate when a user error has been discovered and when the database cannot be returned to a prior point in time. In the unlikely event that you need to use tablespace point-in-time recovery and because of the complexity associated with it, you should only perform this task with the assistance of Oracle Worldwide Support Services.

tag

A user-specified character string that acts as a symbolic name for a backup set or image copy. A tag can be specified when using the **RESTORE** or **CHANGE** command. A tag is limited to 30 characters.

target database

A database that requires the backup, restore, or recovery operations when using RMAN.

time-based recovery

An incomplete recovery type that enables the DBA to terminate the recovery process at a desired point in time in the past after the database has committed all changes up to the desired point in time.

trace file

A file created by the Oracle background processes when a problem or exceptional condition is encountered. It is also known as a *dump file*. The file contains information useful in diagnosing the problem.

unused block compression

The process of copying only used data blocks into RMAN backup sets. When RMAN creates data file backup sets, it only includes blocks that have been used, omitting unused blocks.

user mode EXPORT

An EXPORT mode in which all objects owned by a given schema are exported and written to the export dump file. Grants and indexes created by users other than the owner are not exported. Privileged database users, including the DBA, can export all objects owned by one or more schemas.

user mode IMPORT

An IMPORT mode in which all database objects in the operating user's schema are imported. A privileged database user, such as the DBA, can import all database objects owned by one or more schema users.

user process

A process that is created when a tool, such as SQL*Plus, Oracle Forms, and the like, is invoked by the user. A user process could exist on the client machine or the server machine. User processes provide the interface for database users to interact with the database.

V$BACKUP_CORRUPTION

This data dictionary view provides information about corruptions in data file backups from the control file. Corruptions are not allowed in the control file and archived log file backups.

V$COPY_CORRUPTION

This data dictionary view provides information about data file copy corruptions from the control file.

V$LOG_HISTORY

This data dictionary view provides log history information from the control file.

V$RECOVER_FILE

This data dictionary view provides the status of files needing media recovery.

V$RECOVERY_FILE_STATUS

This data dictionary view provides status information on each data file associated with the specified RE-COVER command. This information is viewable only to the Oracle process doing the recovery. **V$RECOVERY_FILE_STATUS** views will be empty to all other Oracle users.

V$RECOVERY_LOG

This view provides information about archived logs that are needed to complete media recovery. This information is derived from the **V$LOG_HISTORY** view. The relevant information provided by this view is only for the Oracle process doing the recovery. The **V$RECOVERY_LOG** view will be empty to all other Oracle users.

V$RECOVERY_STATUS

This data dictionary view provides statistics of the current recovery process. This information is useful only for the Oracle process doing the recovery. The **V$RECOVERY_STATUS** view will be empty to all other Oracle users.

whole backup

An RMAN backup composed of the control file and all data files.

Index

W